The Sixty Thousand–Dollar Dog

Author's Note

I have observed elsewhere that there is a significant difference between the truth of experience and the facts of everyday life. What I write about in these pages is often emotive, what I experienced, observed, and felt in different parts of my life. Some of the details I've forgotten (and occasionally I make note of that in the text, as with the date of a tragic fire in chapter 3), and some I've remembered, perhaps, imperfectly. So I may not have all the facts in perfect order, but I have no doubt about the truth of these stories.

Books by Lauren Slater

Blue Beyond Blue
Opening Skinner's Box
Love Works Like This
Lying
Prozac Diary
Welcome to My Country

Edited by Lauren Slater

The Complete Guide to Mental Health for Women
The Best American Essays 2006

The Sixty Thousand–Dollar Dog

My Life with Animals

Lauren Slater

BEACON PRESS, BOSTON

Beacon Press
25 Beacon Street
Boston, Massachusetts 02108-2892
www.beacon.org

Beacon Press books
are published under the auspices of
the Unitarian Universalist Association of Congregations.

15 14 13 12   8 7 6 5 4 3 2 1

Parts of some chapters in this book were previously published in different forms in *Creative Nonfiction*, *Family Therapy Networker*, *O Magazine*, *Self*, and *Gulf Coast*.

This book is printed on acid-free paper that meets the uncoated paper ANSI/NISO specifications for permanence as revised in 1992.

Text design by Ruth Maassen

Some names of individuals, dates, and other identifying details mentioned in this book have been changed.

Library of Congress Cataloging-in-Publication Data

Slater, Lauren.
  The sixty thousand–dollar dog : my life with animals / Lauren Slater.
    p. cm.
  ISBN 978-0-8070-0187-5 (alk. paper)
  1. Slater, Lauren. 2. Human-animal relationships—United States. 3. Authors, American—21st century—Biography. 4. Psychologists—United States—Biography. I. Title.
  QL85.S55 2012
  590.92--dc23
  [B]
                            2012020732

For Evans Huber

The Sixty Thousand–Dollar Dog

Contents

1

The Egg

I grew up in a place called the Golden Ghetto, where people sang Hatikvah in the swept streets, celebrating another war won in the homeland. As children we were told our superior Jewish spirit would lift us up, if we were willing to try. *Look around you,* everyone said; *see how wealthy we are?* Back then I believed this, but now I see the story differently. I see rows of modest homes, the interiors often dim, with washed linoleum floors and heavy curtains hanging. On Fridays, at sundown, in the summertime, when the windows were lifted, we could hear sung prayers spooling through the air, the melodies merging with ours as we too blessed our bounty, tearing into the challa's buttery braid. At the head of the table my father carved a kosher bird cooked in a garland of onions and coins of carrots flashing orange and floating in the broth. When I was eight years old I began to sense that the Golden Ghetto and our supposedly superior Jewish spirit were more wish than fact. I knew, for instance, that I could be kidnapped. I knew every bone was breakable. I put this information in some cut-off corner of my mind. What I wanted was a world I could wade in, some sort of perpetual summer. In such a season—the streets deserted in the heat, sun-drenched and silent—I could follow the path of an ant for hours, crouching on the baking curb while watching the insect zig and zag, the black bead of its body ascending a stem, then dropping into the open cup of a wayward poppy rooted in the cracked concrete.

As I remember it, in those afternoons I was often alone on the street, at the peak of the summer heat, when people drew their blinds so the inside of almost every home was submerged in shadow, as if sunk to the bottom of the sea, the brilliant white light visible only as it seeped between the slatted blinds and spread across the sills like oil. Once the sun set, our neighbors emerged, the children in their pressed shorts, the women sitting on the stoops, a kerchief tied around the curlers in their hair, the husbands dragging the coiled hose from its reel and then the sudden spray drenching the parched ground, puddling on the scorched surface before slowly sinking in. For me, the ghetto's gardens tell the story of this place, all the hedges trimmed, every flower staked and noosed at its neck. Our streets were spare, with hardly any trees, the town's Holocaust survivors—and there were many, old and bent-backed—frightened by all that branching, seeing in a single sapling—(quickly yanked from its socket)—the huge forests they'd hid in, escaping Hitler's grip. In those forests, they said, towering larches had crosshatched the sky, making scraping sounds when the wind blew. The ghetto's grandparents had seen vipers living in the shadows cast by trees and had known animals with too many teeth use the yews for cover and for camouflage Our ninety-year-old neighbor, Mr. Eller, said he had seen people hung from low branches, their necks snapped in a second, the tongue taking longer to turn blue.

Despite its stark seasons, its steeply silent Sabbaths, its sadness and its fear, the Golden Ghetto was good enough for a child. Some days, when the heat rose so high the black tar melted, we would stamp our hands into the streets, so when you looked out your window you saw your road smattered with palm prints, as if primates had been let loose in the night. On Fridays, Erev Shabbat, we all sang the same songs in synagogue; then we all went home to bless our fruits and eat our ruddy roasts, this kind of neighborhood communing unusual, perhaps priceless, and yet, it left me longing. I never said to myself, *I am longing*; that feeling lived at a level below language, but nevertheless I knew it because of how I saw things, my mother unloading the toppling market bags, pulling out packages of marbled meat, or the charged color of a wet carrot, my mother with her apron on, her blade whisking away the tough skin, the rind coming off in curls and fragrant shavings I collected in my cupped hands, lifting them to my nose and breathing in that wild and rustic tang.

When I was young there was my world and then, as I grew, came thoughts of what was beyond us. At night, radio towers blinked on distant hills. I could hear from the environs of town the gunning of motors, the boom of a backfire. Sometimes late at night or early, early in the morning, when the summer mist lay like milk just above the grass, I heard my mother crying, and when I crept closer, I could see she always pressed a crumpled Kleenex to her mouth. Once she saw me see. She tossed her Kleenex in the trash and walked off, her high heels tapping on our polished floor. I wondered if her crying had to do with where we were, or where we weren't. I didn't know. I wasn't sure. In sleep I sometimes heard, from far away, a lady knocking on a giant door, the door a mighty wedge of wood, her dress frothing around her feet, as snow fell. In the real world, the daytime world, the seasons switched, and the snow fell and fell and refused to stop, despite our expectations. Snow crept over our ground level windows and darkened the house. Snow turned the quotidian into a question mark, so the Ellers' house next door, a house I'd seen every day of my eight years on earth, suddenly looked utterly unlike itself, fangs of ice hanging off the gutters, a pole snapped in half lying across their drowning roof. School closed for ten days and the roads were all impassable. As the shreds fell from the blank but spilling sky, I saw two policemen ride down our street on huge horses, the horses high stepping in the mounds and drifts. The horses were white and as they melted into the distance it seemed as if the animals became a part of the swirling storm, their massive bodies breaking up into flakes and dancing down the drafts of wind, a sight so beautiful, so foreign, so *impossible* I felt a kind of deep and wild want, but for what I couldn't say.

And then, just like that, the snow stopped. The sky cleared. Spring came. The clouds shook themselves out and, as if embarrassed by their excess, appeared against their common blue background all fleecy and preened. The winter had been long and wet, and it did something odd to the earth. The earth was juicer and darker than usual, and pink worms were everywhere, wriggling with abandon, their bodies translucent, our science teacher holding one up to the light and showing us the dark sac of the stomach and the small smear of the brain. My birthday came on March 21, the first day of spring, my sign the ram with her white horns in a thicket.

I don't know if my parents sensed my sensing. My father, for sure, saw my excitement when the police horses had passed through as I, throwing open the second-floor window, my hands thrust out into the blinding white, yelled out the only thing I could think to say in such a situation: "Hey! Hey!" The horses didn't stop. The snow did. Bulbs, long buried beneath the close-cropped lawns, put forth their serpent skulls. For my birthday that year I got a bike. On its wicker basket were plastic tulips, and the handlebars sported purple and silver streamers, sparkles scattered in the seat. A Schwinn. "A Schwinn!" I shouted out. The bell had a sharp sound, a *brrrrring*, like someone shivering, from excitement or from fear, it wasn't clear.

I was only nine, but my father worked downtown, his hours long, and my mother was consumed with some rage-filled sadness that became, over days and weeks, like her own little ghetto, its color, in my mind, always changing like the lipsticks she wore, a melancholy mauve, a bitter red, a punch pink; who knew why, or when? I couldn't understand her and because I couldn't understand her I couldn't claim her; she wasn't mine. The bike was mine. The snow was gone. The neighborhood was safe, so what was there to watch, really? I was just another nine-year-old on a stingray seat, my wicker basket full of dandelions, snapped stems oozing milk. My brother and sisters went one way, I went another, and that was that. At first I rode around the block and then I rode around two blocks and before the week was through I rode beyond the Golden Ghetto, pedaling furiously, wind in my hair, my eyes tearing from the sharp spring air, my chest at once flung open with excitement even as it was compressed with want. Where were those policemen? Was it possible that their horses lived near here? The next town over was almost just like ours, the same red-brick schoolhouse, the same patriotic post office, the same butcher with his fresh cuts hanging on hooks in the window. I rode farther still. I found a barber on a side street, his pole twisted twirls of color, his scissors flashing as he cut the white locks off an old man's hair. I stopped to see. The barber worked so gently, draping a hank across his palm and then softly snipping, the floor floss-soft with fallings. The barber kept his combs in bowls of sudsy water and the old man, bibbed to his chin, slept with his head lolling in the sunlight pouring through the wall-sized window through which I watched. The barber beckoned me in. I lowered my kickstand and pushed open the door. The spring air still carried the winter's chill, but in here it was toasty and the old man softly snored. "What's a girl like you doing without a scarf?" the barber asked, his glasses down on his nose, his eyes a rich blue. "Who's cold?" I said, although in fact, now that I was in here, I realized that I was. A sudden sleepiness came over me and it occurred to me I could be dreaming this scene, asleep in my bed, the *snap snap* of the scissors suddenly charged with misty meaning, the pouring sunlight infusing the room with the golden color of heaven. I wanted to leave and I wanted to stay at the same time, aware that, real or not, this was a world beyond my own, and anything could happen here. "Your name?" the barber asked, and I said "Lauren," its sound for some reason all wrong, not mine; *Lauren Lauren Lauren* and a jolt went through me, hard to explain, the sudden awareness that I existed, separate from my surroundings.

"Lauren," said the barber and chuckled. "Why don't you take a scarf from the rack over there and return it next time you ride by?" He pointed with his scissors to a series of hooks affixed to the wall: mittens, hats, scarves, hanging from them. "Customers leave half themselves behind almost every time," the barber said. "Most never return for their things," and he shook his head at the wrongness, the waste, which I went towards, one scarf in particular catching my eye, made not of wool but of feathers—sunset pink, and soft, too, when I touched them. I took the scarf from the hook and wrapped it round my neck and saw myself in the glass, a bird girl. The barber smiled. "It's you," he said, and I said, "Thanks," and then I left, the day darkening now, the windows of restaurants starting to glow as I headed home, feathers flying.

It was March when I got my Schwinn. By June, after school let out, I was riding farther each day. I rode under bridges where pigeons clustered in the rafters above me, chirring softly or sleeping with heads beneath wings. I rode over highways and dipped down into towns where stores lined the streets, displaying their wares on the sidewalk, banners of silk and chimes. Every day I pushed on just a little farther, the houses at last becoming scarce, lawns giving way to meadow where wild turkeys pecked at seeds. I was after something here, but if you had asked me what it was I could not have told you. In my mind I saw those police horses, in the blizzard, atomizing into particles of white. I sought, perhaps, to assemble something. I sought, perhaps, the experience of distance itself, learning each day that I could create it, imagining as I rode that a long red ribbon spooled from my pocket, marking my forward progress while, in reverse, it pointed me towards home, when the darkness came. The ghetto's cropped and careful lawns gave way to messy meadows, and the messy meadows became fields, and as they did I drew closer to what it was. A place without look-alike houses. A place where my mother's sadness did not suffuse—even the smallest things—so whatever you saw or touched or tasted had her in it, to such a point that it sometimes seemed like the whole world was a woman with her name on it. I sought something separate.

The country. I was miles from home when I finally found it. The country came to me first as a distant but distinct odor: Sweet decaying dung piled high by paddocks. And then there were novel sounds, like the *kunk kunk* of a woman hoeing her earth or the squeal of a big barn door opening slowly for a spotted cow to pass through. Red barns blazed at the far fringes of fields and, roadside, the occasional house listed left or right.

Now that I'd found the country, I ceased riding without reason and, every day that summer I mounted my bike and pointed myself in a precise direction. What I knew was that people disappeared, if you went far enough, and then there was just you and the enormous yolk of sun and the cows with their heads hanging over their low fencing. At first I fed the cows grass I pulled from the roadside, their limber lips pulling in green, munching and munching while foam collected at the corners of their mouths. Then I touched their mouths—a buttery, leathery softness—and then, without thinking, I scooted beneath the fence and found myself inside a whole new kind of box, the biggest box I'd ever seen, the fenced field sloping down to a clot of trees and bramble bushes sporting exorbitant pink platters of flowers. I stood still, listening, but it seemed I was the only human sound around. I whistled and heard my echo bounce around, and as it dissipated, the cows, one by one, began to go down, sleepy, all of a sudden, their front legs buckling first, then their hind sides, their long-lashed eyes closing in the summer sun, big mounds of breathing I touched with the flat of my palm, feeling their sleep rise up into me, and then the ache of exhaustion came over me, too, and, and so I, too, slid down on my seat and put my head against the haunches of a mottled female, hearing her insides tick and gurgle, feeling her shift and stretch with the rhythm of her dreams, and then my dreams, how long they lasted I'm not sure, but when I woke I was still against her side and the sun was still in the sky. I stood. Beneath me she slept on, her udder rising and falling with her breath. I knelt down then, right next to those four fatty teats, as long as my fingers, but boneless. As gently as I could I placed my hand on her milk bag, surprised by how hot it was, by how hard, despite her gentle easy sleep. I enclosed one teat in my fist and gave the softest, most tentative tug, a spritz of milk spraying me in the face; I stumbled backwards. The cow lowed. She opened one enormous eye and looked at me, and then lowed again, long and sonorous. From the distance I heard someone call and then I saw him, a man coming up the hill, his broad-brimmed hat bobbing as he walked. I scuttled back under the fence, hopped on my bike and pedaled as fast as I could in the direction of home, which was far from here, the light going now, my heart clattering in its cage as if I'd stolen something—milk—and then, mile by mile, my whole body slowing, a sad sort of sinking as the rural retreated and I smelled the suburbs coming closer, barbecues and gasoline. Maybe an hour passed before I dared look behind me, at what I'd left. By then, of course, there was nothing to see, the farmland too deep in the distance, my hands sticky with milk, and sweet to the taste when I lifted them to my lips.

She sensed something but could not say what it was. I was slipping from her, and rather than grieve, she became angry. "Where do you go every day?" my mother asked me, and I shrugged and said, "Just around." Once I saw her in the laundry room. She held my shirt by the shoulders and slowly brought it to her nose and then, with a quick flick of her wrist, she dropped it in the washer. At nine my body was a board, my chest flat, the nipples so pale they were barely there. But she sensed, I think, some subtle shift, not yet here but near. I had dirt beneath my fingernails and briars in my hair. After we were all supposed to be asleep my parents argued, and sometimes they said my name—*Lauren, Lauren*—so I knew I was part of the problem, but which part, and which problem? When he left her each time she was crying, always crying in her Kleenex, the trashcan piled high with crumpled tissue. By night her tears softened her and she leaked like any other mammal, but by day her face was a mask tied tightly to her skull. The evening I came home after touching the teat, she looked at me darkly, as if she knew. "Wash up for dinner," she snapped, and I did, soaping my arms up to their elbows, rubbing my face with suds, but some essential smell was on me now. We ate at the dining room table and when I went to reach for the peas I knocked my milk glass over, and the liquid dripped off the table edge, darkening the carpet below. "Goddamnit!" my mother said, her voice all wrong, too tight, and when I looked into her face I saw it had cracked, the way land cracks in the high heat; she had a zig-zag rent running from her forehead to her chin and from the rent came a red light. "Calm down, Barbara," my father said while my brother and sisters sat silent. "Calm down?" my mother spat back at him, a question he couldn't answer. He shook his head slowly and, with his napkin, began to mop up the mess. "You," my mother said, pointing at us with her fork. "You think he's so sweet? Dear old dad," she said, and then laughed. "You'll never know," she said, "what it means to live like this." That night, in bed, her words were in my head. To live like what? I wondered.

The next morning, at breakfast, still wondering and paying no attention, I spilled my milk again and she hit the side of my face so hard a bruise formed atop my cheekbone, where my hair hung down so no one could see. That day I rode fast to the country, fast to the cows, but when I got there they were gone, the pasture empty. For four days I came back, in search of milk I could spill, and for four days I found just sun-baked land, the goldenrod thick on the banks by the low fence. I began to think it was a dream, no dung, nothing, to prove otherwise.

And so I went on. I pushed past that pasture and found others, but the cows were always on the far side and they ignored me, rebuffed me, even when I held out bunches of greens. In some ways it didn't matter because I was surrounded, out there, surrounded by hip-high grasses and lime-colored crickets poised on oval leaves. The air was packed with a complex jumble of scents I learned, over time, to separate into segments; the dung, the sweat, the hay, the loam, the flower-packed fields, the pigs in their pen, the dense smell of slop in a rubber bucket. I found a wild grapevine, the bulbous fruits taut, dark juice spurting when I bit into their bodies, the seeds, which I spit into my palm, afloat in a light green gel.

The vine, which grew along an unkempt fence, was so ridden and rife with fruit that it took me days of eating to follow its trail around a corner, up a small hill, and into a cove where all of a sudden the daylight vanished, the trees here packed together, trunk to trunk, their enormous branches creaking when the breezes blew. Tacked to one of the trunks was a rusted tilted sign: "Private Way," and, indeed, when I looked down at my feet I saw they were on some sort of rutted path, overgrown with brambles and barely visible, but a path nonetheless.

Private Way. My parents had many private ways, their clues just crumpled tissues or dagger glances tossed across our heads, as though we would not notice. My mother had her private ways, that rent I'd seen in her face, the red light coming from the rip there, suggesting that her insides were bright and quite possibly too much to bear. The bruise on my cheek was a private way, hidden by my hair, a stamp, a suggestion, a clue for someone to find, but no one found it. I was sick of secrets. Thus I decided to discard the sign, not literally, but to discard it nonetheless. I was going to go here, where I was not wanted. I parked my bike by the base of a tree and, following the private path, made my way into those woods.

Darkness. Deep suede shade. Vines twirled around tree trunks, disappearing into the uppermost level of leaves, which clapped when the wind blew, as if I had an audience—eyes—watching. I looked left, then right, trying to see who saw, catching a gleam, hearing a hoot, and then gone. I found, in the dense undergrowth, a rusted tractor, its body orange, its tires flattened, the seat ripped open so its coils sprung free. The tractor glowed in the dank forest, a machine long lost but as if alive. It was hunkered down so silently, its silence suggesting something strange about it, as if at any moment its engine might leap into life. As I crept closer I stumbled across a large bug-eaten boot and then a sound—sudden—surrounding me, this high humming, someone else here, but where? Again I looked, left, then right, up, then down, the sound intensifying as I neared the broken, radiant machine, the humming hard to describe; it made my ears ache and yet it called me closer, the sound of a thousand voices or of just one, a girl perhaps, a single girl singing in a tree above the tractor.

I called out then: *Helloooooo,* and I swear the humming ceased for a second and then started again. The tractor had two enormous headlights, and the sun slanting through the trees made the bulbs beneath the lenses look lit. I reached out to touch the lens, and for some reason I saw myself then, standing in the kitchen, my mother crying, I, reaching out to touch the lens of her eye, which in my mind was stilled, gone to glass, beyond blinking. I saw myself in the snap of a second touching her where one never would and finding a terrible fixed stillness as she stared at me like a doll, and then my own eyes went wet from a sadness much too unwieldy to put in some package, the humming now higher, now harder, and coming from . . . *here.* In an instant I saw the spot, in the busted fluff of the machine's ripped seat. I craned my neck out, looked over the lip of leather, and discovered, in the seat, the squirm and throb of thousands. A nest it was, a whole humming home in there. I picked up a stick, then, and, surprised by the coldness of my curiosity, I used it to poke and prod. The humming went wild in response. I saw the glint of wings, too big for bees, the wings flexed and fluttered and then, one by one, from deep in the center of the tractor's torn seat, dragonflies, hundreds of dragonflies, rose like royalty into the air, hovered briefly above me, and then swerved up steeply, disappearing into the tops of trees. I dropped the stick. I'd seen dragonflies before, of course, but these were different, because their electric blue bodies throbbed in the draped forest; because they were en masse and audible, and because their presence in a place I was not supposed to be saturated them with significance, turned them to Tinker Bells, or eerie fairies. On and on they went, ascending from the seat, carving paths in the dark air, going up, diving down, swinging around, around, and around. Yes. I was with wings.

That summer, and thanks to my Schwinn, the Private Way became for me a place where I could question. Looking back on it now I wonder why it didn't occur to me to be scared—a girl alone in the woods and crimes happening everywhere, all the time, but I wasn't scared, not then, anyway. That was the summer a girl named Emma Gin disappeared, her parents appearing on TV, making pleas, and not long after pieces of her found in the Wayland woods, and yet I wasn't scared. I wasn't in the Wayland woods, but even if I had been I don't think it would have mattered. What scared me were houses, things too carefully cut, or the shining aisles of the supermarket where meats were packed in plastic. What scared me were dinner times and the tongue my mother served one night, the tastebuds visible. *Taste it*, she said; *it's kosher.* I put the tongue on my tongue and felt trapped, then, in the absurdity of an experience where there were no words to define or even describe. We ate the tongue with our tongues, under orders. My father, trying to back my mother or maybe just a dedicated meat eater, said it was delicious. The meat was a livid pink, a plank on my plate, *all gone.* First in the fields, and then in the forest, following the overgrown path of someone's private way, things seemed possible again, enchanting, chantable, each unusual item explicable and attached to some scheme I sensed made sense, even if I hadn't yet grasped it. When my mother cried, there was no answer to her tears, but the high humming had revealed itself to me as an insect with a name and a place. At home, in the "D" volume of our encyclopedia, I looked up dragonflies and learned that they had large compound eyes that saw in every direction all at once. Small now, they had once, in the Jurassic era, been as big as birds, darting and diving over ponds where dinosaurs drank. I put the "D" volume back on the shelf and pulled out the "Z," fanning the pages, each one gilt edged, the pictures blurring by; I saw zebras and zygotes and zeniths, and I felt as if someone were stirring a stick in the center of me, awakening within me my own high humming, my own need for naming, describing, defining, while also becoming aware, right then and there, that knowing was not the same as answering. If you had asked me who my mother was I could have answered you. Yet I knew nothing of her. I did, however, know something about those dragonflies, their enormous eyes, their pupae, that they were born in water and grew wings only at the very end of their lives, learning to fly just as they were about to die.

Thirty, forty feet into the private way was a small pond, the clear water the color of deeply steeped tea, surrounded by cattails and gracile grasses. I lay on my belly on the moist bank and watched the watery world beneath me. Frogs, I noticed, uncurled their long tongues to which flies got stuck, and then swallowed. These amphibian animals lay their eggs in clusters of opaque sacs that floated just below the surface of the water and then bloomed into tiny translucent tadpoles whose pulsing hearts were visible, fast, violet flutters. I observed a spider making her waxy web, and then saw that web go to work as all manner of minute insects got trapped within its sticky strands. I learned, from a library book, that spiders have mouths, tiny hinged maws that they use to devour their prey, mercilessly, sometimes over a series of days, the prey losing its life in the worst way, bit by tiny bit, an elongated torture that could have, perhaps should have, suggested to me that animals, at least sometimes, are cruel.

And yet the spider didn't seem cruel to me, and if you'd asked me why, at nine, I would have told you it was because the spider was acting the way it was supposed to. When she slammed me upside the cheek, or, worse, when, during wars, humans hung others from branches, asphyxiating them slowly so as to prolong their pain, people were acting *outside the alphabet*. This was the phrase that came to me, at nine, and now, at forty eight, I'm still not sure what it means. The animal world worked its spell on me in part because it could be spelled, full of mysteries, yes, but absurdities, no. Amongst animals one was grounded, tethered to the raveled rope that held us together as humans, but when you separated yourself from animals you separated yourself also from your own skin, and forgot what it was you, as a person, were supposed to do, or be. You made a fake face or gassed your young and instead of spelling stories you spread silence, which was *outside the alphabet*. I cannot say much more than this. All around me in those woods were alphabets, from the croaking of the frogs to the high hummings of the dragonflies to the callings of coyotes, as night neared, and the pond water darkened, and reflected back to me the stone in the sky.

July crept on, the whole earth, it seemed, baking in the heavy heat, and the animals of the forest grew drowsy, snakes sunning themselves on rotted logs. I found snake skins on the ground, amazed by their intricate patterns, which I started to sketch in a book I bought with my allowance money. I'd put the sketchbook in my bike basket and bring it down the private way with me and sketch the spiders I saw, the plants I saw, observing how they changed shape when water was near. At home I checked more and more books out of the library, my knowledge deepening even as my answers floated away. At nine, I didn't mind the floating feeling, and if there is anything I wish I could hang on to from that time it is this: the ability to stay suspended in space, living the liminal, in a place where there was no such thing as stink. I often thought of her holding my shirt, bringing it up to her nose, and then tossing it into the wash the way she did. Animals can attack you but they will never, ever revile you. Only humans can do that.

As the forest grew around me and inside me, my own home began to fall away. It was as if the walls were coming down, one by one. The crying fights at night turned into screaming, my mother screaming in the hall, her hands clenched. *What is ON you?* she sometimes asked me, prodding at me with her sharply shaped fingernail. She aimed her eye on me much more than on my siblings, who either faded from her view or grew as proportionally precious to her as I was wrong. All wrong. Sometimes she sunk her nails into my skin and I dreamt they went right through me, her hands entering my entrails, pulling them out, string by string. At home, I began to be scared all the time. My older sister whispered to me that my mother was ill and would soon be going to a hospital. What at the age of nine did I know about mental illness and the genetic liability she passed on? I believed I'd found an escape. I had no inkling that over time my mother's grief would become mine, and that eventually, years hence, I'd lose the capacity for comfort only to find it again, when I was a mother myself.

I learned partly by book, partly by eyes alone. Snakes with printed skins, their bodies cool to the touch. Deer prints looked like this, coyote prints like that. Down here was the scat of a brown bear. Chipmunks lived in that old stone wall, six of them, shy no matter how softly you sang. Squirrels, however, had harder hearts and would come for an acorn if you sat still enough, day after day after day. Moles ran by, blinded. Wrens sang just so. Starlings were harder to hear but prettier to the ears. I filled the basket of my bike with my sketching notebook and wrinkled raisins and curled cashews taken from the mirrored bar where their liquor bottles were. My mother drank the liquor, pouring a clear scorching liquid over crackling ice, lifting the glass to her lips and tossing it back. Sometimes, then, she sang, the sound not pretty. We listened to her lying in our beds, and then the song would stop and she'd start to talk; *you,* she'd say, *shed in the sheets; you,* she'd say, *put the keys in the hanging closet.* Sometimes my father was there but other times he wasn't, and she went on anyway, talking to the walls, the window, the world itself, her first finger flexed and pointed, accusingly, at the moon.

I largely forgot about her in the forest, or at least it seemed I did. I didn't know then that the mind, like the earth, has several layers: a crust, a mantle, a boiling core. I stayed up on top. I saw holes in the ground, ragged circles that went down, dark. I knelt and smelled something rank and alive in there. I planted the nuts from my parent's liquor bar all the way around the entrance to those holes and then sat back, waiting in the shade. At last foxes appeared, their pointy faces popping up, their scrappy paws swiping the nuts down into their dens. I did this for days, and then stopped. Instead, now, I put the nuts on the forest floor, in a small pile, and then sat back against a tree, the food just a few feet from me. How close, I wanted to know, could we come? The foxes saw me and smelled the treats and knew what I was up to. In the earth below me I listened to their language, a panoply of chirps and gurgles and quick, high barks. They debated and decided, their heads poking up, dropping down, overtaken by ambivalence, until at last what looked like a large male made his way towards the pile, nose to the ground, his eyes all amber. *Click click*, with my tongue. The fox stopped, cocked his head, then started again. I got quiet in a way I'd never been before. I entered into stillness. The fox kept coming, his movements both slinky and slow, five curled cashews, crystalled with the grit of sparkling salt, midway between us. As he approached I could see his whiskers, the slope of his snout, the dark dots of his nostrils. It took some time, a long, long time, but at last he crept so close I could hear his breath and see him take the nuts with his teeth, his jaw working as he chewed, fast, then bent his head for more. He eyed me the whole time and then, when he was done, he turned away and trotted back into the forest.

It wasn't until August that I found the egg. It lay in the forest on a little patch of grass, entirely alone, no bird near here. I scanned the sky between the branches but saw just chinks of blue and the faintest fingernail of an afternoon moon. I looked straight up the trunk of the nearest tree and then the tree after that and the tree after that, but there was no nest in sight. It appeared that this egg had been dropped straight from some solar system, perhaps carried down to the ground by a winged thing that had borne it but could not bear it, and so wanted to pass it on.

I picked up the egg. It was more delicate and perfect than anything I'd ever held and I knew, immediately, that I would keep
it, that I would bring it back with me, into the Golden Ghetto.
I pressed the orb to my ear and thought I heard, from within, a
small slosh, and I pictured a thimble-sized being turning round and
round, flexing its fleecy wings, opening and shutting its ruby beak
as it readied itself for its enormous task, based entirely on faith,
cracking the caul of your gorgeous surround in search of something still finer.

That day I filled my bike basket with leaves and grasses to
cushion the egg on the long way home, and, for the first time,
I brought a piece of the forest back with me, into the Golden
Ghetto. Right from the start the egg made it seem like anything
here could happen, and I believed this all the more when I showed
it to my mother, carrying it into the kitchen, which was growing dark as the evening arrived, her silhouette, I remember, and
my words: *Look, look,* my voice strangely soft, my hands cupped
closed, my very being emanating a mystery she could not resist.
"At what?" my mother asked, turning from the window towards
me now, her own voice suddenly soft, too, mirroring mine, as if
we were, indeed, under some spell, entirely transformed, I no longer with stink, she coming quietly across the kitchen floor to *look,
look,* and when she was close I opened the hub of my hands and she
saw resting down deep in my joined palms the tiny perfect orb of
the egg and she said, *Oh. Oh.*

And we two stood there for a second and I swear I saw her *oh*'s
leave her mouth and drift off into the air, floating up like bubbles
and breaking painlessly above us, the first *oh* rising, then the second *oh* following the first, and I said, "An egg, Mom, from the forest," and she said, "What kind?" her voice rising up at the end of
her question as voices often do, and so we were risen, even as we
were, for the first time in a long time, tethered to the ground by
quotidian conversation. *An egg, Mom. What kind?*

"I don't know," I said. "I'm going to look it up. Find out. A car-
dinal maybe." I paused then. "Can I keep it?"

She leaned over again, to peer down into her daughter's dark
hands, where the egg lay, and I saw things stream across her face

then, feelings, but I don't know what those feelings were. With one finger she reached out and softly stroked the side of the egg and I watched, entranced, her finger going back, now forth, that finger from the same hand that had slammed me, and yet here she was, her second self, a gentler self rising to the surface of her skin, cracked open in kindness, or maybe by memory; I said, "*Mom*."

Mom. I wasn't calling her, or questioning her. *Mom.* I'd meant it as a chime but she took it as a "can I" question and stumbled backwards a bit and then said, as if confused, "Yes. Yes. We'll make it a nest." And then she paused. She was over by the sink now, leaning against it. I watched her. Years of tensions had crisscrossed her face and made her mouth crimped at its corners, but at just that moment I could see a second face behind the first, a face from long ago, a face from perhaps before she was even born, and this face was plain and open, the skin smooth and moist. It was like looking at her through a translucent shell she was trapped in, and how had that happened to her? To all the Golden Ghetto? "Yes, yes," she said again, and again, that look of confusion, coming over her. She turned, looked back out the window over the sink. It was dark now, completely dark, and cicadas shrieked in the lawns. "How," she asked, "will we keep it warm?"

My father found a shoebox, my sister a small desk light that we shone on it, for warmth. I placed the box on my bureau, across from my bed. That night they fought, as usual, and she cried, as usual, but instead of hearing her tears I kept hearing her question in my mind, and how her voice went up at the end, like a little wisp rising. I kept seeing her finger, unfurling, stroking the tiny egg, and I wondered if, when I was a baby, she had ever touched me like that. Was I once, I wondered, perfect to her, and as soon as the question formed it was followed by a kind of crushing grief, the sort for which there are no tears, and so you stare, dry eyed, out at your surroundings. Which was the Golden Ghetto and the treeless streets and the strict squares of neighboring windows. I didn't know it then but I had just come up against a question that let loose within me the most primeval ache, and it could not be permanently packed away ever again, no matter how hard I tried, and I did try, again and again, for years. *Was I once perfect to her?* I saw myself as if from above, my cranky curls, scum on my skin, my chest now mounded ever so slightly, a pain when I pressed there, a deep pink singeing.

In our photo album was a picture of me at one year or younger, in a sailor's dress and tied white toddler shoes, perched on her knees, her one arm around me, in her other hand a cigarette coiling silvery smoke. Fresh from my own little egg, she had held me with care, or even love, but then time took me, touched me, made me, somehow, all together *other*, a creature without classification. I saw her as she saw me, with scum on my skin, and a little window inside me shut and the shades were drawn and a darkness came, and I couldn't come out of it. I walked to the sill, the grief settling like silt, and for years I would feel that wordless grief, casting its pall over everything—the tree, the chair, the chimney—and then, when it went, as it often did, coming and going, going and coming, my returned world was all the more beautiful to me. *The dividends of darkness*, I would later write in an essay about depression for which I found a treatment when I was in my twenties, another orb filled with a chemical concoction; it helped some days and then some days it didn't. It all started, I think, that night, when I was nine. On my bureau I saw the box all aglow; the egg was warm inside. And why could that not comfort me? I should have slept soundly but, as it turns out, the light kept me up most of those nights, which grew cooler and cooler, autumn now right around the corner, school starting soon, the egg here, the forest there, and that was that.

In a perfect world full of perfect people who are exactly as they are meant to be and not who they become—shape shifted by cruelty, or terror, or simply rote repetition—in a perfect world, the egg would have cracked soon after I'd taken it home and from its shattered shell would have stepped a bird just as I'd dreamt her, singing like a strummed harp. But of course no world is perfect, neither those we build with our own hands, nor those we find for ourselves, full of foxes and moles and soft-stepping deer.

School started, fifth grade, which meant I could not go back to
the forest, and my father put my bike away, hung it from a hook in
the garage, its wheels suspended off the ground, caked mud falling from its treads and clumping on the concrete. During the day,
now, I was in math class or English class, and I wondered why
none of it had any interest for me, why the words, the worlds, in
my fifth-grade books fell flat, while all through the summer I'd
read avidly, as though transported by some spell. I remember that,
in history, we read a book called *Medieval Days and Ways*. In Latin
we declined nouns and verbs. Yom Kippur came and the rabbi read
off the long list of the dead while the grandparents of the Golden
Ghetto davened back and forth, and we sang "Kol Nidre," a sacred
song I have always loved for the way it transforms deep grief into
a thing of beauty, the voices swelling in the sanctuary, and then
the cantor lifting the horn to his lips and bellowing into, or rather
against, the blackness beyond the windows.

Have a happy New Year, everyone said when it was over, kissing
each cheek, in the lobby the old people holding my hands in theirs,
gripping me hard as if to say, *Stay. Stay*. There were plates set out
on long tables, and platters of diced apples and bowls of golden
honey. My mother said to Sadie Rosenblum and the Ellers, "Do
you know my daughter has an egg she found in the forest?" People
perked up and came to ask me questions. *Right on a patch of grass,*
I said. *Small and silvery. No, not even a crack. In a box, with a lamp,
to keep it warm*. For some reason the egg invoked a kind of curiosity in the old ones, the survivors, who, soon after the New Year,
came around to see. The Ellers, the Rosenblums, the Schwartzes,
the Loves, they rang our bell and, pair by pair, on different days,
climbed our carpeted stairs to peer inside the shoebox. I watched
them watch, tiny tremors in their hands, veins like smashed grapes
blotching their burdened legs, the blue tattoos covered with gloves
or exposed to the cold, the skin there chafed and hairless. The old
survivor Hassids, their lives governed by religious rules that left little room for the sudden, the surprise, well, they leaned over, into,
the shoebox and stared, murmuring *remarkable, splendid, l'chaim,*
but it wasn't what they said that mattered. It was what went across

their faces, or appeared in their eyes, a whole history they'd cordoned off, cracking through the cauls they'd wrapped around themselves. A tiny piece of the forest they'd once hid in had found its way to the Golden Ghetto, only this time they weren't scared. This time they were with want, missing. I could see it by how long they stared, how softly they murmured, how gently they touched the tiny sphere. The earth has a hold on us, no matter what our memories.

Sometimes a question comes over you so completely you become it. It is like being draped, and there is darkness over everything except the question. The question ceases to be a grammatical occurrence and becomes, instead, a throbbing thing, a *must*. When, oh when, would my egg hatch? Day after day I inspected it for signs, and day after day it stayed immutably stubbornly smooth, and the days passed into weeks and the weeks became a month, and the leaves fell from our few pruned trees, saffron hands passing by my window on their way down to the ground. The clock ticking on my mantle sounded like high heels, *click tick click*, coming closer, now receding, my heart flapping fast from a fear with no name, the egg, its surface so smooth and blank. With no forest to escape to, and trapped in the grid of the ghetto and the rote repetition of school, I lost touch with my meaning. I forgot there were cows with hot, hard bags and lacy sprays of milk. I forgot there was a pond held in a scoop of land, the water tea-colored, transparent, the tiny tadpoles swerving between fronds. I forgot the foxes even, and how they'd come for nuts and candy. My dreams were full of fog. I woke up to the sound of the talking ticking clock and I was claimed by the question, jumping from bed, peering over the lip of the box—no change, no change, no change—and this is how it happened, how the egg went from a silvery sphere of luck to this terrible ovoid *if*.

Daylight savings came, which meant the streets became blue earlier each day, shadows flocking the house, from floor to ceiling. Even when the sun was out it was different from the summer sun, which had been radiant and wet, spreading across its pink background in spectacular shows of setting. The November sun was the size of a diamond in the dim sky, its glint meager, its light entering your eye and passing through, so pale you couldn't feel it.

My mother felt it. She had not been well for a long, long time, but this autumn sent her falling farther and faster than usual: the lack of light, the silent streets, her alabaster children and then the one with scum on her skin. Her husband, who wounded her in ways we might very well never know; I tried to tell, to see him as she might see him, watching him now as he walked the hall, a perennially pale person, every Shabbat his yarmulke tilted and attached with a clip to his thinning hair, his scalp exposing itself, almost indecently, the skin there pink as pork, its surface scaly, flakes falling off him as he shuffled from here to there. To us he was nothing but kind, if a little absent minded, but to her he was almost evil, and sometimes it seemed I could see it, this flaming lady married to a man who was more ghost than flesh, not enough for her, no authority, and she, even as she reared up and roared, wanting in some part of her mind to be tacked and tethered, strapped to a safety he would never provide.

That autumn—severed from the forest and waiting on my egg, time for the first time making its appearance in my life, its terrible persistent *tick* taking you nowhere so slowly you wanted to scream—that autumn my parents ceased fighting and a silence filled our house, and the silence could not be broken even when it was. You could speak, but the silence swallowed your words before they'd made a mark, and so it seemed none of us could hear each other, and we were all confused, stumbling around, our mother standing by the kitchen window and petting her neck, up and down and around and around, petting her neck as if it was something separate from her.

When the bird came, I would bring it to her, just as I'd brought the egg. Over and over I played the scene in my increasingly agitated mind. The egg would crack perfectly in half and from its broken shell would step a feisty ready-to-fly baby bird. Cupping it in my hands, which were now a second sort of shell, I'd come into the kitchen and say, "*Mom*," and something in my voice would put its soft hook in her and pull her towards me, and together we'd bend our heads and view the baby bird. And with one finger now unfurling she would stroke its feathered skull, her gentleness evident, her touch so true I'd feel my own head held, as if by her, she looking at me with pride, because see what I—her second daughter—had brought back from the forest?

This is the scene I played over and over in my mind, and as I pictured it I'd stare at the damn dumb egg, which was at once crucial to my fantasy even as it made its fulfillment impossible. "It takes time for eggs to gestate," my father said, but weeks had gone by, a season had changed, and this egg was still in a slumber so steep it seemed it might never awaken. *When when when when* morphed into *if if if*, the question mark finally clasping me too tightly to its curve, I drawing in draughts of air, my heart going so fast I felt it might breach my chest and throb along outside me. In school I stared out the window where every day I saw a tiny plane flying by at precisely 11:03 a.m. If only I had a for-sure—a time when the egg would hatch, some sort of schedule, an obvious endpoint—that would make it easier. It could be a year from now, or today, just something definite, the cruel curve of the question mark becoming the calming point of a period.

I wasn't crazy. I was anxious, but definitely not crazy, but how was I to know that, at nine years of age, my body doing its own little dance utterly apart from my notions or desire, the sensitized mounds mounding more and the nipples now swelling and going dark as nutmeg. I ceased sleeping well, the lamplight over the egg blazing too brightly in the dark, and the sound of her pacing in the halls, dragging her manicured nails across the plaster so it snowed on the margins of our carpets, white plaster dust rising up and coating the silver-rimmed mirror in the hall.

Then one day, a Saturday, November now, my mother left the house just after sundown, Shabbat over, she tying a kerchief around her head and pulling on a big black coat and when we asked her where she was going, she said, simply, "Out."

"Barbara," my father said, and she said, "Every man needs a little mystery," and then she left, closing the door behind her. I went to my room, looked in on my egg. Exhausted—the lamp light and my nattering mind making sleep difficult every night now—I lay on my bed—one hour, two hours—and was just slipping over the rim when I heard her car crunch into the driveway, and then the engine turning off. I sat up, waiting to hear the slamming of the car door, her steps on our walkway, the front door handle turning, but there were no sounds, nothing. I went to my window and saw the car below, its interior lit, she just sitting behind the wheel, in a sealed space.

She came in at last. I heard the car door open, close, and then our front door open, close, and then my father, his voice unusually loud, almost a shout; "*Barbara*," he said, and she laughed a strange little laugh that went up and down the scales, girlish, tinkling. "*Barbara*," my father said again, and then a series of sharp rapid barks. I opened the door to my room then and went down the hall, down the stairs, and there she stood, her coat still on, pink-streaked cheeks, her usually sprayed hair windblown, in her arms a teacup dog, a miniature greyhound, its skin slack over its bony body, its eyes bulbous and alarmed. *Tiny*, my mother pronounced, holding him to her, pressing the bony beast to her chest and smooching his hide with her lips. "His name is Tiny," she said, staring at my father, who stared at the dog, his eyes wide, his scalp glistening, as if oiled. And then, before he could say anything else, she thrust the dog at my father, forcing Tiny into his arms, the beast beginning to howl as my father fumbled, stumbled, clasped the now-panicked, scrabbling canine scratching feebly at his face.

"Barbara," he gasped as the dog twisted and flung about, and she laughed a wicked wretched laugh and stood back, saying, "Look at you there. Just look at you." My brother and two sisters were in the living room, I standing on the last, the lowest step in the hall. We all, on cue, looked at my hapless father, Tiny overpowering him by thrashing wildly and swiping his face so finally he dropped the dog and said, "Jesus."

"He's nowhere around here," my mother said, turning to me, and then swiveling towards my siblings and saying, "See. Do you see it now? Do you?"

The four of us stood, frozen. Our father. We saw. We saw his naked pork-pink scalp, his alarmed eyes, his kindness, and his clumsiness. But, in the end, we saw him as his children, not his spouse, so what were failings in her eyes were mere idiosyncrasies in ours. "You," my mother said, turning and then pointing to me. "Do you see?"

Then I knew, in an instant, why she wouldn't love me, couldn't love me, even as I blazed before her, brighter than her others. I knew what she wanted me to say, but her words were not my words, never. *Stubborn*, she had always claimed, but now I'm not so sure. It isn't as if I insisted on being me; it felt more as if I simply had no choice. At some basic level, you do not pick your views; it's just the opposite. They claim you, and the only question is what you will decide to do with them. "Do you?" she said again. "Do you see?"

I looked at my father, my mother, my father, the dog sprawled on the floor between them. "No," I said. "I do not see." Her eyes narrowed and sparked. We stared at one another and when the stare got too hard, too sharp I turned away. Quickly, then, she looked to my siblings, the three of them standing in a row by the piano. She made some sound, a kind of gargling, warped little sound, or was it a word? "Do you see?" she said to them. Frightened, they gave barely perceptible nods of assent while my father stepped back, shaking his head, his whole scalp burning as he brushed greyhound hair from his clothes.

Tiny, as it turned out, was an animal as anxious as we were, and to make matters worse he was nocturnal in nature, howling whole nights away, keeping each one of us not only awake but keyed up, my senses heightened so it seemed I could smell and hear and see prismatically, every facet of existence honed to a keen gleam. In the darkness, after midnight, Tiny's howls rattled the whole house while we tossed and turned. Strangely, only my mother seemed peaceful. Tiny's distress had a paradoxical effect on her; it seemed to calm her, at least for the first few days when she sat up all night long, soothing him on the living room couch, the television on even when there were no shows, at 3 a.m., 4 a.m., the screen filled with static as she stroked the little animal and I watched from the hall, where she could not see me, her murmurs audible, the static sizzling, his howls finally giving way to whimpers just as the domed surface of the sky cracked with the first line of light. The house was finally silent, Tiny and my mother dreaming on the living room couch, surrounded by piles of blankets and opened boxes of biscuits and bones, white bones as big as my fist, stuffed with crimson meat. I'd turn off the television then and climb between my sheets, and fall into an hour or two of fitful slumber until the alarm burned through my dreams of trees and toads. It was time for school.

And so we went along, Tiny howling out some sort of hurt or rage, some essential insult, my mother now suddenly, noxiously, soothing, the egg sleeping through the whole hurrah, until Friday came around again; "Shabbat," my mother announced. "A time of rest." Before sundown that Friday afternoon, my mother drove to the drugstore and came back with a bottle of Nyquil which, after our Shabbat meal, she fed to the dog by a dropper. Tiny liked the taste and so my mother gave him more, filling the glass dropper again to the top and squirting it into his happy mouth. Within the half hour the dog was stumbling around like a drunkard and I had a bad feeling. "Look at him!" my mother said as he rolled onto his back, his four paws dangling uselessly in the air; he fell asleep there, in that posture, his sleep so deep he didn't stir even when my brother stuck a straw up his nose and blew in. "Thank god," my father said. "Let's all get some rest," and he turned in by nine o'clock, my mother curled on the couch with a comatose Tiny in her arms. That night I fell down a deep and dreamless hole, the lamplight glowing over the egg—which I did not once get up to check, as had been my practice over the weeks—the clock talking its endless ticks—none of it mattered as exhaustion grabbed me by the cuff and hauled me straight away to sleep land. I slept like someone pulled under a dock, the darkness complete, the next thing I knew my window rosy with anemic November light.

I jerked awake then, sat straight up in bed, and when I stood I swore I felt a slight tilt to the floors, as if we were keeling with a wave. Something, I knew, had happened, but what it was, or wasn't, I couldn't say. There was no noise anywhere, not inside, not outside where, in the dim dawn, a truck glided by without a sound, and down the street I saw the dark shape of a hunched figure opening his mailbox and from its innards a spill of brilliant white light, illuminating his hands as he reached in and pulled out a stack of letters. I tapped on the glass and with each tap I saw a spark—a pale prick of light—as my nail flicked the slick window, icy and beaded from the long moist night. I shoved my feet into slippers and peered in at my egg, looking over the rim of the shoebox, the box itself all off, de-squared, as if the long dark night had somehow wrenched what was supposed to be just a little to the left, so everything in our world was suddenly slanted. The box looked like a parallelogram, and it too was emanating light, like the mailbox had, and a rich roar of excitement went through me because maybe this all meant the egg was at its end.

I sometimes think that hope is a kill switch, ensuring that precisely what you want you will not get, some sort of punishment from god for desiring beyond your borders. I also think that hope is a hook, its point dipped deep in a toxin which, once its lodged in you, fills you with an ache that erases the sound and shapes of the world, so you lose sight of whatever it is you have in your hands, and the more sight you lose, the harder you hope, and so you go round in your barbed circle. Hoping, I looked over the warped lip of the box and saw in an instant that nothing in there had changed, and that the morning's odd roar and tilt was either all in my mind or signaling some other event. The egg, clearly, was not the event. It seemed so smug in its solid shape, so sure of its own solidity, so happy to mock my desire, and then I let my eyes go lax and brought the box up close to my face so the egg doubled, two times the taunt; I put the box down. I picked a pencil up off my desk and then, holding the egg in my palm, I tapped twice on its shell with the blunt rubber end, thinking as I did of how my doctor tapped on my knee with his red rubber hammer and how my knee moved, no matter how hard I tried to keep still. Holding the egg now at a distance from my face I tapped twice more, bringing the pink eraser down hard on the speckled shell and then, to my shock, a crack appeared, a zigzag crack just *appeared*, all at once, materializing instantaneously, and the crack was leaking light, the same brilliant light that had spilled from the mailbox down the street and from the shoebox on my dresser and now from the body of the egg itself. I put the egg down, quickly, walked a swift circle around my room, and then picked the egg back up again, balancing it on my palm, closing one eye and looking at the orb with the other, and the zigzag crack, *right in front of my eye*, closed up, sucking its saffron light back into itself, *poof.* I held my breath and then gave the shell three hard raps with the nub of the eraser and the crack, so hairline, so deeply delicate, again appeared on the shell's surface, this time larger, webbing its flank. "Do you see?" I said, for some reason using my mother's question when she'd brought Tiny home. "Do you see now?" I said out loud. My voice, like everything else that morning, seemed all wrong in the quiet dawn, my sounds hollow, somehow false, a bit British, and I suddenly saw myself on a stage, people watching me. A red flush fell over my face. The crack closed up.

Who could I tell this to? No one, of course. I was old enough to know I would be mocked—*a magic egg?*—and besides, there were other obvious explanations, the scrawl of a shadow, my own tired eyes playing tricks on me; *do you see?* I adjusted the desk lamp and left my room, the morning sun now risen, beneath me the streets of the Golden Ghetto filled with cars.

The dog was dead. Like me, like the rest of us, he too had fallen down the steep slope of sleep, dragged under some dock, only he didn't come up for air. He was lying on his side on the couch, and when my father put his palm right up at the animal's snout, he could not feel any air. Strangely, my mother seemed unaffected by the unhappy event. She stood at the stove, frying an egg in a pan. "You were cruel to him," she said, looking from the pan to my father, who leaned in the entryway to the kitchen. "I'm not the one," my father said in a low stern voice, "who chose to give him Nyquil."

"I'm not the one," my mother responded, "who let him fall to the floor, too inept to hold him." And then, as if to prove her point, she slid the spatula beneath the egg, the intact yolk warbling and beaming bright as she gently, skillfully, flipped it all over without any spill or seepage. "Perfect," she said, sliding the egg onto a plate, its lacy edges browned, its golden center whole.

Two days later, when I got home from school, Tiny was gone, along with his bowl and leash. Gone too were the antics of my egg; it sat innocently in its padding as if nothing had ever happened and maybe nothing had. My mother's boastful mood was also over; she was sitting at the dining room table, before her, hundreds of keys of all different shapes and sizes, some so small I could not imagine what sort of door they would open, others large and thick, edged with chunky serrations. "I bet you kids never knew I had a key collection," she said to all of us, gathered round the table, still holding our book bags, and we shook our heads no, we'd never known. "This key," she said, holding one up, "this key goes to the Shah of Iran's stable. Do you want to know how I got it?"

We all nodded. Suddenly her face fell. It was as if someone had come along and simply swiped something central and essential from her, and she fell inwards and silent. She shook her head. "I forget," she said.

The four of us stood there, looking at the keys, then at one another, then at the keys, then at her face, which seemed to be dissolving right before our eyes. "What about this key?" my older sister said, grabbing one from the table, holding it up, turning it in the sunlight, her voice loud and full of forced cheer. "Tell us about this key, Mom."

My mother looked up then, glanced at the key, and then suddenly she raised her hand and knocked it from my sister's grip so it clattered to the floor, bouncing twice and then lying, still, on its side. I looked down. It was a bronzed key, a car key maybe, threaded on thin wire with a tiny tag attached to it and on the tag some script too faded to read. "What about this key?" I asked, hearing something desperate in my voice, reaching for the littlest one she'd sifted off to the side, raising it up in the air and turning it. The key was silver, smaller than my pinkie, and it hung from a frayed red ribbon, and I said, "It's beautiful, Mom." She swiveled her head then, in my direction, her swivel all wrong, though, so slow we could practically hear the creak and crank of gears beneath the supposedly solid surface of her skin. And now she squinted up at me and then started shaking her head, back and forth, back and forth, back and forth, and I said, "What, Mom?" and she said, "So many keys!" and before we could stop her she, in a single motion, swept them all onto the floor, hundreds of keys falling from the table and crashing at our feet, a sea of keys, she with her face in her cupped hands now, crying softly. We all stood still, not knowing what to say, and then with one hand she started it up again, petting and then scratching her neck, digging deep in, the skin there flushed and beginning to bleed, and we all said stop it, but she wouldn't even look at us, never mind listen.

We gathered, then, in my oldest sister's room while she called my father from the upstairs hall. My father came home from work, and we kids sat on the hall steps, listening to them murmur behind the closed kitchen door. Eventually my father opened the door, his face all haggard, and, as he walked up stairs, motioning for us to follow he said, "She's agreed to go to a hospital," and I said, "When?" and he said, "There'll be a bed available in three days." I didn't quite understand that and saw in my mind a bed with wings floating aimlessly in the air, my mother's bed, coming to us from across the sea, a trip that took some time.

Now that Tiny was gone, or maybe now that she knew she was going away, or maybe simply because some switch had flicked in her brain—the darkness coming earlier every day now, and on the East Coast, where we lived, there was very little light in mostly gray days, a hard and bare time of the year when the burst of autumn is long gone but the snow has yet to brighten the browned-out beds where flowers still stand on their stalks, all shriveled—her outbursts ceased entirely and a different demon came over my mother, one I'd never seen before. I can't recall who cleaned up the keys; in my memory they are there, they stay there, scattered and heaped on the dining room floor for years and years to come, but that could not be true. I know I woke up that night late, the clock clicking in my ear, the second hand sailing around its flat lit face, and

I couldn't hear her. There was something about the quality of the silence in the house that suggested danger, but despite that sense I got out of bed, magnetically pulled, it seemed, by some strings from the sky, making my way down the pitch dark hall, feeling for the switch on the sconce but then pulled forward before I could find it, suddenly the stairs beneath me, lowering me by levels, and then a line of faint light at the base of the closed kitchen door. *Do not open that door,* a voice inside my head said, but the strings on my marionette body did differently, or maybe to say they were strings is all wrong, and I'm talking about a terrible urge, the need to know, to crack the casing, to come to the red-hot heart of the matter, where scum and stink live. *Do not open that door,* I said to myself, but Lauren was layered and the commands coming from the crust of my mind had no bearing on the urges of my mantle, my core. On the surface of our land we have houses and highways, our intentions spelled out in what we've built, even as, beneath us, the earth has a whole other agenda, its giant plates crunching up against each other, the core licking.

I opened the door and saw her almost clear as day in the iced light from a whole moon visible through the bay window, on the one hand just a woman sitting simply at a table, but if you looked a little deeper, something deeply wrong with the sunken stillness in the body, her head on her hand on her elbow, the posture frozen, she sitting so still, as though she could not move. "Mom?" I said, and, indeed, she did not move, not even a twitch to acknowledge my presence. "Mom!" I said again, and then, angry all of a sudden, I reached way forward and yanked her hand away from her face, and the hand fell to her lap, her face staying still, as if her hand were still there supporting it. And even though everything in me told me to keep my distance, I crept closer still, and suddenly I was back in the forest, crouched down on the needled ground, the trees all touching above me and above that the here-and-there chinks of sky. Now, crouching down, I held out my hand and the animal in my mother came alive, woke up; she moved her head and watched me with the sort of suspicion I'd seen before in the faces of fox and deer deciding whether to take whatever it was I offered on the platter of my palm, only now my palm was empty, or, rather, slick with sweat, lined with my whole life, all I had to offer her, and it seemed to work, sort of, she coming closer now, edging towards me in her seat, I with my palm held out and then a clicking came from my mouth, a *here, here* that is uttered simply through sound, and every animal knows it, and she knew it too, and her forehead fell into my outstretched palms, and I was holding her head there, like that, her hair hanging down around me, she just sitting with her head in my hands, and when the weight was just too much I slowly let her go, removing one hand, then the other, and instead of sitting up she sunk still deeper down, her head between her knees, I, not knowing what to do, her stillness much scarier than her sounds. I clicked again, but this time it seemed she didn't hear, or refused to respond, such surrender a terrible thing to see, the psychic spine snapped. In school the next day a nurse came to inspect all of our spines for abnormal curvatures, and when it was my turn I knelt over the desk in the gym teacher's office and held my breath as the powdered professional hands pressed the supposedly solid rod that held me up. The exam seemed to take a long time, the nurse's fingers pressing down between my vertebrae, pushing at the pieces of me.

I came home from school that day, the feeling of hands all over my back. I opened the front door and looked left, towards the kitchen, the door ajar just as I'd left it the night before and somehow I knew she was still sitting there, in the same seat in the same way, and I didn't want to see it. I tiptoed past the door and up the stairs, throwing my books onto my bed and looking in on my egg, as I'd done every day now for too many months, picking it up and turning it round and round, and then pressing it to my ear and hearing in there a second silence, and then eyeing the egg, so perfectly formed, so opposite us, with our keys clattering and our heads hanging down and a dead dog and our faces rumpled from fatigue and fear and everything else that goes along with being human. The egg was mocking me and at the same time the egg was calling me forward into a world that was shaped as it should be, the only thing between me and it this hard but slippery shell that I tapped on—*tap tap*—and then I picked up that pencil again and, again, using the pink teat of the eraser, I pressed down on this sphere of silence, and as I pressed an urge came over me to press again, and harder still, to drill down and through the silent shell, so I did, searching for the center, the living gel, the animate animus, the liquid life that is poured into the bottle of every body so deer dance and foxes prance and wrens sing in trees, and I kept going, putting the pencil down now and enclosing the sphere with my whole hot fist, bringing it to me, consumed, suddenly, with the urge to know what was in there, ready or not, I had had it, could no longer live in the liminal and needed, besides that, the shock of the shatter against my chest where the grief had settled like silt, so I pressed and I pressed and heard from within my fist a most satisfying crunch and crackle, and a concomitant loosening in the shell of my own skin, so I could cry, finally, about everything and nothing, about the faraway forest and the fact that I was almost ten and that she didn't have a bed yet, the tears coming freely from my eyes, and on my desk a letter from the nurse to my parents because my spine went a little to the left and imperfections in the human form should be fixed.

And then I was done. I opened my clenched fist to find shattered shell but . . . but . . . that was it. Just shattered shell. Where was the golden goo, the yolk, the embryo or fetus or half-formed winged thing? Where was it? WHERE WAS IT? Not here. I clapped my hands together and the scraps of shell fell from my hands to the carpet, flecks and pieces, all of them dry. The egg, it appeared, had been empty all of this time. Later I'd read at the library that sometimes this happens, when fertilization doesn't occur or when the developing embryo for some reason ceases to proceed, its genetic code wrongly wired so maybe all that grows is a wing, or in my case a tiny tine that looked to be the beginnings of a beak, and a few white chips that could have been bone. Not all eggs, as it turns out, are good eggs, which I'd already known anyway.

It was a disappointment, of course, but I was surprised, after all this Sturm und Drang, by how little of one it was. Had I, after all, ever really believed in a golden feathered friend? When I'd found the egg I was nine, but that was months ago and now I was nine going on ten. I kept seeing my hands, in my mind, shattering that shell, and I remembered feeling the hot hard urge, and how I kept going, couldn't stop, believing there was life in there, and able, obviously, to kill it out of pure and cold curiosity, or compulsion, the pulsing movement of my muscles, what I was capable of, her hands, my hands, whose hands? Would I grow up outside the alphabet, a person who did harm, harboring her rage and waxy whiteness? Or, perhaps, it was the other way around, and I'd been the bad egg, somehow infecting her with a wrath that was mine first, from the very beginning, the wrath kicked into existence once my first cell split. The keys lay for a long time on the living room floor, but I picked up the egg shells right away, combing the carpet for every last fleck, trying to come away clean. I tossed the shoebox in the trash and stored the warming light in my closet, way up high. Now my nights were dark again, the only glow from the moon or the streetlamp right outside my window, casting an elongated triangle of light on my floor and flooding one small section of my wall. My hands looked huge in the shadows there. I could flap them like wings, clap them like cymbals, ball them like bombs, bursting five fingered and angry into the air while beneath me, below me, around me, the night pedaled on, the sun punched through, and then the Golden Ghetto hummed away another blunted day.

These were different times. Nowadays, if you go into a hospital for depression or even psychosis, they'll patch you up with medicines and send you back down the slide into society just as fast as they can. But when my mother went in, it was in the early '70s, and what the doctors lacked in chemical concoctions they made up for in time, and talk. I don't remember ever visiting her there, although I do recall going by the building in our car and my father pointing out to us what floor she was on. Four weeks later she came back home, on some medicine that made a difference. Color had returned to her skin and the sooty shadows under her eyes had faded away, replaced with something smooth and almost clear, the veins there visible, tiny tendrils. She went back to doing what she'd done before, like making our lunches and talking to a friend or two on the phone, even laughing now and then, a normal laughter that seemed to set things straight in our jumbled-up house. It's not like all was well, but much was better. She never talked about Tiny and when his little collar turned up under the couch cushions one day, about two weeks after she'd returned, she held it before her face with a wrinkled brow, reading the small, silver, heart-shaped tag that said *Tiny* with our phone number inscribed beneath it. "Tiny," she said out loud, her head cocked as if listening to something far, far away, and we all got quiet, not knowing what she knew and afraid that a memory might send her down the slide, back to blackness again.

"Yes, Tiny," my father said then, his voice brisker and louder than usual, and he leaned forward and plucked the collar from her. "That was all a while ago," he said, and we nodded, and she looked at us, her four children, and then nodded too. "You," she said to me, "need a haircut. And your room cleaned up. Now."

I cleaned up my room, *now*, and two days later she took me for a haircut, instructing the stylist to chop off the curls that came whenever my hair grew out, the floor beneath my feet littered with large locks and maple swirls, the scissors clipping and clipping and my mother saying "more" until, in the end, the floor was a sea of hirsute waves and I looked nearly bald, the hair cut so close to my skull it appeared to be clinging to it, like a cap that might blow away in a brisk wind. While my mother paid I sat in the seat and watched a woman sweep me up, my whole head, it seemed, tossed into the trash and my neck now bare to the breezes outside, so I shivered. Lying in bed that night I could feel the bareness of my neck, feel the palpable shadows flickering and stroking, and it wasn't until I hunkered down deep in the sheets, a blanket bunched up to my chin, that I could finally fall safely asleep.

We had a snowless winter that year, the ground hard and brown while my nine-going-on-ten body seemed to think it was spring, ripening, the curls she's tried to cut out of me appearing, as if by magic, in other parts of my body, my waistline changing, my legs growing longer and covered with curly fuzz. Just as the smoothness of the egg had seemed to mock me, my dancing, springy body seemed to mock her, although I never meant it that way. When, I wonder now, had she ceased seeing me as a good egg and started seeing my shape as wrong, as an intended attack? Although the forest was far away there was always an animal between my mother and me; she said she could smell me and insisted I wear deodorant. Her hands strapping me into a bra were invasive, intense, her snout sniffing me out, no matter where I went. The whole thing was hard, over the top, perpetually painful, and yet we seemed to need it, this primitive battle we fought in a moist mythical forest of towering trees and pure white owls and tufts of vivid moss growing in dark delicious hollows; we needed it.

At forty-eight years of age I am five feet tall with hands and feet so petite I can wear my twelve-year-old daughter's sandals. It always surprises me, to see my feet slip into these narrow flats or to pull child-sized mittens easily over my hands. It shocks me, really, that I'm so small, because in the mythical forest where I've lived with my mother for most of my life, I tower and stink, my huge hands ripping trees out by their roots or crushing stumps and eggs, egged on by a barbed need to know. I can't calculate my ratio of gentleness to cruelty, can't claim for sure that my teeth aren't fanged in my mouth. I don't know where the beast in me begins and the human ends, or what sort of centaur I am. On my good days I feel the animal in me is a sign of strength and speed, a gift to give the daughter who is right now around the age I was then, when this all happened. On my bad days the animal in me becomes a beast and then the beast a burden I'm not sure how to hold, as I go about my business.

For my tenth birthday that March I got a flute, with its lean, long body, my mother insisting I learn to play. She hired a private instructor named Mrs. Rodoway, a tall lady who came to our house twice a week and stood over me turning the pages of the music book on the stand of walnut wood. I'd pick up this gorgeous, complexly keyed instrument with the oval hole for blowing, and I'd blow, trying to curve the air just so, trying to coax melody from this slender shining shape. My first sounds were all squawks and screeches and so loud my face flushed and I'd put the flute down on the ground. "No, no," Mrs. Rodoway would say, "you can't give it up like that," but of course she didn't understand it wasn't the flute

I wanted to give up; it was me—the self that made the sounds and smashed the silver egg.

I practiced, under my mother's strict gaze, for thirty minutes every day, and despite the fact that I learned how to keep a whole new kind of time—2/4, 4/4—and despite the fact that I learned to play some Bach and simple songs like "Gay Tarantella," I couldn't come to a different image of myself. When June arrived and school let out for the summer, I put the flute away in its velvet-lined case, breaking its body down into three separate segments and laying each piece in the space it was supposed to go, and then closing the case and putting the instrument under my bed, Mrs. Rodoway gone until school started again. Unlike the summer before, when I'd been free to ride as I wished, this summer my mother signed us all up for swimming camp and we got Speedo suits. I hated to swim, hated the cold concrete pool with its narrow lap lines and chemical smell. I had one week off between swimming and school and, with my flute packed away and my Speedo suit folded in my drawer, I took my Schwinn from the hook it hung on in the garage, ratcheted the seat up a notch, and rode off, out of the Golden Ghetto, over the highways where, beneath me, cars streamed by, fast and free; I kept riding and riding until the streets narrowed and the red barns blazed and the cows meandered in the churned-up pastures rich with rotting loam. I didn't stop for the cows or for a pink drink; I didn't stop until I reached the Private Way, at which point I leaned my bike up against a tree and, for the first time in almost a year, entered, once more, my forest.

Birds screamed. Creatures flapped past, so close it seemed their feathers brushed my face. The pond, so clear last year, looked brackish and dark now, surrounded on all sides by enormous bump-backed toads. I looked left, then right, stepped here, then there, trying to affirm that, yes, this was the forest I'd so loved and it was, it was, *the same* forest, only this year it scared me whereas last year it had enchanted me.

I could have run, but instead I stayed on the path, vines hanging down, bright berries bleeding on the ground. My feet looked huge to me, my hands hanging from the rims of my wrists downright dangerous. They'd never caught the killer of the girl named Emma Gin—the one taken by a stranger and then found part by part. I'd seen it on TV, here a hand, there a leg, wrapped in a cloth and put into a car. Would my mother, I wondered, love me if I were brought to her like that, in pieces, something she could assemble just as she saw fit? Sometimes, now, a fatigue came over me, so encompassing I couldn't move. And right then and there the fatigue came down like a cloth covering me, and I sat on the forest ground, my back against a tree. The tree's roots broke the crust of the earth and tiny white flowers thrived at its base. I picked one of those flowers and, with my fingers, flicked off its head. The sun crossed the treetops and began to descend on the other end of the day. It was 2, then 3, then 4 p.m., the forest edging into night so slowly, just slipping in as one might slowly slip into a cool pool. I, then, entered into stillness again, and as I did I heard the songs of the starlings. Deep in the distance I could make out the moving blur of deer and then, closer by, I saw those holes in the ground, and now I heard the chirps and gurgles of foxes just waking from their naps. I didn't have any treats and would they even remember me? It appeared they did. First came what I guessed was the large male, climbing out of his hole, and then some slightly smaller ones and then behind them some could-be cubs. Now the male circled the tree, coming closer, the others following him, and then—in a dream I had—came more foxes from more holes, so I was soon surrounded by dozens, then hundreds, then thousands of foxes, all flickering in the late light as they circled me and circled me, and I recalled, then, how once I was a child in an airplane that circled the city for hours while I looked on, my face pressed up against the bubble window, and beneath me the whole world made more beautiful by my distance from it, the cars as tiny as toys, my longing to land growing only larger the more time we were aloft. And so it was with the foxes, inching closer by nearly invisible increments, and I held out my hands so they could see who I was, what I was, and they approved, or so it seemed, because even with no nuts for them they still circled and circled for who knows how many minutes or days or years—this in a dream I had—and then

I *click clicked* with my mouth, and all those foxes stopped, turned towards me, sniffing and snuffling, taking in my jumbled scents, for so long, they couldn't stop, sniffing my palms, my knees, the curves of my calves, sniffing and sniffing and coming back, each time, to my upturned hands, my scrawled lifelines and finding—was it possible?—something sweet.

2

Sugaring the Bit

1: Girls, on Horses

My daughter, fallen for a horse. My girl, at eight years of age, asking why we can't take Pegasus home with us, our urban backyard big enough, she claims, for a pasture. This is what horse craze does to a child, stretches the perimeter of the possible.

My daughter, Clara, loves her lessons and all the accoutrements that go with it: bridles and bits, hoof picks and crops and currying combs, jodhpurs with suede patches and long black boots with over one hundred eye hooks, total. My daughter has taken the time to count them and lingers when she laces, her cider-colored hair falling all around her as she leans over, lost in a world I know so well, having been there myself, my own black boots long gone now, by the time I was through the leather so soft it slumped.

My daughter, like me, loves the smell of the stable: dirt floors, wood shavings, wildflowers growing in the cracked corners. My teacher's name was Rose, and I'll get to her, but first there's Amy, Clara's new instructor, no more than twenty years of age, a ponytail pulled high off her fresh face, her body lean, molded muscles visible when she moves. Each of Clara's lessons start the same way. With the halter slung over her shoulder, Amy leads my daughter and me to the wire that fences the forty acres of field the horses graze on. If it's morning there's mist floating just above the grass in scraps of white; if it's evening the land looks blue, its hollows filled with shadows.

We three stand by the fence and Amy calls for the horses. She calls for the whole herd, even though Clara will only ride one, and each time I'm tempted to say, "Could I, might I, possibly try riding today, too?" I thought I'd long lost my love, but here it is, as intact as ever, returned to me though my daughter, who now becomes my tether to the past as well as my funnel into the future.

When we three arrive at the fence, the visible parts of the pasture are always empty, the horses down and around. The sky sprawls above us, everything quiet, as though waiting for some show to start, and it does; it always does. Amy takes each pinkie and pulls back the corners of her mouth so a keen whistle sluices through the air and makes its way over the land, a whistle so strong you can almost see it, dipping down and around the curves, sliding over the modest mounds, racing between rocks, and eventually reaching the horses, whose sensitive ears fork forward as they rise up from grazing, turn their majestic necks towards the call, their bodies, all at once, breaking into a trot, and then a canter, the whole herd of them, thirty, no forty, galloping towards the sound so we always hear the horses first before we see them, or rather we *feel* them first, through our feet, the ground vibrating, the thunder building, building to its breaking point just as they round the bend and burst into view, silvers and bays, chestnuts and golds, their bodies surging as though they are one mass moving, as though they will not, cannot, stop; they pound towards us with no sign of ceasing, and each time Clara and I start to step back—an instinct, a preservationist impulse—and each time Amy says *no.* "Stay still," she commands and so we do, putting our faith in her and the herd, who are now no more than thirty, then twenty, then ten feet away, their necks extended as their hooves lift and hit the ground, closer and closer, our hearts in our throats as the whole hustling lot of them screech to a bunched, sudden stop right at that electric line, their huge chests heaving, their long faces hanging over the wire. Laughing, we open our hands and offer them carrots and apples, loving the ways their dry, rippled lips search our skin for more. We love the huge pools of their eyes. We love the veins visible in their faces. We love their wild gallop just as we love how the chosen one demurely, politely, lowers his head for the halter Amy slips on him, Clara now holding the rope as the horse walks behind her. I stand back and watch. All three—Amy, Clara, and horse—enter the darkness of the barn, the horse flecked with dirt and streaming sweat from his run. Five minutes later the three reappear on the concrete path, the horse totally transformed in his tack, gone domestic, it seems, in a matter of moments. A clip and a clop and my daughter's chosen mount now stands obediently in the center of the ring as Amy tightens the girth, pulling up the saddle straps so they cinch the horse hard; he doesn't protest, never protests, and then the stirrup proffered, Clara's booted foot slipped in, and, with a boost from her teacher she's up and over, sitting straight—remade, my daughter is—taking on height that isn't hers.

And as I watch the lesson progress I wonder what sense we might make of this sport and the undeniable draw it has for millions of girls growing into adolescence. Does it have something to do with the paradox at the heart of being female in our time and place, girls told to stay strong and yet to be soft, this contradictory message reflected in the body of a horse, with his mixture of power and delicacy, size and fragility, animals who inspire fear even as—pure prey—they are full of it themselves? *How powerful your daughter must feel up there*, some feminist might proffer, an unfulfilling explanation, too easy, too pat, the flip side of the horse-as-phallus theory that, from what I can see, most people buy into without much reflection.

Like Clara, my own love of horses was paired with a desire to ride, and when there were no horses available, I spent my time locked away in my room with equine novels and plastic ponies, my fascination eclipsing every other childhood interest: the Schwinn bike I'd so loved and on which I'd pedaled my way out of the Golden Ghetto, now hung on a hook in our garage, its sparkling seat furred with dust. I don't know what became of that bike, or the box I used to warm the egg I found in the forest. I have not carried those things with me into my adulthood, hanging on hard to my ribbons only, in pinks and reds and glory blues.

By the time I was old enough to understand the prevailing theory about females and equines, I was already sliding off the saddle and on to other adventures. For my daughter, though, I suspect riding will be a lifelong love, if only because we have bought a house in the country and will be moving there soon, the antique barn equipped with stalls, all ready for the pony we plan to purchase. My parents never encouraged my riding, believing it to be a fundamentally dirty sport, but for Clara, well, the case is very different, and it won't be long before she's old enough to understand, and worse internalize, the psychoanalytic viewpoint that I believe brings shame to the prismatic and fundamentally irreducible love a girl has for her horse.

I want alternative theories for my daughter. I believe the current understanding—the horse as phallus, the horse as practice for later heterosexual love—is not only wrong but—more problematically—damaging, transmogrifying a relationship packed with profundity of a highly unusual sort. And yet I've no choice but to admit that when I try to express what this profundity is, I come up tongue tied, stuttering, my head swirling with disparate images from my past; Rose riding Mr. K in the pasture stacked with cubes of hay; the glitter of the trees we raced towards; the flash of a stirrup, the resounding crack of her crop, rain on the roof of the barn, a deep-green show jacket lined with luminous yellow silk—thousands of images but nothing of substance to offer my daughter or any horse-loving girl. See her there, riding round and round the ring? See her, going in circles?

As for me, how odd to rediscover this love in my middle age, when I was so sure it had disappeared. Sometimes, during my daughter's lesson, I sneak off to the barn and whisper to the piebald pony, combing his blond mane with my weathered fingers. And then sometimes I simply walk the aisles, reading the nameplates affixed to each stall door. I have always delighted in the way we name our equines: *Smokey Raindrops. Pride's Starlight Tanya. A. M. White Night. Praise Be. World Peace. Lay Me Down. Amen.* And my favorite: *Sweet Revenge.* What do these names tell us? There are fourteen domesticated large land mammals—alpaca, cow, cat, goat, pig—to name a few, and I have never heard any of them referred to in such a, a . . . magisterial manner. Can you imagine a sheep called "Praise Be" or a dog called "World Peace"? The horse is the only domesticated mammal that can carry his ceremonial title; on

any other it sounds absurd; it breaks the back. Were the bond primarily sexual would not a girl pick a designation that reflected lust
rather than reverence? But what is this reverence made of, and why
do boys in the presence of horses seem not to feel it, or to feel it
less? I need to ride my mind back, and back, trying to find, in the
scraps of my own particular past, alternative explanations for the
bond between girls and horses.

So here I am, a girl of ten, then eleven, then twelve, a girl who
saw in the hugeness of a horse terror and beauty both, a girl who felt,
sitting up in that saddle, and only on my best days, that she had some
kind of connection with an absolute *other*, and the elation that went
with that, my body a bridge over which it seemed all the animals
could come. And they did come, Clara, in some dream sense they
did, and then later, back down on the ground, the ride now over,
I'd open my hand clutching carrot peels, apple halves, or even a dark
chunk of chocolate, the horse's limber lips taking it in, *all gone*, but
that small smear on my skin somehow proving it had happened,
proving I'd been freed, if only for a moment, from the prison that
a person is, my human halter off, my whole self dilated, trees and
teeth, fur and wind and every kind of weather pouring through me.

2: Fire

According to myth, Pegasus lived a brief and noble life on earth
before ascending to the sky, whereupon he atomized into a spray
of stars that bear his name as an immortal constellation. Thus, on
any clear night, you can look up and find him, his sequined eyes
staring at you from a vast blackness in which he is either trapped or
forever free, depending upon your view of infinity.

I find it ironic that the horse of all horses does not gallop on the
ground but rather lives his life amongst celestials, in a dark field of
silver florals. Because to me, in my mind, and for my body, horses
were the one, if not the *only*, way to tether my broken being to the
earth, from which it always seemed I was drifting, disassociated,
radically severed from self and soil.

Surely I was not born this way. I arrived on March 21, 1963. Of
my very early childhood I recall little, or little I wish to mention

here, for in this story of horses and history, my life, it seems, started one spring evening. I don't remember the date, but let's call it May 28, 1973, ten years after my actual birth and just at the cusp of the sweetest season—June—when the gardens drop their modesty and begin their driven bloomings.

I know on that evening I smelled summer coming right around the corner. At ten, I was cradled in the stage called latency, a peaceful time well past the throes of infancy and long enough before the next leap into adolescence.

And I was playing that evening in the church's empty parking lot, as I often did, with the children from a few streets over, let me call them the Callahans, a Catholic family and thus an oddity in the Golden Ghetto.

The Callahan kids were six in all, ranging in age from Mary, fifteen, who smoked and sulked in a corner of the lot, watching us younger ones with the slight sneer that teenagers perfect, to Joey, aged three, his face a splatter of Irish freckles, slurry always running from his nose.

We had a red wagon. It must have been the Callahans, and they must have left it behind in a hurry that evening because days later, after what happened had happened, the police found the wagon with Mary's bracelet inside it, her name inscribed on the silver plate.

The wagon had a long, black pull handle, and the body was rusted here and there. One wheel was loose on its axis, so it clattered crazily on the church's bumpy asphalt. Each kid took his or her turn pulling while the rest of us crammed into the cart and screamed with delight as we ricocheted around and around the empty church lot, the split-level houses across the street so silent, so stubbornly suburban, with their little lawns and little windows and dark doors. The world, it seemed, was emptied of everyone except the Callahan children and me, one kid pulling the rest, stuffed into the rusted red wagon circling the asphalt beneath a fiery sky, the streaked clouds painted pink and welt.

We had no notion that anything was or might soon be askew. Presiding over us was the gothic church with its windows of gorgeous glass that soared to the uppermost story, windows everyone in the Golden Ghetto, regardless of their religion, admired for

their artistry and size, windows we all presumed were fixed because they seemed far too big to open and close, and much too special for such prosaic purposes.

It was a Thursday. It could not have been much past 6 p.m.,
because I recall the setting sun, the svelte shadows on the cracked
concrete of the lot. Soon, we knew, our mothers would call us in
and so—would it be fair to say—we sensed our time was short?
We were, all of us—minus Mary blowing smoke O's into the cool-
ing air—crammed into this rusted wagon, the loose wheel making such a very loud sound, the person pulling (was it Andrea's
turn?) making a show of our enormous weight and her enormous
strength, groaning and spitting as she used all of her horsepower to
propel this mass of youth and laughter over the wrecked asphalt of
the empty lot.

And thus it was that we did not immediately hear the strange
sound, nor notice that one of those gargantuan and supposedly
forever-frozen stained-glass windows was moving, yes, *moving*,
inching out, and out, accompanied by a series of rusty bronchial
screeches that suggested, in retrospect, hidden, unused hinges on
every one of those supersized works of art.

"What's that?" I recall someone said, and then a "shhh," and
then, "Goddamn it, guys, *shut up*." That did it. Andrea stopped her
Clydesdale imitation, and, as if on cue, we all looked up, searching
for the source of this strange sound. And that is when we saw it,
the ten-, maybe fifteen-foot panel opening above us with a crackling, sickly creak that was still somehow strong enough to move a
giant Jesus through the air, his crown and cross captured in the cut
of glass and careful curves of lead.

I was sitting smushed up against slurry-nosed baby Joe, who
right then and there wet his pants, my pants soaking up his seepage and his smell. "Shhhh," someone said again as the window
kept coming, moving slowly out, and out, the late light landing
on the colored glass, inflaming it. "God," Andrea said, meaning,
I think, that she thought God was making the window move, but
I thought I saw the dark shadow of a person and a hand clutching
what could have been—must have been—a crank, and then the
crank cranked up and released the most unearthly rasp, a sound

arthritic and scraping, as though the Jesus pictured on the moving panel had begun to speak of his agony in the only way he could.

And the last of the light turned the blood of that approaching Jesus dark and darker still, until finally Jesus's blood was the color of gravy falling from his form. We all froze solid fear. Mary, who had been standing the entire time smoking and sneering in the corner of the lot, dropped her cigarette, just let it fall from her hand and then held her hand there, in the same stuck posture.

And now, appearing in the open window, the upper half of an old, old man, only a few wispy whites on his scraped scalp. The old, old man was wearing, I could see, a stiff white yoke around his neck, and when he stretched his arms towards us, his black robes billowed in the breeze. "Mary," the man said, and Mary's sneer fell from her face so quickly and completely I could practically hear it hit the ground, and her face turned soft and scared, both at the same time. "Joseph," the man now said to the boy crammed next to me, and then one by one he recited the names of those six Roman Catholic Callahan kids—his congregants every Sunday—from his ledge on high, the man's hands on the sill of a window gone wide, so Jesus entered the Golden Ghetto with all his horror and none of his purported peace. The old, old man pronounced the six names of the children he must have baptized at their beginnings, articulating each name with a purpose so pure and so mysterious that the names kept echoing in my mind all that evening, the man pointing with one rickety finger to each child as he titled them, declared them, and then, when he was done, his finger found me—the singular Jew and, for a reason I still today cannot say, a great fear filled me, perhaps because I did not want to be declared, could not be called by a man in billowing black, his finger fixing me to some barbed spot. I sensed danger—what danger? why danger?—the stained glass burning in the last of the light as he pointed straight at me, his eyes beaming blue beams until a bird blew by, breaking his gaze with a sound I could almost hear: sweet snap. I was free.

I ran. I ran away. I was at the edge of the parking lot when I heard the priest say to his congregation of children, articulating, again, each and every name as though their lives depended upon it: "Mary, Jim, Mark, Grace, Andrea, Joseph, go home. Go home now. It is late. Your mother must be worried."

Late, late that night I awoke to the smell of char, the sound of sirens, striped lights swinging across my wall. I fell back into the fastness of sleep.

The next morning, in school, our teacher told us that a fire had taken the Callahans' house and everyone in it as well. Only the mother, not home that night, had survived. Later, over days, the story seeped out. The children's bodies had been found by the windows, which were not double hung, but crank operated, the aluminum handles too hot to touch, melted beyond shape or function.

All gone. Every single child, plus their father, gone. Mary, Jim, Mark, Grace, Andrea, Joseph. I was ten years old, in the third grade, my mind too small for these six singular facts, and yet not so small that I could slam shut some door, or window. Their names. Mary's sneer. The pond-warm pee of a boy next to me. Gone now. And worse than gone, the going. How they must have clawed at the glass, flame-licked. The depth of human terror. Its persistent possibility.

For years after that I walked, once a month or so, by the site where their house had been, and, in my mind, a window all wrong, a man in black billows, a bird blowing by, my name not called, not called, not called. If every childhood has its defining event, this perhaps was mine, not the fire, not the enormity of the loss, although those figure in, believe me, they do. But the defining event, in the end, is not what happened, but rather what did not, and how close it came to being otherwise. My name not called. Myself, and yours, just a few little letters away from going Pegasus, who began as flesh but ended up astral. I was ten but also ten no longer.

I'm sure there are a thousand reasons for the fears that came to define me as definitively as my skin or my signature. I came of age in the 1970s and am old enough to recall the ending of the Vietnam War and the beginning of the nuclear era, missiles lining the banks of Europe, the threats, the button, a world emptied of people, a war where no one touches yet everyone dies.

Yes, a thousand reasons for the fears that waxed and waned but never left and instead, in their perpetual presence, became the beat by which I marched my way through life. For me, starting at the age of ten, life was about a *not*, a near miss, and thus I ricocheted between dodging dangers real and imagined while concomitantly clutching at whatever I believed could keep me safe. By the age of twelve I could list every elevator crash since 1923. I knew the date on which Charles Manson had become eligible for parole. I walked in fear and yet knew enough to mock myself, and thus my peers thought me quirky enough to be *almost* (but not quite) cool. In junior high's homeroom, during attendance time, when we were all sitting in rows, I would not infrequently whip out a thermometer and take my temperature just to get the giggles, making comedy out of neuroses too severe to stuff down.

Two years after the Callahan fire, my father received his inheritance, and we moved from the Golden Ghetto to a much plusher place, 219 Chestnut Street. There, we had a butler and a burglar alarm that included what were called panic buttons positioned at calculated intervals along the corridors. The panic buttons glowed at night, mandarin bars of light we were told to never, ever push unless there was an emergency. The panic buttons presented me with a continuous unsolvable philosophical quandary that to this day I have not solved: *unless there is an emergency*. The panic button presumes that there is life on the one hand, crisis on the other. I had a more integrated approach. Panic did not exist apart from life. It *was* life, and to this day I swear I'm right. The sheer *number* of ways things can go wrong in a trillion-celled human body held together by gossamer threads of good luck confirm for me my stance. There are no freak accidents in life, and how could there be if the entirety of life is *itself* the most outrageous incredible freak event we will all never truly understand, even as we stumble through it, doing our best to dodge the dangers. And in my mind there is always a priest in billows of black leaning out over the sill of a window. *Go home. Your mother must be worried.*

Amen.

On the subject of god, as a child, I was skeptical, but my mother was not. Where I wavered, she stood strong. Where I wondered, she knew. If personalities can be described as punctuation points, I was a question mark, half erased. She was an exclamation point, typed in toner so dark it bled through and blackened the fingers.

As for god's particulars, these my mother also knew. In fact, when she spoke of God it seemed she was so intimate with him that they'd just gone golfing or had a dinner out at the Capitol Grill. When there were wars—and the 1970s were *full* of wars or hijackings or kidnappings in the Holy Land or about the Holy Land—God, like Santa, always knew who was wrong and who was right, and he always told my mother, who always told us. Despite my doubts, I never went to bed unless I'd recited the Schmah at least twenty three times, in Hebrew, lights out.

This, I know, has nothing to do with horses, at least not on the surface. But beneath the surface, it was Judaism, or more specifically Zionism, that brought horses to me and also, ironically, prevented me from becoming the rider I so wanted to be, because, as my mother often repeated once the great affair had begun, "Lauren [all exasperation], Jewish people *do not* ride horses. They play tennis or golf."

There's probably some truth to this statement in the aggregate, but here's the problem: I was not the aggregate but rather some speck spinning within it. And the particular speck called Lauren (and *not* Mary, Jim, Mark, Grace, Andrea, Joseph) one day, sometime around the age of twelve, two years after the fire, well, that speck began to burn in a whole new way.

We travelled to Israel, my brother, two sisters, parents, and me, sometime after the Yom Kippur War. I don't remember much from this trip except a vague boredom and the tinted windows of tour buses. I do recall landing at the airport and how my mother, so stern, so *fisted*, how she bent down to kiss the ground and told us to do the same. I remember kissing Jewish ground, the smell of smog and soil combined. I remember seeing horses on the highways, so odd, the dusty, plodding equines side by side with peppy cars whizzing and tooting hysterically. This was Tel Aviv. The war was over, but still the streets were full of soldiers and Red Cross cars. My brother and I collected bullet casings on the Golan Heights, where the fighting had been fiercest. Inside one casing mysteriously speckled with black, I found a ladybug. I fed her from a secret stash of leaves. I brought her home within her home, snuck her through the airport search on one side, customs on the other. A few days later, back in the States, when I looked into the casing, there was not one ladybug but hundreds. How could this be? The bugs were tiny, each bright being the size of a pencil point, but growing day by day. I brought my cornucopia to the science teacher. She put her glasses on, peered inside and announced, "Babies," as though this were the most common thing in the world. Babies in a bullet shell. Babies from another world. Babies that had survived against all odds, in a place devoid of resources. At recess I took the shell outside and, kneeling at the far end of the schoolyard field, where the woods began, I tipped the bullet-nest downward, tapped on its copper bottom, and, after several delicate thumps, the whole infant galaxy slid into the moss. I couldn't find the mother though. I said an improvised prayer—*Good luck. Schmah y'Israel.* When I came back to check the next day, they weren't there.

When I think of Israel now, from the graying, worried age of forty-eight, I think of ladybugs in a desert. I think of blooms in bullet shells and the Golan Heights. I think of the bedouins we met, people in a warp, untouched by time. They wore long white shirts that billowed in the desert winds; they seemed to sail on the Sahara sand. They had horses.

I first fell in love with horses near the end of that trip, right before I'd found the ladybugs, so the two are entwined in my mind—*miraculous* and *equine*.

The bedouins' horses were unlike those we have here in over-fed, glossy America, where even our beasts gleam as though they've stepped from a Clairol commercial, their coats blow-dried and scented. The bedouin horses were predominantly tired, and when you touched their hides you felt matted fur. Flies sizzled in their eyes, covering the rims and lids. The bedouins offered tourists' children the chance to ride, for a shekel or two. In fact, if I'm remembering correctly, something like two shekels got you a camel ride; one shekel, a plain old pony. I wanted the camel, and we had the money, but on that particular day, the camel was tied up, quite literally, to a post, and for some reason out of commission. Thus I got my first ever horseback ride by default.

We waited, my mother, siblings, father and I, we waited for my turn by the flapping bedouin tents. The wind was roaring. Army planes flew in formation overhead. They flew wing to wing, made mischief with the clouds, darting in and out. Somewhere someone was singing, the sound so slender it could barely be heard. To the side of the tent clusters, a bedouin woman was washing fabric in a bucket and then smacking the drenched garments on stone. Why was she smacking the stone? Why did the planes fly above? Why do the clouds stay up but the branches fall down? Nothing seemed sure except a certain singular fact—the balance beam we're always on.

And there we waited for the bedouin to bring me the paid-for pony, my parents, my siblings, myself standing sun-struck in the desert, so still, we were, as though made mute by the intensity of the Sahara light, the heat, the white tents pinned to posts in the sand but nevertheless sagging and flapping in the wind while the woman fished bolt after bolt of bright cloth from a bucket, pulling from a seemingly endless source, like a magician coaxing handkerchiefs from his hat; the fabric kept coming. She kept wringing, as did my mother in our washroom at home, wringing the dirt from my soiled shirts, furious that it was there, wringing hanks of my hair, furious that they were there; wringing her two hands after one more fight with my father, furious that he was here, all of us kids gone mute, blinded by the bright light from the ice landscaping their marriage.

Where oh where was my horse? We waited by the white tents. I heard a tinny little tune but could not see its source. I felt a familiar leaden deadness smack in the center of myself. My breath rasped, in and out. Where oh where was my horse?

And then from behind the bedouin tent came a piercing cry, a continuous whinny that kept reaching its crescendo only to shatter the ceiling of sound and go higher still; some rage this horse had; I heard before I saw. And when the bedouin finally approached, he was not leading the horse so much as dragging him, the animal sitting back hard on all four heels. His equine legs were ramrod straight, his nostrils flaring. The horse was drenched in sweat, so wet the beast looked oiled, unreal, and when he came up close he let out a second kind of sound, a high pitched plea it seemed, a long, up-spiraling whinny of a cry, and from all four corners of the desert the answers bounded back.

And then, only moments later, the Sahara settled into silence again. "Ma neesh nah?" the bedouin asked, tapping on the monstrous saddle, but I'd changed my mind; no thanks. This was a horse who'd woken up on the wrong side of the stable, clearly, his eye rolling loose in his huge head. "Ma neesh nah?" the bedouin said again. "Lo," I replied, Hebrew for "no." But then the washing woman—she'd been watching the whole time I think—now she stopped her smacking and came over to me, her hands dripping, and in my memory my parents and siblings just go away, and that woman, well, she lifts me like a baby, her dripping hands under my arms, lifting me as though I am light and easy, she swinging me onto the saddle as someone whistles and we are off. I am hanging on hard to the greasy mane and, though it couldn't have been more than a slow trot, what I feel is the world break up in a bounce, the immutable, rock-solid stuckness of things become otherwise, the landscape chunked and piecemeal from the clunky gait, and my mind, for once my worried nattering *what will happen* mind, resolved into a particular point of concern, or concentration. All that mattered was to do what I would later learn the phrase for: *keep your seat.* That was it, sum total. All that mattered to that girl back then—and to maybe my girl now and, if I extend myself still further, maybe to so many of the girls groomed to groom, loving horses—all that mattered was to root myself to the animal, graft my rhythm to his, or vice versa. The concern is not over who gives, who takes, who leaves, who stays; the point is simply stay*ing* with, stay*ing* here; *here.* And suddenly there was a here, and the future fell away, what could or would or may, and truly time stood still.

"Did you have fun?" my father later asked. Did I have fun? *Fun?* No, I did not have fun. I was sore and chafed. I was gripped and gripping. I wanted one thing only and that was to try this thing again, this perched-on-a-precipice-hang-on-hard sport. This getting off the ground, and the subsequent return, refueled, full of thanks, enough so you could, of your own free will, become bendable, kneel down, and put your mouth to the mud in a kiss that no one called for.

But my mother—she was not happy. She had brought her brood to Israel for certain reasons. She had wanted us to improve our Hebrew and experience the feverish pace of a country determined to irrigate the desert. My father, although a paler creature than she, also had these hopes. My brother brought back from Israel an embroidered yarmulke, my eldest sister a prayer shawl, my youngest sister a miniature menorah. I brought back ladybugs no one knew about and an Arabian saddle blanket made by bedouins, who, of course, are *not Jewish*, never mind the Semitic similarities. My mother tried to toss that blanket. I insisted on sleeping beneath it.

Jews play tennis or golf, my mother always said. For this reason she forbade me riding lessons at first, hoping I'd come out East Coast-Jewish-country-club style. Perhaps the fact that I am ambidextrous is why that never happened.

I was a terrible tennis player. My siblings all got good at the sport, but, being ambidextrous by nature, I couldn't decide which hand to hold the racket in, and thus I didn't get past step one. While the other students at the country club progressed, I was simply stuck between two equally possible grips. When the coach quit on me, my mother must have seen her options dwindle.

The coach quit in March, and in April overnight camp material arrived in the mail. My sister chose a sleep-away called Ben Davide, the promo material picturing girls singing at the edge of a beach, their eyes all fastened on a colossal menorah adrift in a row boat on a large lake.

There were no menorahs anywhere in the pamphlets for the Red Fox Riding Academy or the Salisbury Hunt Club, both describing eight weeks filled with black boots and blue ribbons from the riding competitions that were at the heart of the camps' missions. My mother shuffled through these materials, shaking her head. I shuffled through, also shaking my head. Then Flat Rock Farm appeared in the pile. No fancy binders or calligraphed letterhead. *Flat Rock Farm* was typed on plain white paper spiral-bound into a simple notebook. I turned the page. Four or so cabins scattered on a grassy knoll. A red barn overlooking a field bordered by birches. A girl leading a pony by a raveled rope. Three girls bareback on a horse high-stepping through a rock-strewn stream, each girl hugging, the one in front hugging the horse hard, her ear pressed to a floss-soft mane, mink black. Slick stones. Sun slant.

There.

3: Flat Rock Farm

Here, the summer of 1974. The summer after the series of blizzards that buried the East Coast under so much snow. When the melt finally arrived, we found the pavement buckled and, come summer, cosmos bloomed in those cracks. In Maine, where Flat Rock Farm was, the fields were saturated all through July.

Flat Rock Farm. The entire camp consisted of twelve girls in a single cabin below the main farmhouse where Alice lived with her husband, Hank, and their daughter, Rose, the riding instructor and stable manager.

We went there in the Cadillac Seville. I recall a long, rutted road, tree-lined and shadowy, an arrow nailed to a post—*left here*— and then, quite suddenly, *space.* Verdant pastures as far as the eye could see. Mounded hills and horses high on them, the air so clear I could see across the acreage the blond plume of a palomino's tail, a Welsh star, a pair of stark white socks on lean legs.

We parked in a clearing and each of us emerged from the car's interior. My older sister, fifteen, her hair in a high ponytail, had come along for the ride. I saw her peer around, squinty eyed. Her tennis sneakers seemed a shining white against this verdant back-drop otherwise known as *where we stood*. A space of hills and horses and grass all headed to hay.

And everywhere, running about this space, swerving here and there, dashing around my sister and parents and me as though we were mere obstacles in an agility course—my sister and mother flinching when the contact came too close—were horse girls gone giddy from the thought of eight weeks immersed in saddles and straw, girls with scabbed knees and sloppy, unlaced sneakers laugh-ing, calling, pulling from their parents' well-kept cars stuffed duf-fle bags and knapsacks. The girls stomped across the soil in their muddy shoes, jodhpurs, and fancy show jackets slung over their arms. I heard new words: *Friesian*; *dressage*; *snaffle*. These words felt good in my mouth when I whispered them.

My mother, however, did not look good. My father seemed lost, just peering about, staying still in his spot. All around us were flies feasting on clods of fresh manure. Alice, wife of Hank and mother of Rose, was serving punch from a bowl on the lawn. My first view of Rose, I recall, was unremarkable. She was leaning lan-guidly against a fence post, her hemp-colored hair in a long braid over one shoulder. Rose looked young and lovely, the way you'd want your teacher to be. Meanwhile Alice ladled four drinks into Dixie cups for the clot of family we were, standing so tightly to-gether we must have seemed sealed.

"I take it you're Lauren," Alice said, and before I could answer she'd pressed a nametag to my chest.

I felt her hand against me. I saw her face, roughed up from wind and weather, somehow the skin still soft.

My mother set her the Dixie cup on the table. My sister peered inside hers. "There's a fly in here," my sister said. I looked. Yes, there were. Two flies, alive and struggling. Alice laughed.

"They won't harm you" Alice said. She looked at my sister. She looked at me. "Nothing here will harm you," Alice repeated.

Turns out, she was half right.

We had lessons twice a day, three hours in the early morning, two hours in the late afternoon, when the coolings came. The fact that I often recall less about those lessons than the events surrounding them speaks to the strangeness of the situation I would soon discover I was in. Our sheets were dewy each evening when we climbed into bed. The tarnished bell in the paint-peeled cupola tongued out the time when Hank tugged the old rope. The old rope, the old desk in the old office in the old barn with its closet beneath the hayloft, the door as dark as the wall, so it was almost invisible. Opening that closet door to get at its innards; the glycerin block for washing the tack; the fresh girths, the deep tin scoops with which to dole out grain for the feed buckets affixed to the stalls, their doors brass plated and inscribed with the twenty names of the twenty horses, many of whom I still recall: *One Precious Dot*, *Splash*, *Mister K* (Rose's favorite), and, yes, even Pegasus himself, all white except his withers, which where splattered with astral debris—splotches, spots, moons; on his haunches he carried an impression of the world's biggest bang—a horse with history on his hide.

Both Pegasus and Mr. K had dental issues and thus in that closet was also stored a separate equine toothbrush for each animal, the toothbrushes the size of pot scrubbers, plus an enormous tube of toothpaste flavored like sunflower seeds, a fact that we confirmed empirically. Twice a day Rose required that we brush K's and P's teeth, or get some other horse a new girth, or do this or that, so we were always hustling to and from that closet. This is why it did not take us long to find, hanging in the closet's back, an old show jacket lined with silk, silk slippery and cool no matter how high the heat. Who would not want to touch such fabric or not want to open the accompanying, and by contrast plain, plastic bag crammed with first-place ribbons in every hue of blue. Later, when I learned more, I imagined Rose shoving in the ribbons, punching them in in a fit of rage. Each ribbon we fished free stayed spastic, the kinks resisting the smoothing press of our palms. On their backs—Rose's name, a date scribbled on decades ago, but we never put our twos and twos together. Rose's blues in 1952. And then Rose now, in 1974, so lyrically lovely, especially in the evenings when she wore tank tops that showed her freckled shoulders.

Who could forget Rose? We guessed she was twenty-five, maybe twenty-six, but beyond that the guessing got hard. A boyfriend? College? She was princess pretty, with her long Rapunzel braid she'd at times let loose so we could comb the rippling river of her hair. "Girls," she'd sometimes say, apropos of nothing, "girls, I don't want to see you ever in makeup. You should let your natural self shine through."

As for Rose, she wore jeans ripped just right, and when she wasn't in boots she went barefoot, her nails nacreous against her trim tan feet. She could be in great good moods, laugh uproariously, tell us ghost stories, lend us her head and her hair, and at night we whispered about her boyfriends, who they were, and if they ever came around once we were asleep. We tried to picture Rose in cars with their soft tops down, above her the sky spattered with stars, or at college in a library by stacks of books, but no matter how hard you thought about Rose, there were always curves you couldn't get around. Almost every day, before breakfast, she would ride her favorite horse, Mr. K, through the fields, the sun a spotlight following them as they galloped, serpentining the spools of hay. One of the first stories Rose told us that summer, and then kept retelling us, was how she'd raised Mr. K from infancy. "I almost saw him born," Rose would say. "Eight years ago. I had a monitor by my bed, and I kept running to the barn every time the mare moved in this way. And each time, false alarm. I finally brought my blanket out there and slept in the straw so I wouldn't miss the birth. But I'd been up so many nights," Rose would tell us, "that, you know what, girls?" she'd ask, for the fifth, the sixth time. "You know what?" Rose would say and we'd all lean forward—*what?*—even though we knew.

"Mr. K was well on his way before I woke up. I was sleeping right there in the straw and I didn't hear a thing. And when I opened my eyes, there he was, more than halfway here."

We loved hearing Rose talk about Mr. K; how he whinnied before his hips were even freed, how the mare's milk bag was full but she kicked him away every time he tried to nurse, how he persevered and how, relieved of the pressure from her swollen teats, the mare relented, and love came, all mixed up with milk. But more than these specific stories, we loved that Rose loved to tell them, standing by the stall, Mr. K's heavy head resting in the crook of her arm, how she stroked his nose in time to the words, how he sometimes snoozed there. We loved to see this. And we loved to see Rose ride Mr. K, because it seemed incredible, how he changed from a sweet sleepy mammal to all elegance in his bridled attire, ears forked forward, tail held high as he raced the fields. Rose could take Mr. K from a squared stop to a full gallop with one simple word: *Now.* She had trained him to trot sideways, to pounce and pivot—human predator and equine prey flung from their fixed roles and deciding to dance together; for me it was proof that if—rule number one—the universe could be impossibly bad, then—rule number two—it could also be impossibly good.

And then there was rule number three: rules were unruly if you peeled back the bark and kept going. Nothing stayed still.

At night we often listened to their fights. "This is *insanity,* and that f'ing *garlic,* my god, Mother." Silence. Silence. Sile—"AND WOULD YOU STOP WITH YOUR HIGHER POWER?" In the listing farmhouse where Rose lived with her parents, we could often hear her voice, the snippets senseless and all the more riveting because they were so. Garlic? Higher power? We could hear Rose's father, Hank, like a plodding donkey: *"Let's respect each other now—"* and Alice: *"How could you? Why would you? That's IT."*

Our bunk, located just below their kitchen windows, meant for us front-row seats to a B-grade movie we had, at that point, no ability to really rate. As the summer progressed, so too did that family's misery. Twelve girls, we'd put our chins on the sills and listen.

As times passed, we learned the tempos. Sometimes the battles screeched to a stop, a brief beat of silence, and then hearty laughter, odd in its abruptness. Other times the opposite; on and on the fighting went, deep into the night, the pauses between outbursts growing longer, and then longer still, as though Alice, Hank, and Rose all had mechanical packs in their backs, the batteries running down until at last the charge was lost. Then an ominous silence settled over the house, and in the cabin, we'd eye each other with worry. I'd picture the family slumped in their separate chairs, resting like rag dolls.

We tried to guess why, the guesses growing wilder and wilder still. Now, thirty-some years later, I can't recall our tall tales; what's stayed with me are the details: Hank's slippers next to his reclining chair, Alice's crocheted pads arranged almost desperately on every armrest. Their staircase curved up into a shadowed second floor we were not invited to explore, and once a week the family's clothes dried on the line, Alice's incredibly large underpants, Hank's jeans, Rose's red bras and teensy panties flirting with the wind until Alice plucked them down, her mouth a tight line as she hurried inside, balancing the laundry basket on her hip. What's stayed with me is Rose's face the many mornings after a battle gone really bad, her skin the color of some sidewalk. She was in such a state the first time I saw her kick the paint pony, camp only one week old, and then also the next time, when she whipped the Welsh mare so hard a red seam opened in her hide. The high cry of pain. The pony, trapped on the lead line, rearing back, front legs dangling down: *Stop.* Rose stopped.

Except she didn't. Some horses were so scarred from her whip work that they had sunken spots in their hides where you could fit your finger in. We began to understand: these beatings happened, like wind or weather. We started to scan the sky.

We were twelve girls with twelve tongues, girls thick with gossip and giggles, but about the beatings, we did not speak.

I remember Splash, a large, baby-faced gelding who, smelling dinner on our very first trail ride, took off towards the barn no matter how hard Jenny yelled, "Ho there, Horse!" Back at the stable, Rose undressed Splash. She unbuckled his girth, slid the bit from his maw, slipped his halter over his head, hitching that halter to a hook anchored deep in the barn's main beam.

"What a bad, bad horse you are," Rose said.

At these kinds of times, her voice took on a little lilt, and she tongued the dentures she'd showed us just days before, when, without warning and during a ghost story she'd popped them into her palm, enjoying our sudden shock.

And now, with Splash, we could see her tongue her teeth; slip them from their sockets, the brief gap in her gum line, the sudden snap back in.

We knew. The horse knew. Rose brought out a long crop and flicked it towards Splash's face. His anus let go. "Stinker," Rose said. And then she did what she did, but this time no touch, Rose coming closer, slashing sideways so the horse must have felt that buzzing breeze, the edge of expectation sharper than any actual instrument. *Could* is such a wide word, composed completely of corners. Rose kept the crop at him, but always a skin-shaving away, here and there, now here. As for Splash, he wept, but not from pain—from *could*. He wept sweat and droppings. And we just stood there, dangled dryly. On and on Rose went, toying with this . . . pure possibility.

And all that night our sleep was slashed. I saw an angel in an orange grove. Her wings made a buzzing sound as she rose into the sky, mouth full of pulp; I snapped awake. The cabin was dusky with dawn just coming on; in the other beds were the bulky forms of girls on the move, girls deeply dreaming, troubled, tossing here and there.

Splash, huge in stature but delicate in psyche, got sick after that. We were, by then, ten days into camp—at most. But already every one of us girls had grown frightened of Rose, while we were also equally enchanted, numbed by some spell, the feeling as if for forever. Splash circled in his stall. He stopped eating. Dr. Fascal came out in her van. She put her ear to Splash's heft and listened. She pressed his sides and stomach. She used her stethoscope and let us hear his insides, the secret sounds of horses. "Maybe a torsion?" the vet said, clearly confused. Splash's bedding was matted and stunk from slurpy shit.

"Has his diet changed?" Dr. Fascal asked Rose. "Don't know, I mean, no. No," Rose said, stumbling in a way that was all wrong for her, eyes cast down. The vet left, with instructions. For the next twenty-four hours Rose massaged Splash's sides, sang him songs, slept in the straw so she could walk him on the hour. Had she answered Dr. Fascal smoothly, had she not slept in the straw, had she sailed instead of stumbled, we could have simply hated her.

Rose. Nothing simple. Sweetly pretty. She slept in the straw. She loved Mr. K. Every evening she bathed her horses; hose on, loofah sponge; she massaged each animal, humming as she worked, her feet bare in the sudsy runoff. She was a woman lovely to look at then, pale and vivid both.

It didn't take me long to map out Flat Rock Farm. Within days I knew how to find the pond, the pastures, the far field. Within the first week I'd seen the whip work and adjusted to my mandates. The goal, Rose told us over and over during the group lessons that dominated the day (we were taught all together despite differences in our abilities, and I was the least experienced rider at the camp), the goal for every rider was to practice balance by finding the body's core. One must not grip the mane or reins: balance was *ultimately* a matter of mind.

And also, I discovered, a matter of physical work, so different from the cerebral pursuits of school. Each dawn at Flat Rock Farm Alice fed us warm biscuits, then sent us to the stable for scheduled chores just as the day became blue. We took up pitchforks, wheelbarrows, brooms. Balance could also be found in labor, in the repetition of small tasks that occupied the body as they freed the mind. We learned to wash the tack. We climbed ladders, crawled into the cupola with a rag and a tin bucket. Once inside that cupola, I found an intact but dead dragonfly. Its body glinted green, like the ones I'd seen in the woods. The wings were netted and reminded me of the nylons my mother wore. How odd, something similar between two species that shared next to nothing. And yet, maybe the spaces between them were not so great. Weeks went by. I learned to balance on the broad back of a horse. As I did I found I could do more than just hold on. I found I could talk to the horse with my legs, my hands, my weight, and that the horse, in turn, could talk to me.

Reassuring, yes. Apparently nature had these built-in bridges, and who knew how far they could go? If a thousand-pound, hard-hoofed beast could understand you, and vice versa, well then, who or what could not? Horses proved that there was no such thing as an impossible conversation.

I think we came to Flat Rock Farm for this impossibly possible talk. We were all girls between eleven and sixteen, but the gaps in age were irrelevant here. All the ordinary dividing lines dissolved: old/young/fat/thin/pretty/ugly/well-dressed/slob/rich/poor. Here all girls were equaled by shoveling shit and putting in bits. When everyone stinks, no one does.

While Freudians posit that girls are drawn to horses as a form of heterosexual practice (in both its private and public manifestations), maybe the opposite is the case. Perhaps girls are drawn to horses because these grand animals provide girls a rare opportunity to be together, as females, *unsaddled* by cultural conventions. At Flat Rock Farm, Jenny, the fat girl, was friends with Theresa, the prom queen. I remember one rest hour going to the barn, all twelve of us girls, and finding there in the back tack room an old trunk.

"Open it up," Emily whispered.

Outside it was high noon, glaring and hot, but inside the tack room the air was dark and quiet, the saddles on their mounts looking haunted, their shape suggesting a rider we couldn't see.

We opened the trunk. It was from another century, lined with crumbling floral paper. In there we found a black-and-white photograph of a stern, slim woman sitting high on her high horse. With one hand she held the reins, in the other a bouquet of roses. Beneath her a judge was pinning a ribbon and rose to her horse's bridle.

We found flouncy skirts held up by hoops; jodhpurs padded with threadbare suede; boots that laced up the front with tiny tarnished fishhooks; a postcard showing a massive ship, its prow raised above the wild waters of what must have been the Atlantic, on the backside someone's spidery script, impossible to read except the end: *Love to you all, to the farm, to Lady—Moi.*

"'Moi'?" whispered Amy.

"'Me' in French," whispered Jenny, holding the card, turning it over and over.

"Why are we whispering?" shouted Theresa.

All twelve of us girls jumped as though we'd been stuck with a cattle prod.

"Shhhhhhhhhhhhh!" said Jane. "Jesus!"

"Look at this," said Elizabeth, and she pulled from the trunk a straw hat banded by a cucumber-colored ribbon; she put it on.

That was the beginning. Someone else pulled on the old black boots, another girl the once-white skirts. That trunk had no end; from its interior came more and more clothes, came pearls and brooches, hard hats and sun hats, multiple corsets with ribbon and eyehooks, crumpled kid gloves. Despite the heat, we shucked our standard uniform and dressed ourselves right out of this world, and when we were done, we walked around, bowing to one another, admiring.

Not long ago, Amy Brisbee, a girl who'd been at Flat Rock Farm during the same summers I was, e-mailed me a picture of us dressed up in the mystery clothes from the old trunk. "Remember this?" Amy wrote. "I found it in my dresser drawer." The picture, scanned in, was grainy but unmistakable; there we were in various stages of Victorian regalia, behind us the saddles and the sunbeams through the shuttered windows, our real clothes visible in piles on the floor. "Who could forget?" I e-mailed back. But there is one part I did forget, or maybe never knew: Who had taken that picture? Not Amy, because I found her. I found everyone, following form after form with my finger. All twelve of us accounted for. "Who gave you the photo?" I asked Amy, and she wrote back, "Don't know." Was someone looking in on us from outside, perhaps peering between the shutters; someone spying. Hank? Rose? Someone seeing.

That picture is remarkable for the way it captures a group of girls at play, in whim, but it is more remarkable if you realize we were so absorbed we never knew we were being watched. Or if we knew, we didn't care, and thus forgot. We were twelve girls learning to do the work of womanhood—the shit-smeared feeding, cleaning, muscle-aching labor of loving an animal dependent upon you and *not* losing yourself in the animal. In fact finding yourself in the animal and all the associated tasks of care, shaping as you were shaped.

Practicing. Twelve in all. Girls, learning our mothers' lives were not our future's only form, and that, unlike those older women, we need not be diminished by the need to nurture. Twelve girls. Washing the tack on Sundays, cleaning the cupola on Mondays. We grew so strong those summers. Twelve girls freed in our faux corsets. Standing sure, we were. Learning. "My, you look lovely, madame."

That I was the worst rider at camp seemed more a matter of character than skill, a fact that I accepted with an odd equanimity. My heels flew up; my reins tangled. I kicked when I should have squeezed, squeezed when I should have kicked. When the other girls cantered, I had to move my mount to the center and stand idle. Sometimes my mounts, probably bored beyond reason, would lift their heads and let loose a plaintive whinny, or a deep soft nicker, as though chuckling to themselves over me, the clumsy one who belonged in a Schul, not a saddle.

The fact is, my bloodline was entirely irrelevant. Religion did not hold me back; philosophy did. I rode like I lived, and vice versa: in a state of foreboding. What so scared me up there? Was it that I could feel, though the thick wedge of saddle, the orchestration of many muscles moving me, so I was moved, a passive person, a rider only in name? Or was it simply the gap between me and the ground, that descent decorated night after night with tales of horse lore as we lay in our beds; someone knew someone who had died going down, her neck snapped when the horse bucked her off, or worse, *had we heard*, or still worse, *there had been . . .* In the dark girls swapped stories, the purpose of which seemed to be to tether us to horses through terror, like a frightening film one can't wait to see. I'd cover my eyes one second, peek out the next.

What is the purpose of loving what haunts you, of returning, time and again, to terror, or its kinder cousin, fear? What is the story here? Well, for starters, there appears to be no single story when it comes to girls and equines. Terror on the one hand, reassurance on the other, and then we run out of hands, but not contradictions. What is wild and domestic both? How can you find the ground by learning to leap? How can you hate what you love? Some researchers posit that the female brain has a thicker corpus callosum than does the male brain. What might this mean? In the female brain there could be more fibers connecting the separate hemispheres, so left and right swap stories, blend concepts, come closer. Male brains, in a vastly generalized sense, are better at keeping their twin bins on separate sides of the shelf, verbal here, spatial there, image to the right, logic the left, tears east, talk west. Male brains in general don't court inconsistencies, while the female brain seems to be built for these. Obviously there are abundant exceptions, but let's look for a moment at the mass. Horses, their mass, one thousand pounds on average. Horses, piebald or chestnut, stubborn or sweet, stallion or mare—either way all this bulk and its associated contradictions may fit with more ease inside the circle of female skull.

Maybe this is why—short on talent, constantly criticized—I still went back (we still went back), lesson after lesson. Possessing a brain built to perceive paradox, females, or some subset, may find a resonant focus in the horse. In my own particular case, add in the sole certainty of uncertainty that is part and parcel of every equine encounter, along with an entrenched tendency to see a universe ringed by risk, and what better way to practice my perseverance, to entertain my compulsions?

But what I was mostly chasing up there, I think, was what I'd found that first day on the Bedouin pony—a total concentration, both a focus *and* a frame for my fear. And when that happened— focus and frame—I got just what I wanted. The click came. I cantered and forgot to call it cantering. There were two beings but one beat. I started streaming.

And when the ride stopped, the horse stopped, the rhythm stopped, when I slid off the animal and slipped back into the singular, then for a little while objects appeared brighter, sounds suggestive of worlds beyond themselves, a simple sip of water—like drinking diamond. It is hard to hold such joy. Its brimming feels nearly painful, but not quite. No one else knows. The day is as ordinary as country cotton. The milk is as it always is, tinged bluish in the bottle. And yet you look here and there you see new angles in the day, every person a prism. The grass a thick impasto. Horses look different too when you are saturated with such joy, already leaving now, its life span shorter than a fruit fly's but still enough so you can see the animal anew.

"Doesn't it seem weird," I said to Aggy as we stood by the pasture fence, the lesson over, the click clicked, "doesn't it seem really weird that horses could kill us in a second if they wanted to?"

"Yeah," said Aggy, her hard hat still on. She took it off, dangled it by its strap.

"Every single time we tack up, and ride a horse, they could trample us, or buck us off; they could kill us in a second," I repeated. I paused. The wind made the sweat on my scalp tingle in a wonderful way. "But they don't," I said. "I mean, even though they have the strength to really harm us, they hardly ever do. We put on their saddles, put in their bits, tighten the girths, sit on their backs, even a two-hundred-pound man could plunk down on their backs, and in just a second any of these horses . . . they could decide to just throw us off and stomp us to pieces. It would be so easy for them. But for some reason, they, every time, they don't do that. . . . Instead of killing us," I said, trying again, "horses choose to . . ." I couldn't find the word.

"Move us," Aggy said.

"Yes," I said. Precisely.

There were two babies—Jack and Jill—who, said Rose, were ready for "breaking." I had scant knowledge of what "breaking" meant, how, for years men had believed the best way to tame a horse was to sap its spirit. In pursuit of this, men used—and many still do—methods that make one wince, the pictures preserved in books. Here is a mare with her lips sewn shut, here a stallion, hung upside down, his eyes full of terror, his hoofs pawing at air.

Humans have used great cruelty in trying to tame the horse, this despite the great gifts the animal has given. For the thousands of years since horse and human first struck up a relationship, we have been blessed with a beast that, while of nature, has enabled culture to proceed in ways that would have otherwise have been impossible. Horses have aided people in thousands of ways that include ameliorating autism to enriching the soil from which our nation's crops grow, year after year after year. A single horse daily sustains its massive bulk on a mere eight hundred calories of stringy vegetation otherwise known as weeds and then, from its internal factory, spins out, *daily, reliably,* pounds of manure so rich in organic matter it can practically turn friable asbestos into a rich and rot-black loam. And anyone who has ever tilled manure into a failing field, and seen it yield a crop of pungent lacy herbs and scarlet vegetables knows, they know, what a horse is worth in this world.

Surely Rose knew, because her family survived in part by farming; Flat Rock Farm's pastures were ringed by harrowed fields from which Hank grew and sold broccoli, squash, corn whose husks you could peel back before the time was right and see the pale kernel pattern slowly going saffron, ripening in late July. We'd tasted this corn, husked it when the cobs were much too tiny, eating these starchy embryos with only the frailest tang of what would soon be its sweetness.

On July 15, 1974, Rose pulled on fringed batwing chaps and a showy platter of an oversized cowboy hat—an outfit entirely out of character as in general she was a hunt seat rider—and, along with Hank in steel-toed boots (how odd, his sudden switch)—they went in search of the colt Jack, whose turn it was for "training." "Rope 'im in, Dad," Rose screamed that day as Jack fought the knot that brought him to his knees. Together Hank and Rose tied Jack up in what Hank called a Scotch Hobble, bringing the hind leg up and tying the rope to a post so Jack couldn't move or change positions: pinned, he was, in place. And so the horse stood there, trembling on three legs while Rose and Hank left him like that and we girls whispered, watching from the tree line: *let him go, how, no why when,* and too soon the heat claimed the day completely so by noon the colt was drenched in sweat and they came back. Hank untied Jack, distracting him with his escape-about-to-be while Rose sidled up and jammed the bit into his soft maw. Jack's eyes rolled up, his slab of tongue clamped completely down under this bit made especially for breaking, studded with small tacks. For four days Jack, a breaking-to-bridle horse, wore this bit so when it came out his tongue was toughened and his mouth was ready for snaffles, kurbs, cumberwics, hackamores, or any of the other hundreds of possible bit types without which control would not be possible. For four days we heard Jack's cries, watched as he was roped and reeled, hour after hour, Rose's face blank, her eyes oddly empty as she cracked the crop so hard Jack's hide opened up and red ran down his withers.

On July 15, Jack got broken. On August 15, one month away, Jill would follow. We dreaded this date, but maybe because we were children, or maybe because we were immersed in our chosen passion, we trotted on, centaurs, slipping between forms and foci.

As for time, it turned over. Our faces tanned; our muscles thickened. I was still the weakest rider, even as I got stronger. I learned to trot, and then at last to canter, more or less. Three days after Jack, Rose scrawled a star on the stable's whiteboard, which held our schedule: *July 21st.* No explanation written beneath. What? we wanted to know. "That's the day," Rose said to us, "when you all will learn the secret and *essential* equestrian skill."

What secret skill? Why essential? And were we really *all* going to learn it, or only the advanced riders?

"Every one of you," Rose said. "The secret skill does not depend *upon* experience. It *creates* experience." Beyond that, Rose wouldn't drop a clue.

July 21 came, breakfast as usual, barn as usual, tacking up, riding into the ring, all as usual, but then, once we'd assembled, Rose walked to the far end of the ring, unlatched the back end gate, the one we never used, kicking hard so it swung open on screechy hinges, rasping the unmowed meadow beyond. We never entered that meadow, unkempt, clotted with vines, lined with cherry trees and their droplets of red fruit. But now, without saying a word, Rose walked into this thick field as she beckoned over her shoulder for us on our horses to follow. Bees fussed with flowers. Rose kept beckoning. The grasses were hip high, and when we rode through the whole world was filled with silken sounds.

And then, at last, our teacher stopped, and when she spoke her voice seemed thin in the hugeness of the space. "Form a circle around me, girls." We did, maneuvering our horses into position. "Now," Rose said, standing in the center so we could hear her better, "you can't really learn to fly unless you learn to fall." She paused for a moment, as though to let this statement sink in, her hands clasped dramatically beneath her chin, and that's when I noticed she was wearing her hard hat, uncommon only because she wasn't riding, so why would she have it on?

"Know what I mean?" asked Rose.

"I've fallen plenty of times," said Aggy.

"I'm sure you have," said Rose. "But have those falls been orchestrated? Or have they been just . . ." and here Rose paused, searching for the words, "just chaotic attempts to cope?" Again Rose paused, appeared to be thinking and then added one word: "Retrospective."

Rose and Aggy stared at one another for a few moments, and then Aggy shrugged.

"Come on" said Rose, suddenly striding over to Aggy, who was riding Oh Gosh! that day. "Down with you," Rose said. "Time for a demonstration." And now Rose gently knocked one of Aggy's feet from the stirrups. "C'mon," Rose said again. "I'm going to show everyone how."

This was a rare event, an illustration during a lesson. For Rose, riding seemed to be an essentially private activity, mostly between her and her beloved Mr. K. It seemed to be like praying, her church the mowed fields behind our bunk, where the spools of hay were.

Aggy dismounted, went to sit on a nearby rock, while in a seemingly effortless little leap Rose cleared the back of the fifteen-hand gelding and settled herself into the saddle like it was an easy chair, getting deep down in it, angling back, then stretching her hands high, high towards the sky, fingers interlaced, the clear cracking sound of knuckles and neck. "Feels good up here," Rose said and smiled at us. That was the first I noticed it, something off, or wrong about her smile, something slightly tilted, like a bike when it begins to wobble.

Now, Rose patted Oh Gosh's neck, then picked up the reins. "It's been a long time since riding you, buddy," Rose said to the horse. The horse seemed unsure of what to think. His ears went forward, then back. Rose poked them with her crop. "Don't pull an attitude on me, my man," Rose said. At that, Oh Gosh's ears shot forward and the horse—you could practically see the ripple of transformation, his slack muscles tensing, his head lifting, his eyes filling up with fear and focus both. His tail, swishing back and forth. Back and forth.

We moved our horses off to the side. Rose picked up the reins. "Now," she said, "you can *always* fall off a horse." She smiled, looked at me. "That's what makes it fun, right?"

I smiled, nodded yes, felt no. Something had shifted the moment Rose got on that horse, but what or why I couldn't say. My lips were cracked and dry.

"It's possible to fall when you're at a walk," Rose continued, now walking a highly alert, energized, anxious Oh Gosh! in circles. "It's not likely," she continued, "but the horse might stumble and you might—" and then, with a whoosh, Rose slipped from the saddle and landed, feet first, on the ground—". . . fall," Rose said, ending her sentence on two feet. "If you fall at a walk, you've got time to go feet first, or what I like to call birth backwards." She smiled.

She climbed back on Oh Gosh! "I was born backwards," Rose said. "I came into this world and landed right on my feet. Almost killed my ma," she said and laughed a harsh, brief laugh, and then stopped, suddenly. "All right girls," she said, "enough about that. It's the trotting, cantering, or galloping falls that really matter. Fact is," Rose said, "the human head is a highly important piece of the machinery, so you gotta protect it. If you land on your head and don't kill yourself, you could wind up no better than a string bean. Hats are good," Rose said, "but not enough when you're coming off an animal going up to forty miles per hour.

"Unless you like string beans, of course," Rose said, and then laughed again, looked up, her mouth slightly open, as though swallowing some sun.

We were all listening, looking, lined up, quiet on our mounts. "Falls never happen in a snap," Rose said. "They're a *process*. Do you understand? A *process*. First, your feet come out of the stirrups. Or

maybe you lose one stirrup, and then the other. This isn't like falling from a tree, or a building. A fall from a horse is *unique* because
you have *prior clues*, and so you always have the chance to *plan* it."

All the time Rose was talking she was walking Oh Gosh! in
fast circles before us. She seemed to be talking half to us, half to
herself. She was grinning, enjoying her lecture, almost tickled, you
got the feeling. "How lucky is that?" said Rose, turning her head
towards us. "How often do you get to plan your own downfall,
huh?"

Now, Rose moved Oh Gosh! into a slow, tight trot, working
her reins on him, drawing his whole body up and inwards, insisting on both intense energy and its fierce control. The horse was
starting to sweat, high stepping, Rose sitting deep down in the
saddle, keeping contact, conversation through her slow seat and intricate rein work. "And because you can plan your fall," Rose said,
her voice trotting right along with her body, "you've got time to
remember to put your arm out to the side of your head, like you're
sleeping on it, so when you hit the ground, you break your funny
bone but not your brain." She pulled Oh Gosh! to an abrupt stop.
"Got that?" she said, eyeing us one by one down the line. "Is this
making sense to you?"

We all nodded. Yes. It was.

"Let me tell you a little story," said Rose. "Horses are in my
blood. My family's been riding all the way back to my great-great-
great-granddaddy Lindquist, a German."

"A German," Rose repeated, as though this had some special
significance. My great-great-great-granddaddy Lindquist had a
terrible temper, so I've heard, and wound up an old man screaming
at invisible elves. But he was supposedly one heck of a rider when
he was still a gentleman, and that talent got passed on down and
down until it was Alice's turn to take it on. Bet you didn't know
that. My mama, Alice, was nearly Olympic," Rose said. She was
talking, and then she urged her horse forward again with a velvety
cluck, a quick tight trot, Rose looking at us as she circled, checking our faces, seeing we were rapt.

"Nearly," said Rose, huffing a little now. "As it turns out, *nearly*
is as far on the map from *is* as North to South. So when I was born,

and I got the gift, Alice wanted me to take her *nearly* North life and find my way South, to the *is-land* of the Olympics," said Rose. "And I got the gift."

Then Rose paused for a long time in her tale, kept riding the horse round and round, posting up and down, her jaw working, tense. "Thing is, girls," Rose finally shouted as she went round, "thing is, you can have the gift, but that's got not a lot to do with *the prize*. Prizes and gifts, they're different things. Alice trained me from my first cry to go Olympic, but I got tired of the training, got tired of the winning, because you know what's on the other side of winning?" Rose asked, and then, before we could answer she yelled, "Losing. I got high up there, got a lot of ribbons, all blues, mostly. I even went to England, but I was going gold," said Rose. Her voice kept rising with every slow circle she trotted. "Going gold, like Midas himself, ever heard of that story? I couldn't see my life. I wanted a life, you know, college, clothes. Of course, a horse, too. But just for me and . . . my kids," Rose said. "Horses are huge, but riders, they come in different sizes. I didn't want to be huge. But I didn't want to let Alice down either," Rose said. "She's makes damn good biscuits, but she's a bitch to disappoint, let me tell you, girls. You don't cross Alice; you don't mess with her doilies. So, know what I did? I learned how to fall off a horse going fast, so I had a guaranteed goof at the Olympic tryouts. And it worked. It worked!" She laughed in a choppy, all-wrong way.

And then, she pulled Oh Gosh! in, squared him to another tense stop. "It worked," she said again, softly. "I'm living proof."

"Wow," said Jenny.

Rose bent into a small bow atop Oh Gosh! "Good story, huh?" she said.

"Great story," said Jenny. "The is-land."

"You like?" said Rose. "I've been told I have a way with words."

We all nodded then, fast and hard.

"South, North, nearly, the story, the symbols . . . they're kind of clever," Rose said. "I sometimes think I should write about my life. She turned to me. "What do you think, Slater?" she said. She'd seen me scribbling in my notebooks.

I opened my mouth, but nothing came out. "So," I finally said, "so you were gonna go Olympic?"

"Is that what I said?" Rose asked, narrowing her eyes on me.

"Yes," I said, my heart skittering around. "You could have gone Olympic." And then, suddenly, I found what words I wanted. "You could have, Rose," I said. "Maybe you didn't want to, but you could have. I can see that. I can tell; you're *that* good. I bet you always have been."

Suddenly, something swerved in Rose's face, a subcutaneous shadow. "Is that what you see?" she said softly. She touched her face then, pressed the bone beneath the eye, as though trying to sense something about herself. Then she gestured widely. "Girls," she announced, "don't believe a word I say."

We heard her say that. We heard the wind teasing the trees, the squirrels bothering the bark, their nails tap tapping the thick skin of the oaks as they scampered.

"Come on," said Jenny. "No fair."

"I'm not here to be fair," said Rose. "I'm here to teach."

"Teachers tell the truth," said Em, who, at eleven and three-quarters, was the youngest in our group.

"That's right, Emily," Rose said, gently now. "They do. So let's get back on track. Let's stop with the stories. Cleverness is a distraction."

And then, Rose pushed with her seat and Oh Gosh! began his high, hard walking again.

"Back to falling," Rose said. "Here's how it happens."

Theresa raised her hand.

"Yes, ma'am?" said Rose.

"So, you're going to show us how . . . right now?" said Theresa.

"How what?" said Rose.

"How to fall," said Theresa.

"Right now," said Rose

And then Rose pushed Oh Gosh! back into a slow trot. "But as long as I'm demonstrating this for you," said Rose as she posted past us, her voice rising and falling with her body, "I'm gonna go full force. Because I'm only gonna show this once. This isn't the sort of thing you do every day," she said, and now she had Oh

Gosh! extended into a canter, so in order to speak to us she had to shout as she streaked by, and still, her voice seemed like glass, smooth and unbroken, her sound and her skin separate, one on the run, one standing, terribly tethered. And as the horse kept cantering, she reached up with one hand, unsnapped her hat, and tossed it to us like we were bridesmaids catching a bouquet.

Except we weren't. And the hat, it sailed well over our heads. We heard it thunk down somewhere deep in the distance of the field behind us.

"That's against the rules," yelled Aggy.

"You're right," Rose yelled back, because she was clear across the field now. "But I'm at a point in my life where I make the rules, so I can break them."

Rose slowed Oh Gosh! down now, brought him back to where we were, still mounted on our horses in a line, Oh Gosh! trotting a tight tiny circle in front of us. "I'm doing this just to show you how possible it is to be totally head-safe on a horse, if you've got your technique correct. The hat's gravy," Rose said, squeezing with her legs so Oh Gosh! cracked into a canter again, and she streamed, yelling backwards, "What's essential is your know-how."

I heard her cluck, then, and Oh Gosh! stretched into a still faster canter, and then, somehow, at some point hard to define, he crossed the line into a full-fledged gallop, the pounding sound, the blur of her body passing, faster and faster they went, circling, Rose urging him on, high up on his neck like a jockey, flicking her whip just enough to tease him into terror, he flew, that horse, and we sat there, stone silent, overtaken, our own fear rising now, because she was going to do this, somehow, without a hat. She'd said she would but when? When? When? They kept circling, and just when it seemed there could be no more speed they acquired yet one more measure of it, the gelding's legs almost entirely off the ground, and then she did it, pitched off, curled up, arm out, she didn't fall first; she flew first, pushing herself off the horse so she soared for some number of feet, she was *flying*, I swear, I saw a person fly without wings, and then she went down, landing without a sound in the plushest part of the grass fifty, one hundred feet from where we were, Rose going down in the deepest blades and bachelors buttons at the other end of the meadow, in a field so thick with growth we couldn't see her, and Oh Gosh! raced on until he realized he'd lost her, and then he slowed, slowed, slowly stopped, stood still, his head cocked, confused.

"Rose," Emily called.

No answer. "Rose!" she called again, louder now.

Again, no answer.

"Holy shit," said Jenny.

We kept staring at the place we'd seen her fall, who knew how many yards from us, from where we were, in that high meadow grass. We kept waiting, like when you see a person go under water, waiting for them to come up, and if they don't, and if you love them, you also don't come up, for a long, long time.

Without speaking, almost as if driven by a singular force, we each and every one of us dismounted. We knew, *knew*, a person doesn't fall off a galloping horse, no hard hat even, and be okay. Be even alive. And as one, a single line of girls, we left our horses standing still, reins slack, stirrups down, we left our horses standing there and moved across the meadow to where we'd seen her soar and then sink, and then we were there, in those high green and golden grasses, which we parted—no Rose—and then again—no Rose—and then again, increasingly frantic, parting the grasses over and over to finally find, down at the cooler base of the blades, not Rose, but just one lone black boot.

Now, this was starting to seem . . . what? Without talking, again, as one mind, we moved forward, parting the waist-high water of meadow *again*, only no Rose, no Rose, no Rose, and it wasn't until we started making sound, real sound, screaming "Rose! Rose! Rose!" that we heard her relaxed, velvety chuckle, and we whipped our heads around. "Rose? Rose?"

Again, that chuckle. Jenny was holding the single black boot by its rim. Rose was sitting on a rotting log at the edge of the field, eating an apple. At first, all I could think was, "Where did she get that apple?" And then she stood up and stretched in a casual way and said, "See how fine I am? Where's Oh Gosh!?" At which point Jenny hurled the black boot at her and Rose caught it, expertly. "Don't be crabby," Rose said.

"You scared the *fuck* out of us," said Jenny, her voice low and serious in a way I didn't know she could sound.

Scared. Scared the fuck. The fuck. Scared. And finally the extraneous curse word dropped away and the core word remained, repeating in my head: *scared.* I kept saying that word to myself and at the same time hearing it was already in the past tense. The *ed* of its ending was a footfall, an underline. The past tense. And it was at that moment I realized I hadn't really felt afraid, until now. *My* fear was in the present tense, even as for the other girls it moved into the background as Rose explained her trick, explained it was a well-practiced move, aiming herself for the softest spot in a field she knew as well as the palm of her hand, having lived by it all her life, protecting her head with the bushels of hay she'd laid down, and her own arm, of course. As for the boot, well, she'd slid it off and crept to the log, under the cover of the tall grasses, her form diminished by distance.

The girls began to laugh. Far, far away from us, we saw all our abandoned horses, still in tack, lazily munching the meadow. Rose had made her point. You could survive almost any speed, almost any situation, with enough practice and finesse.

We brought our horses back to the barn, untacked, ate lunch, lay down in our bunks to rest. "Oh my god," the girls kept saying. They whispered words like "talent," "incredible," "outstanding." Jenny, leaning over her top bunk and talking to Theresa on the bottom, was explaining that great riding was like any great art, which was frequently accomplished through superior insanity, Van Gogh's severed ear a case in point. Aggy, more cynical, said, "I think she'd bite off a horse's ear before she'd whack off her own, if she went totally crazy," and Theresa said, "Kids, she already *is* totally crazy, which contributes to her genius." For the first time, I felt separated from those girls. I wasn't impressed. I may have been enraged. In my head, I got the point. But in my heart, I kept seeing that single black boot, the shock of her absence, how the space where she should have been seemed to pulse, even ooze, with sunlight. I kept hearing her throaty, undulating chuckle, the rich, velvet creep of it on me. In me. I kept seeing how she popped up where she should not have been, at the edge of a field, on a soft rotting log, and that's what kept going through my mind, this phrase: *Where she should not have been. Where she should not have been.*

I knew what was coming next. Next, we'd all have to learn to fall, at the speed appropriate for our skill level. And all the girls would learn to do it, because that's the way they were. Except for me. I knew I'd flat-out refuse, in flat-out fear, but also because of other things. Stubbornness. Anger, maybe. Maybe even rage. All mixed up with wanting.

I was right. The next day, and the day after that too, the girls minus me, going after genius, or simply trying to please, the girls went down to the ground, stood, shook, the dust flying from their clothes, their hats, their hair. A giddiness rippled through the camp. At night, in the cabin, the horse stories changed. They were no longer about death, but about situations survived. For the first time in a long time I thought of the Callahans' fire, two, three years behind me now, something not survived. The sound of the sirens at night. The smell of char. Six children clawing at the windows. Six children and their father falling deeply into death. Every once in a while, after all their deaths, I'd caught sight of Mrs. Callahan walking through town, totally alone now, her coat blowing open, her devastated face drained. Over the years, the mother of those six seemed to grow paler in skin while her hair turned preternaturally dark, her lips more vivid. Eventually, we stopped seeing her. She must have moved, maybe to Florida, my mother had said. Or to Texas.

"What's up, Lauren," Aggy finally said to me one night, late.

"Yeah," said the others. "What's wrong? You used to always talk." I could hear them rustling up on their elbows, looking towards me in the dark.

"You'll get it after a while," said Theresa. "I mean, we've been riding for years."

"Yeah," said Jenny. "You'll get the falling trick. And as soon as you do, you'll go intermediate. Personally, I wish someone had taught that to me way back when I was just a beginner."

"You'll get it," the other girls said.

"I know," I said. But I didn't. I didn't know much. I didn't know why I'd dreamt about an angel with buzzing wings, or why air, which you needed to live, fanned fires that killed you to a crisp, or why I kept seeing that single black boot in the space where she should have been but wasn't. I didn't know why I was affected one way, everyone else another. I didn't know then that some people are just that much more likely to see in a shared story darkness, where others see stars. I didn't know that, nature or nurture, some bodies, some brains, are prone to feeling unsteady about their unsteadiness, a kind of tinnitus of the soul. For a long time, much later on, in my therapy-believing stage, I blamed my mother for all my fears, and then I blamed my brain, and now I don't have time to blame anyone or anything, because my mandate is just to manage. But it's taken me a long, long time to land here, where I am right now, typing these words, in the house where I live with my own daughter who is close to the age I was when I first fell for horses but couldn't fall off them and went through all that a person does, all that tumbling otherwise referred to as growing up, and looking around, and if you are lucky finding in the world a single soft spot where you can rest your head, no joke, no punches pulled, a place you maybe first see from the sky, or on some speeding being, and gradually get to, despite the constant fog, touching down on the ground—no joke.

"I don't know," I said again, and I really didn't. I had no way of knowing it would be years before I'd learn touchdown my way, my style, in the house I have here, with my husband and my soulmate son and my so-special-to-me daughter who loves horses with me.

Outside, in Westminster, right now, next to the country house where we spend our weekends, and where we will soon move to full time, is a field we will seed with alfalfa and timothy. The moon tosses some meager light on the moss-padded stones that are centuries old and, piled high, define the borders of what we own. The dogs are in for the night because there are coyotes in the woods. "Are there bears?" Clara asks me, and I tell her what I know. "I don't know," I say. And touch her head.

The fields, the meager light of the moon, the timothy and alfalfa, how I lost my mother and left my childhood home—left the

Golden Ghetto when I was still a child, and for forever—how I landed here—all that is a whole other story, a part of this story perhaps, but not now. Not here. Next.

Here. 1974. The summer after the snow storms that covered the whole East Coast, knocked out people and power. "Do it Slater, do it," Rose kept saying, but I didn't. Rose knew my fear, smelled my stubbornness, and her nose twitched. Sleep got difficult, each drop down interrupted—snapped in half—I sitting up, holding tight to my sheet in the night. I didn't do it Tuesday; I didn't do it Wednesday. August came in a blast of black flies .The fields turned tawny in the August heat, and the vernal pools shriveled. The nights were dense, intense. Fireflies and falling stars. I kept clutching—a reasonable response, in my opinion.

She came up close to me then. This was near the end, the last part of summer when the heat's still high but begins to blend with autumn, borrowing bits of it here and there in a cool current that comes and goes so fast you can barely feel the freshness.

And it was during this ending of one time, the beginning of another—*fall fall fall*—when the trees would turn to torches, beautiful one day—apple and rose—ugly the next, infection red—it was during this time when she came up to me in the ring, in the afternoon, during our group lesson. Because I'd refused to *fall fall fall*, every day Rose assigned me ponies, each one smaller than the next, until at last came that day when I was riding the smallest there was, a smelly shaggy Shetland with cracked hooves. Her assignments seemed part out of pity, more out of mockery, but what did I care? In my mind, down is down. Pride is pride. It got all mixed up for me, and for Rose too, I think. "Slater," she said on this particular day, the afternoon lesson half over, I on the shaggy Shetland; she came up to me, leaned in close to me, and then closer still, so we were nearer to each other than we'd ever been before, nearly nose to nose. And what I saw—I have to say it shocked me. Her lashes—they looked different so close, each lash separate and tarred, coiffed in a way it was impossible to notice from even a few feet back. And this close up I could suddenly see that the skin on her face had some sort of film on it, some kind of dun-colored cream, visible in only the slightest streaks not blended. Or was I misperceiving? I had the sort of urge you sometimes get, senseless and difficult to resist, just to reach out a finger and swipe her face, to see if she smeared or came out clean. As for Rose, well, she saw me see and narrowed her eyes at me. Without meaning to, an unconscious response, I narrowed my eyes back.

Rose took one solid step away from me then, put her hands on her hips. I sat as still as I could on my miniature mount, in the middle of that lesson, with the other girls looking on. No one moved. For just a second Rose seemed flustered, somehow caught. She stroked a finger beneath her eye, checked the pad, blew briefly.

"Are you wearing makeup?" I asked. I wasn't meaning to be rude. She just hadn't seemed at all the type. In fact, hadn't she told us more than once that women who wore makeup were fools? Every day she dressed in jeans, her braid slung over one freckled shoulder, her t-shirts a simple washed white. I blinked, and suddenly I could see Rose differently and definitively, her foundation cream, the tiniest but definite marks of black dotting her lower lids, giving her eyes a deepness they did not deserve. "Are you?" I asked again. I leaned out of my saddle a ways, peered at her, and, without meaning to, she instinctively, revealingly, took a second fast step back.

No one could hear us. The other girls on their horses were at the far end of the ring. Rose and I were in a separate sphere. I saw her fast-step back, how it was hiding, what she didn't want us to know. She saw me see.

"You," she said, her voice low and wrong. It was so simple. Campers didn't disobey, didn't question, certainly didn't cut to the quick. That was her job and her job only. We were in this sense like her horses, and sure enough, Rose raised her crop. I did not think she would hit me. I was so sure that under no circumstances would she hit me. She would never go that far because she was only so crazy, right? But what I thought she would do is pull a Splash, send that crop slashing sideways so it would whizz, and I would jerk back, as terrified as I was bold. Bold? Yes. Paradoxes aplenty.

But Rose didn't slash her crop sideways, toying with me as she had so many weeks ago toyed with Splash. Instead, she raised her crop, her face going fiery, her bunched mouth mean—on the barest edge of control Rose was—and just as I was getting ready to jump down and run from her rivulet of rage, Rose did this weird thing. She jerked her arm and her crop away from me, trying to make it look like this had been her plan all along, to just casually place the crop on the highest part of fence post, which she did, laying it up there with a forced, false gentleness, plan B. Obvious to me.

"Plan B," I said.

And then, Rose came in really close to me again. Closer even than before. So close that even if you'd been standing one foot from us you could not have heard her speak. I leaned down to listen.

"Slater," she said, "you think I'd hit you?"

I didn't say anything.

"You think a forty-year-old woman needs to really bother with a rich kid like you?"

I stared straight at her, in shock, but not for the reason she thought.

"You're . . . forty?" I said.

A puzzled look crossed Rose's face. "How old did you think I was?" she asked.

We were whispering this. The girls were still looking on from far across the rink. I shrugged.

"How old?" Rose demanded again.

"I thought you were . . . much younger," I said quickly. "But that's just because you, your, um, your braid, and you live at home, I mean usually old people don't live . . ." I was confused, making mistakes I could hear, Rose smiling a wicked, slow smile.

"So," she said. "You think I'm too old to live at home?"

"I didn't say that."

"You most certainly did," Rose said. Suddenly, she whipped around. "Girls," she shouted, somewhat maniacally. "Girls, Slater here thinks I'm too old to live at home."

The girls on their horses at the other end of the rink didn't say a word.

"How old is too old to live at home?" Rose asked, walking into the center of the ring, equidistant now from us all. She pointed at

Jenny. "How old," Rose repeated, speaking loud so we all could hear, "how old is too old to live at home?"

Jenny shrugged. "I dunno," she said. "Thirty-two?"

"Wouldn't you agree," Rose said, striding back to the fence post, picking up her whip, pointing it at Aggy as she resumed her spot in the ring's sandy center and then repeating: "Wouldn't you agree, Aggy, that a thirty-two, or even a thirty-six year old living at home was a loser?" Rose paused. "Of some sort," she added quickly.

"I guess I'd think that it was weird," said Aggy.

"How old do you think you'll be," asked Rose to Theresa, now pointing the whip towards her. "How old do you think you'll be when you leave home?"

"I want to go to college," said Theresa. "Far away. California,"

"I bet you'll go to Stanford," Rose said, her voice dripping with resentment. "And I'll bet when you're thirty-two you'll have four babies, right?"

"Two?" said Theresa in a small voice.

"Twins," said Rose, her mouth a strained smile, her face collapsed. She scanned all of us. "You girls have all got it made," she said. "You'll all grow up," she said and paused. "You'll all grow up and meet some man and have babies of your own. You'll have your houses and your husbands, maybe not in that order, but you'll have them all right. And then you know what?" she said. "Then you'll spend the rest of your life telling yourself that all that crap was what you really wanted." She turned and looked directly at me.

"You too, Slater," she said. "In the end," she said, "no matter how eccentric you think you are, you with your notebook and neuroses, you're no Emily Dickinson. You'll do nothing different. But I," said Rose, laughing a little, "well, I've done something different all right. I've . . . ." and here her voice trailed off. She stood and stared. Stared and stood. "I've never . . ."

I could, we all could, hear her struggling to find her words. "I plotted my losses," Rose said, at last. "I leapt off, and made it look like something else. I said no to Alice," Rose said, and now it seemed she was speaking to herself, or maybe to Alice, who was there, invisible in the air.

And then Rose turned to me again. "So I'm an oddity, eh?" she said. "That's too true. And in the end, Slater," Rose said, "no matter how unique you think you are, in the end, Slater," Rose said, "you're not an oddity. You'll never say no. You'll be just like the rest."

"And you," I said, overcome, again, by a boldness that simply makes no sense in a life full of fears. "And what will you be like, in the end?"

"Just as I am now," Rose said softly. Her answer seemed to surprise her. "As I was and am and forever will be."

And then, just like that, Rose turned, left us on our horses in the ring; she just walked off, whistling. We watched her cross the field, her form diminishing with distance, then gone.

Overhead, a plane went by, high, high in the sky. It was so tiny, *so* impossible, a minnow stuffed with people.

"What the fuck?" said Aggy.

"She's forty," I said, still on my little Shetland, speaking to all the girls. "She just told me she was forty years old!"

We all twelve looked at each other then. No one moved from where they were. Even the horses stayed silent, stayed still. I kept seeing Rose in my mind as I'd first seen her the day my parents dropped me off here, leaning languidly on the fence, her plump blond braid tied off with a cherry-red ribbon, purple flip-flops and frayed jeans. "Forty," I heard someone say, the word just dangling there. And then, without further discussion, we all solemnly dismounted. The giddiness was gone. So much for learning to fall. What good did that do if you didn't know the ditches?

It was mid-August then. In two more weeks, we were out of here. It started to rain.

It rained and rained. It rained and rained and rained and rained. It rained. The fields filled with puddles, the driveway streamed, the sand in the riding rink gullied and washed off, leaving only what was beneath it behind, bare patches of clay and pavement. It rained on the roof and on our heads and in our eyes when we went out, each drop distinct, the tap of a foreign finger, cool and commanding, appointing, anointing, again and again. It rained on the barn roof, which was white metal in the summer sun but turned slick and sterling in the storm, deepening the red of the barn beneath it, that big building floating on swales of water and hay. It rained.

We stayed in the cabin. Nothing much to do. We played Crazy Eights and Spoons. Our sheets dampened, nearly dripped, our blankets gained weight, the wood walls swelled and split, and when we read, or tried to, the pages of our books stuck together, two or three or four or even five pages of paper clumped, tearing softly, almost luxuriously when you tried to pry the paper apart. And the paper left behind, on our finger tips, the stains of words, of stories we'd never make sense of now.

It rained. It rained and rained and rained and rained. It rained. It rained all over the old, listing farmhouse, and the downspouts couldn't carry all the weight of that water, got choked up, backed up, gurgled, and spit, Hank sprinting out of the house with a folded newspaper over his head and tugging from the downspouts' metal mouths a clot of leaves, a clot of clots. Wiping his hands on his pants while inside the yelling kept coming. It rained. It rained water and voices. Hank hurried outside, pried clots from the downspouts, wiped his hands on his pants, tossed the newspaper down, and stood still in their flooded yard, looking directly, challengingly, but hopelessly up, his face rent open, water coming into his clefts. His eyes.

It rained water and voices. Weather outside and in. The forecast said rain for the foreseeable future, and in their house they kept it coming, too close, perhaps, too tired, too many leaks, too many years; who knew? The pages of books were stuck together, tore softly when we tried to pry them apart, the ink all smudged, so pieces of the story were and would always be wet. Senseless.

The rain came pounding down, but it had the odd effect of amplifying their voices, each distinct drop carrying within it a tiny subwoofer, a speaker, broadcasting their forecast, their weather, their tears, too. I heard crying. I thought maybe Rose was crying, but who could say for sure? Someone cried, perhaps a bird, perhaps a person. Mostly they yelled, as was their custom, their religion, but during those days of rain, the rain following the fall which preceded the discovery of Rose's age. She had assumed we knew, and yet she had also made her mask of makeup, but this wasn't what really hurt her. What really hurt her were just the figures, plain and simple, two digits impossible to fly over or fall from; horses and humans—both tethered. The yelling changed in the house, and the house tilted just a tiny bit more, strained its anchor, so for maybe the first time, the house could consider its options, sense the open sea.

In my mind, when I watched that house, I pictured what it would look like snapping from the anchor that kept it in place and then sailing off, all three stories, what that would feel like from the inside, the sound of it, crisper than anything they'd maybe heard in a long, long time, the feel of it, a sudden little lilt, a lifting, so surprising it would stop them dead, or alive, in their single circling track, and they'd eye each other as they felt their home rising on a small swell, leaning into the wind, not against it but finally with it, all the rooms coming along for the ride, and there they went, whisking. Hi-ho, the Derry-o! I pictured their faces at the windows once they realized the cord was cut, the feared freedom now theirs, by hook or by crook, no choice. Change. Their faces would appear at the windows, one face per window, one circle in one square, each circle smiling, the white hand waving, at once mechanically and ecstatically. Good-bye. Good-bye!

Sometimes I wanted to cry, for no obvious reason. Crazy Eights. How long can that go on?

A long, long time, as I learned that summer of 1974, the summer after the snowstorms that came and killed people with not a single, solitary weapon. Nature's way. Quite cunning.

One thing Alice and Hank and Rose were not was cunning. They were all blunt blades that kept on cutting uselessly. As it rained, they yelled. As it poured, they screamed, all cooped up and crazy. Alice screamed at Rose, the words, the phrases, over and over again: *Underappreciated; not in my home; can't you care? you had your chance; what a slob; you mope and mope; return the ring; my only hope; I didn't try; I tried.*

And, in return, Rose screamed at Alice, the words, the phrases, over and over again: *Mr. K; outta my hair; it was never my life; I feel so bad for Dad; you think it's my fucking fault? I was always first place; you push.*

And the words went singsong in my head, *Feel so bad for Dad return the ring my only hope you mope and mope my only hope*, over and over again, until it seemed I was indeed falling in precisely the way I really feared, the ground completely gone. And then, on the fourth night, the rain came down with a weird, wrong ferocity, a sheer, pounding sheet washing things away, while in that house on that hill they ranted and raved, screamed and shouted, swore and swore at an intensity I had previously believed not possible for them, and that plus the strange rain scared us until it stopped.

In a second it all stopped. It was like God had a big brake, the pedal of which he suddenly pushed down, hard—*enough!!*—God said, and crushed his big brake to the floor of his gazillion-dollar chrome Corvette up there in the sky; he screeched everything to a stop. Red light. *It's over.* Mars—see it shine? Mars is so small and so big at the same time that the confusion could make you cry. And in a second, in a single, simple swoosh, God's housekeeper cleared out the clouds so we could see the sky beneath, and all the stars appeared as though they'd been there the whole time, just waiting, which of course they had been, only tonight they looked unusually bright. They looked festive, as if extrascrubbed for some special show, opening night at The Universe, the whole cast of characters glowing and perfect and pulsing with energy, some shooting, some still, that sky filled and filled with stars streaming back into their rightful place in space. Oh my god your god no god—was it ever something to see.

What I saw: The sky was almost pure pearl, with the occasional black gap called night. And the moon was so flat but bright; in its light I could see tiny toads hopping on the ground and the dark, huge puddles and the barn roof, still soaked and sterling, all agleam, but peaceful now.

The sudden storm, its sudden stop, surprised us all, and for a little while—how long? Six minutes? Six hours?—silence settled over the campground. The main house, too, was silent. We were in our bunks, maybe 9 p.m., peeking out the small screened windows because a sudden silence like that commands your attention and draws out the details you might otherwise miss, so we could hear the peeps of little creatures in the grass, the rustle of the treetops, the bang of a feed bucket in one of the horse's stalls; he was probably searching for food. We heard the whip sound of wings above us and the clank of the corral gate, and in between these sounds was the silence, dense and real and deep, just as in between stars was the night, dense and real and deep, and in between us, Lauren and Aggy, Rose and Alice, Al and Alice—in between all people, every pair—there was a space, dense and real and deep, and I felt that space as a serious problem, a reason to cling to your life. A reason to make a raft, even as you knew it would fail. A sadness, or maybe better described—a raw hurting—came up over me, as sudden as the storm and its stopping.

But before I could give this hurt a name, or draw out its details: BANG! BANG! BANG! The sound of gunshot in the main house. We leapt up, all twelve of us, someone screaming, Rose screaming? And then a second-story window flung open, and in the bright night we saw what we saw, Alice's hands, Alice's arms lathered with moonlight, stunningly bright, heaped with Rose's clothes. Rose's voice, her rude, vituperative tone: "Don't you fucking dare! Mom! I said M-o-m!" Alice dared. We saw Rose's clothes sail out the window, arms and legs and torsos made of silk and cotton swishing in the bright night, dancing their way down, now shorts, now boots, now scarves and hats, now skirts, it just kept coming until it didn't. At some point Rose stopped screaming in protest. Alice didn't stop though. With the window open, she tossed her daughter's garments—the ones we'd seen and the ones we'd never seen—out by the armful, did it through screaming and silence, until there were no more. Then, she snapped the window shut; we heard the lock click, saw the shade drawn, and it was done.

We looked at each other. "Holy shit," said Aggy.

"Should we go out and help pick up?" said Theresa.

The yard, after all, was covered with the contents of a closet, the clothes heaped, sprawled, and soaked on the lawn.

"We could," I said. "But then Alice and Hank will think we're siding with Rose."

Before we could decide, out came Rose. We peeked through the windows. She had a laundry basket with her, one of those plain plastic ones with webbed sides. She picked up her possessions. There were so many, she had to squash them in so they fit. I was surprised she had so many clothes and such fancy ones, too, because all I'd ever seen her in were jeans, jodhpurs, spaghetti-strap tanks, and that huge cowboy hat when she was breaking-to bridle. I saw her pick up long skirts, silk scarves, six-inch high heels. Then she went and sat on the glider on the porch, in her old jeans, frayed holes at the knees, her bare feet, tanned toes, up on the railing. She pulled a cigarette from her pocket, lit the match, drew in deeply. She leaned her head way back, then stretched her neck left, right. She tapped ash into her hand, blew on her hand, scattered the ash. A long time went by. She smoked a second cigarette, then a third.

I felt myself grow sleepy, watching as I was, as we were, twelve chins propped up on the cabin's moist sills, looking out. The night air smelled delicious. My eyes grew heavy. I'm not sure if what I heard next came from dream or life: her voice. "You've seen enough," Rose said, speaking from the shadows, straight into the darkness. "Go to bed now girls," someone said. Rose said. The last thing I heard—her voice.

"Sweet dreams."

When we woke up in the morning, the clothes were gone and so was Alice. Sometime during the night the storm had passed, but everything was dripping. The wind was still whipping. Hank served us our breakfast, looking gaunt. "We got some high-pressure systems coming in across these mountains," he said, peering not at us but out the window, where we could see the weedy space in the driveway where Alice's old station wagon usually sat. Gone. "Too many mountains around here," Hank said, staring at the space his wife had left behind. I didn't know what he meant. There were no mountains around here. But there were gusts. And hills.

We found Rose where she usually was, down at the stable, where huge puddles had seeped straight up through the cracks in the concrete floor. Rose seemed extremely busy. "No lessons today girls," she said, doing this and that, rushing here and there. And she wouldn't face us, instead kept going in and out of stalls, carrying brushes and buckets. She reminded me of my aunt who, one Rosh Hashanah dinner, had lost her crown so she didn't want to smile and kept her mouth shut tight. But you can hide a missing tooth much easier than you can hide a found face.

We milled about, unsure of what to do. We should have left the barn. Had we left, this story could have ended here, not an ideal space for stopping, but maybe good enough.

Instead we stayed. It was clear Rose did not want us there. We must have wanted to be there, perhaps for the horses, perhaps for her hurt, perhaps because we were plain bored of our bunks. I don't know. Even today, so much older, when I'm in a fight with the man I've married, I cannot walk away. I will stay and stay and stay, insist insist insist, long past the point of productivity, unable to cut off the connection, no matter how gnarled, because what could be worse than nothing?

So I stayed. So we all stayed. Without plan or discussion, each of us started in on chores: Sweeping, brushing. We slipped inside stalls, going to groom. The whisk of currying combs. The clink of picks. Silence.

And then, finally, Rose spoke. She spoke from deep inside Oh Gosh's stall, where it sounded like she was bent way over, maybe cleaning his hooves. I don't know which stalls all the other girls were in, but I think we all could hear her, clear and true. "Girls," Rose said, her voice coming out of that black box of a stall like some Oz who's already had it happen, the curtain. "Girls," Rose said. "Today I'm tired."

Her voice, perhaps in part amplified by the damp stall, and perhaps in part for all these other reasons, sounded different. It was so much smaller, yet deeper too. It was, in its own way, very hard to hear.

"Would you mind," Rose said, and then she cleared her throat, seemed to swallow something down, as though trying hard to keep her own rain in. "Would you mind, girls, maybe skipping lessons for the next few days? We have some serious drying out to do."

No, no no, not at all, of course not; let's skip today, tomorrow, the next day, because it's too wet, it's all way way way too wet anyway. And everyone needs a break. An ending.

"Thank you," Rose said, from inside her stall. Pause. "You are all," she said, "good girls."

I was combing my pony, Tanya. I ran my fingers through her honey-colored mane, rested my face against the thick ledge of her neck. I smelled her pony smell, so solid. So strong. I thought *thank you.* I thought, *please.*

And so we all kept doing what it was we were doing, helping I suppose, together in the barn in a weird, quiet way, and this was maybe the closest we came, that summer, a stall separating each one of us.

A few more minutes passed like this, just brushing or mucking or standing still. Just being. With.

And then Rose spoke again. "Girls," she said, and again, I could hear how we all, in our separate stalls, stopped, our brushes, our grooming gear held aloft; we listened closely. Her words were oddly formal.

"You know what I think I need to do?" Rose said.

No one said *what?* It was implied.

"I think I need to ride my Mr. K today. I know it's very wet," Rose said, "but sometimes you need a ride same as a shower or something. It's just what you need. It's the right thing."

"Totally," said Theresa, from wherever she was, in some stall to my right.

"I have watched you ride Mr. K almost every morning," I said from my stall. "It's one of my favorite parts of the day."

"Thanks," Rose said. "I think I'll just throw a saddle on K and take him for a quick run up the hill and back. I'm sure he's bored and would appreciate the chance to stretch."

"They're all bored," said Aggy. "Rain can get very boring."

"You bet," said Rose.

I heard Rose come out of Oh Gosh's stall. One by one then, every girl followed, stepping from her stall, holding some piece of grooming equipment. We stood there, still, in the long barn hallway, stalls on either side. We stood there.

Rose went into the tack room, came back with Mr. K's saddle, his name gold-plated on the back, inscribed in cursive. She had his bridle slung over her shoulder, her hard hat on. She still wouldn't look at us directly. She seemed to be hiding behind her hair, which had been most days done in two childlike braids or a single thick weaving slung over her shoulder. But today her hair was down, mussed, some kind of snarled but pretty curtain hanging halfway over her.

Rose went to Mr. K's stall, slid open the door. From where I stood I couldn't see the horse, just her, paused on this threshold she'd crossed so many times, the line between the human and the horse world. Step into a stall and you've stepped into smells that are pungent; the flies buzz and dive; manure is ripe and rich. But mostly, you are stepping into size, into something so much bigger, and yet smaller (her cupped hands once described for me the size of a horse brain: "No bigger than a golf ball," Rose had once explained, dismissively) than we are. And as I saw Rose pause, as I saw her *hesitate* for a second on the ledge of her horse's home, it occurred to me that she and I shared some fears. We both knew the risk in every equine encounter.

And, seeing that, getting that, I for the first time observed how she did not simply step forward into the stall; she had to push herself forward—an act of will and faith and, who knows, maybe even hope. I saw Rose pause and then cross over, disappearing into darkness. From inside the stall I heard her talking to Mr. K: *Hey there; sweet boy how ya doin'not so good? Tell me 'bout it; wanna go? That's right.* I heard the sound of her currying comb getting the grit out, and I pictured Mr. K loving this, like many horses do, especially at the perpetually itchy, nerve-filled neck. When you brush there, the horse leans way into it, the tines of the tool gathering all the grime and coming clean. If you scritch a horse's neck, the horse will learn to love you. The horse will give you his muzzle, maybe the best part of the body, somehow softer from the threat of teeth mere membranes away.

And then the sound of jangling, huffing, *there there boy*, and Mr. K began to emerge rump first from his stall, Rose invisible, pushing him gently from inside.

Now this horse, Mr. K, he was enormous, over seventeen hands. He was uncommonly large, yet still sleek, sired by the best, born for the track except his heart had derailed him. "Thank god for that," Rose would always say to us whenever the subject of Mr. K's minor birth defect came up. "Had his heart been totally A-plus normal, my baby would've spent his life with no-good gamblers."

Instead, though, the Flat Rock Farm family had not sold the newborn off, as was the plan. Instead they kept the colt for themselves. So what if somewhere in his DNA there was a tiny chip in the china? This horse was a beautiful being, the color of fresh sap, so sunlight didn't bounce off the barrel of his body but rather got absorbed into it; he radiated.

And what a fine horse he had been, right from the start, healthy and huge, the heart defect only so slight. Twice the first summer I was there Dr. Fascal had come out to do her customary pump check, once just by herself, the second time with three other men in the van. The second time they attached suckers to Mr. K's mighty chest and made a picture of his heart in jags and dips. "Same old same old," Dr. Fascal had said, handing Rose the scroll. Rose had studied it. "There it is," Dr. Fascal had said, pointing with her finger to some spot in the squiggles. "See this, girls?" Rose had said, holding up K's EKG, indicating with her thumb. "That's the valve not closing."

And we had clustered around to see such a sight, a horse's heart sketched on a skinny strip of paper. What a disappointment. A bunch of toddler lines. "In a perfectly normal heart," Dr. Fascal had explained to us, "the valve closes all the way, like a door."

"But in Mr. K's heart," Rose had continued, "the valve doesn't quite completely seal, so his door is always open. And that's why he's my sweetheart."

Then Rose and Dr. Fascal, plus the men who had come with her, all laughed, and Dr. Fascal had patted K on his big brunette rump, which was, right this minute, weeks and weeks after Dr. Fascal's last visit, getting ever larger as Rose guided him butt first from the stall he'd been cooped up in for days.

Horses were not made for stalls or boxes of any sort. Some animals, like dogs, are. Their human-made crates mimic their natural inclination for enclosed dens, but horses have not the slightest desire for any sort of shelter, except that which is provided by their coats, their fur layered and waxy so weather slips off them. Some horses, when kept too long in stalls, develop what's called "stall fever." They start to gnaw at the wood, or themselves. Mr. K had plenty of pasture time, so he'd never had stall fever, as far as we knew, except maybe now, after four rained-out days.

As K cleared the stall's door and Rose emerged, pushing on his chest, I turned to view the pasture, those fields, the meadow where she'd done her diving trick. The barn doors were open wide so I could see the sky, too blue, the clouds a mix of stain and sun. The trees swelled and settled. Far up, at the farmhouse, I saw a figure— Hank?—pacing back and forth before the third-floor window. Where oh where was Alice? In the barn, Rose hitched her horse to two lines, one on each wall, so he'd stay still as she tacked him up.

"Look at you," Rose said to Mr. K. She leaned in close, nose to muzzle. We were out of her world now, entirely. She reached up and fluffed Mr. K's mane of bangs, the thatch of hair that grows between the ears and brushes across the wide eyes.

"Getting long," Rose said. She stepped back, as though to better appraise her horse's hair. "Can you even *see?*" she asked Mr. K.

I swear the horse nodded no.

"Neither could I," said Rose, "if I had bangs that low." She fluffed her own hair now. "We both need new do's."

It was charming, watching Rose talk to her horse like this, and yet, I was not charmed. I still had the weather in me, the rain, the sudden sunlight, the splashy drops that kept falling, and then stopping. The weather was unsettled. So was Mr. K. Now that she had her horse, Rose seemed to quiet, but Mr. K, well, he might have had stall fever, because he was pawing at the concrete floor, dancing back and forth on his cross ties, like a child waiting for recess.

From far out across the soaking fields, almost an acre away, I heard the rattle of car coming fast down the dirt road, the sound of its splash and squeal. Mr. K's ears popped forward, his head cocked in question.

"I'm gonna give you a trim," said Rose, "before we go."

A horn sounded then, in the worst way. It was not one long solid sound but rather a series of brief screeching blasts, the kind that could get under anyone's skin. Rose seemed not to hear, or care. The horn kept up. It had no rhythm or reason. It would go *blat blat blat* in a series of rapid, unpredictable exclamations, and then fall into silence, and then start up again, *blat blat*. Long pause. Now over. No. *Blat. Blat blat blat blat*. We all turned towards it. High up at the house I saw a tired old Hank open the porch door, lean into the crazy day of clouds and clearing, and look out, craning, his hand a visor. No car visible. But the horn kept coming. When I turned back, all the horses in all their stalls were now starting to pace and paw, and Mr. K, cross-tied tight, well, I swear I could almost see his whole coat bristle up, billions of tiny tacks.

Rose always kept a pair of shears hanging from a huge hook screwed in one of the barn beams. They were old electric shears, the kind where the cloth cord has long since frayed, exposing the charged veins inside.

Now, Rose reached for the shears, popped the plug into its socket. She depressed the big red button and held up the clippers as they chattered. "Will you look at these?" Rose said, but to whom was she speaking? To Mr. K? No. He was obviously distracted, if not worried, his eyes darting here and there.

Blat. To us? No. She had ceased to register our presence at all, to the point that had we all simultaneously burst into a Latin chant, I doubt she'd have even noticed.

"Will you look at these goddamn clippers," Rose said as they gnashed and clattered. "How many times have I suggested we buy new ones? How many times? Penny pinching, pound foolish," Rose said.

"But you know what, K?" Rose continued. "You know what? Me and you, we can't let old patterns preclude new adventures. We can't continue on as we have. We've gotten stagnant, old K Man," Rose said. "And that's not what we're about."

And with that, Rose lifted the clippers to her own head, and *crick-acrick-acrack,* I saw her cut off a few snarly pieces of her own hair, just strands here and there, blond *S's* and darker *C's* floating to the floor, letters lying there; she looked down. For a few seconds it seemed she was reading her own wispy sentences, or trying to; I don't know. What I do know is what I saw. All of a sudden, and I mean *all* of a sudden, Rose pulled back her leg and gave a swift, vicious kick to her curls.

Rose kicked her curls with the same pent-up rage I'd seen on occasion in my massive mother, and instead of flinching as I might have before I'd come to this camp, I simply stood, knowing: *Not me*. True, I hadn't found a way to fling myself off living ledges, but I could ride a horse bareback while he walked into the water, a second spine now mine, and later on, side by side with this big beast in a stall, I could cradle his foot in my hand and expertly pry dried crap from its innards—and how many people could do that?.

And it was strange, that I should feel this quick surge of pride at just that mad moment, the moment of Rose kicking her curls and the clipper clipping, and then my pride coming, and then my pride going, so it all came down in flakes around me. And I was back in the barn then with nothing but pure plot, the events happening very fast now. Rose kicked her curls, switched off the shears, so for a second there was a blessed silence, and then I saw a brief shudder go all through her; her body just jolted, and she switched those damn shears on again, the blades clacking like mad beaks in front of Mr. K's face, invading his space as she lifted them to his eyes for the quick trim he never said he wanted. What he wanted? Who can say. What he saw? No one knows. This is the saddest part for me, that we will never be able to say, for sure, what happens inside the minds of the four million five hundred thousand other species with whom we share this planet, even as we have our wordless ways of sensing. Still, I cannot say what Mr. K saw or felt as Rose lifted those buzzing blades to his face, but what he *did*, that I can tell you because I was there. Rose lifted the lip-smacking shears to his hair, came close enough to take a single swipe from the strands that fell into his eyes. She aimed those shears directly *at* Mr. K's tethered face, and Mr. K, cooped up and freaked out from the swirl of crazy sounds around him; Mr. K, at once utterly obedient and regally self-possessed—a paradox only he had had the genius to master—Mr. K lost it. He reared back, this massive muscular horse going back high on his hind legs, so strong he snapped the ropes that tethered him and split the barn beams with a satisfying *crrrack*. And for a shaving of a second, Mr. K hovered there, freed, high on his hind legs, a huge but breathing statue of some equine in an ancient war, and I could see, I think, the imperfect pump pumping in his terrified chest. So, perhaps, could Rose. And he stayed there, risen up, his nostrils infernal, his chest sweat-slicked and erratic, and in my memory of this, I ceased entirely to see myself. Like Mr. K, I lost it; we all lost it, our hearts jammed with static while we dangled, waiting for the page to turn.

And then it did. Turn. Mr. K, all one thousand six hundred pounds of him, including his heart and that valve that didn't seal shut—came crashing down to the ground. And as he did, Rose grabbed hold of the broken rope with one hand but she couldn't keep a grip on her horse. He was bucking back and forth now, side to side, unable to get calm, so the rope slipped right through Rose's fist. Really, Rose had no business insisting on intimacy with an animal seventeen times her size and sixty times her strength, at least. She dropped the shears she'd been holding. They circled the floor idiotically, chomping on air.

And then Rose grabbed hold of the rope with her two hands now while the shears clacked and Mr. K reared back again. And this time, when he came down, his front hoof sliced into Rose, so a small smile of blood appeared right above her temple; it was weird, how it appeared. It was as though a dark red smile appeared on her skull, just emerged there on the white wall of her skin, complete and insistent for an instant before dissolving into drips.

I wonder if all warm-blooded mammals have a singular response to the sight of blood. Maybe here is where our perceptions touch together. It was just a little bit, really, a superficial slice, as these things go, but it stopped Mr. K in his tracks. Rose reached out and pressed the cut with the heel of her hand, then looked at the heel of her hand, and the second stretched out to the point of snapping as she studied her blood, the rich smear of it. And then she lifted her hand to her lips, mouthed her own fluids, and a sour-lemon look crossed her face. *But blood is NOT sour,* I wanted to yell, as if that might help the situation I was seeing form right before my eyes. Rose didn't have her whip. The shears had at some point ceased, gone completely to sleep, lying on their side in a drunken coma, the plug pulled out in the melee.

And now, slowly, Rose lifted her arm, palm flat, blood sucked, wound its way back, folded her hand into a fist, and then hurled her grip forward in a blow across the bony bridge of K's face. And Mr. K, well, he hollered, let loose a sound I'd never heard before and have never heard since: pain, shock, insult, betrayal. And then she did it again. Sock. Sharp. Crack. Was that a bone in his head? Or was that her head, breaking up, gone mad for good; good-bye.

Yes, good-bye. Because the force of her wallops made the huge horse stumble backwards, his eyes all bloodshot and startled. And then Mr. K—fantastic, brave, dignified Mr. K—the pain of her punches was such that he did what we'd never seen a horse of his spirit do. He buckled. It was like watching a person who has been hit over the head, or who has had the breath knocked out of him by surprise. You could practically see stars whirling around that horse's stunned, scared face and his heart had always been just a little off, which is maybe why the animal crashed down, all one thousand plus pounds of him, falling first to one knee, then to the other, keeling sideways, the whole stable shuddering as he hit the floor hard, landing on his left side. He lay there, one eye open, the shears next to him, all unplugged. And so still.

Silences come like characters—there are many kinds. Some are sweet, some are sad, or severe. The silence that followed the fall of Mr. K was unlike any of these; it was stunned. Rose held her hand up before her eyes, then let it drop uselessly to her side.

"He's dead," whispered Jenna.

"Shut up," said Aggy, tears squeezing out of her eyes. We were, all twelve of us, pressed back against the far wall. Rose stood frozen, and for a second I thought I'd see her topple right on top of Mr. K, but she didn't. Moments passed. More moments passed. The flies seemed unaware of the atmosphere; they kept right on buzzing, as busy as ever with their germy work. I kept brushing them from my face, my hair. Outside rain began again in those soft loose splashes; we could hear it on the barn's tin roof. "Mr. K?" Rose finally asked, her voice a tiny, barely there question. And then the floodgates broke. "Mr. K," Rose screamed, and she rushed towards the horse she loved and hated to love, and loved to hate, and that voice shattered the spell, and the giant, Mr. K, well, his huge body shuddered and he snorted in air, and then, as though pulled by some puppeteer in the sky he awoke and stood, one leg up, second leg up, steadying on the strings of god, the massive animal moved, lurched back on his haunches, heaved forward, chest to floor, and then, gathering the energy it takes a one-thousand-pound beast to defy gravity (which is why horses rarely lie down), Mr. K heaved himself onto his hoofs and got back into balance.

And now there they were, woman and horse, face to face. I swear, it seemed like Mr. K was staring her down. And then he turned, apparently disgusted, and at his own behest, trotted right out of that barn, neighing high into the hills, his herd answering back from their locked stalls. He was picking up speed now, his gait as magnificent as ever, trotting through the grasses, the mud meaning nothing to him; he'd go as far as he could, as far as the wires would let him, but we could see, as he broke into a canter, we could see the fence was of no consequence to him, because he'd have his dignity back long before he ever reached that point.

And down in the barn now stood Rose, all alone. She stood there silent for a while, and we never saw her face, and then we heard her whisper. "Shit," she said, and walked away.

That evening, the old farmhouse was quiet. Around 7 p.m., Alice's station wagon crunched across the driveway. She got out, kicked the door closed, unlocked the basement door, and slipped inside. Maybe an hour passed before the dinner bell rang. We never ate in the family's dining room, or even in their house for that matter. Alice served us our meals at a long table on the screened-in porch, just as she did that night, the table set as it always was, apron tied around her waist, as it always was. The only differences I could detect: the lipstick she was wearing, a fruity pink that made her mouth stand separate from her whitened face, plus the food she served, fried chicken and butter beans, both unusually good that night. Hank wasn't at that dinner and Rose never came to any meals, instead eating by herself in the stable office. But Alice was there, trying to be bright because that was her way, but something was beyond broken in that family, and we could feel it. "So much *stuff* to do," Alice said. She pointed to the calendar, an exact copy of the one Rose kept at the barn, each box crammed with appointments. We could see large X's drawn through the boxes of the past. The box of tomorrow had a full moon in it and beneath that, a single event scrawled; no surprise. We knew what was up: Jill's turn.

We went to sleep scared, the memory inside me: Mr. K's giant body falling down, shuddering the floor beneath my feet. In sleep, the whole earth shuddered and then I was above, seeing countries falling from the globe like so much scrap—there goes Europe, a jigsaw piece dropping through space. My sleep was fitful. Several times I woke with a thick thirst that could not be slaked. I fumbled for my canteen, drained the warm tin-tasting water to the last drop.

There are stories of shipwrecked sailors drinking the ocean and seeing stars and streamers before they die. If the water in the canteen had been salted, maybe that could account for the oddity of what happened next, could confirm it all as a hallucination stemming from stress. But that water wasn't salted. It was pure, from the well drilled beyond bedrock two hundred and fifty feet down in the Maine ground.

So if it wasn't the water, what else could explain what happened but could not have happened, and if the answer is *nothing*, then what am I left holding, in the end?

The first time I woke up it could not have been later than 10 p.m. My mouth was thick with this strange stubborn thirst and outside the bunk I saw the sky was swirled with stars, the constellations crazy, the farmhouse so dark it seemed nearly snuffed, only its chimney and edges visible here and there. It was as if its occupants had died or collapsed from the intensity of their emotions. The water dribbled down my throat, cooled some spot in me, and sleep came quick and true. The next time I awoke, I snapped out of sleep so fast I heard my own hurdling. I sat up. A bolt in my back.

I could tell we were in the thickest part of the night now, when time takes on texture, a black material plush and drenching both. Outside the bunk everything was submerged, except for the farmhouse, which was, now, completely, inappropriately ablaze, golden lights gushing from every chink and square, lights so glittery I had to keep blinking in order to bear them, and when I closed my eyes my lids lit up, and on those two silk screens I saw vortexes morph into millions of tiny tacks. I fell back asleep once again.

And when I woke for the third time (or was it the fourth; I am not quite sure) all the lights were once again doused, and the farmhouse was sitting hunched and quiet in a damp dawn at the barest beginning of any old day in late summer, the dawn so new that shapes had only recently asserted themselves, in pieces here and there, the fence visible, the barn not yet. And now all the windows in the house were open, gray, and, although there was no wind, although not a single tree stirred, although the meadows were settled and still, every curtain in every window of that house was blowing madly, Alice's white sheers and Swiss polkas and laces. Classical music soared from some room I was sure I'd never seen, some room deep in the core of the home. Complicated crescendos came and went—cellos waltzing with violins vibrating with trombones deep and true. Then the brief beat of a pause—and then, just at the point when you were primed for the crashing of a complex orchestra—instead came the pure simple sound of a lone piccolo. I opened my screen, stuck my hand into the stagnant air while watching all the curtains twist, while listening to the light swift steps of that lone piccolo, and then sleep hit my head again in a swift blow, and I was down for what felt like hours but must have been just a second or so, because next when I next sat up the dawn was just as undecided, the house still hunched, the piccolo still playing. Only now I saw Dr. Fascal walking across the lawn, coming to inquire, it seemed, about Mr. K. She slowly, with immense exhaustion, climbed the porch steps, stood on the stoop at a time too early for a doctor to normally arrive, except this was maybe an emergency. Dr. Fascal tugged on the bell, which I'd never seen before—brand new—some fancy thing Alice must have bought during the twelve or so hours she'd left the farm, after the fight, the night, the clothes coming down. The brand-new bell was skirt-shaped silver, its clapper a girl's lean legs melded at the entwined feet. Now Dr. Fascal pulled on the cord and the bell let out its peals clear and perfect in the dead-still dawn. The door opened.

I saw the door open. But whoever greeted the doctor stood where I could not see, and I only caught her shadow thrown down like a welcome mat. I saw Dr. Fascal shake her head back and forth, back and forth—bad news?—and then she knelt down, in the same exhausted way as she had walked. She set the big black bag she'd come with on the granite stoop, and then, unclasping it, she dumped its contents out and spread them around: mounds of lockets, big silver ones, blue and yellow ones, lockets of glass and gold and turquoise, all twinkling in her heap. "Here, for the horse," Dr. Fascal said, gesturing to the jewelry, and then she walked away. From what seemed to be a second-story window came Rose's voice, unmistakable. "Look up here," Rose said. Then I was asleep because the next time I opened my eyes the day was definite and fully formed. The sky was not strange. The weather was perfect: 85 degrees.

August 21, Jill in a box. Alice served biscuits and eggs for breakfast. Around her neck, dangling by her breasts, was a small golden locket I'd never seen before.

"Where'd you get that necklace?" I asked.

Alice looked down, palmed the piece of jewelry, studied it thoughtfully. I saw a thousand things cross her face then. She looked up at me, her brow all furrowed. "Lauren," she said, "I honestly forget."

Hank appeared in the breakfast room then wearing his breaking-to-bridle-clothes.

"Hank," Alice said, "where'd I get this necklace?" She held it out to him.

Hank came over close. He traced its shape with his thick forefinger. "Guess I must've given it to you," he said.

"You *guess?*" Alice said.

And then Rose came in, *Just passing through, does anyone have some thread?*

"Hey Rose, Rose," Hank said. "Slow down a sec. Where'd Ma get this necklace?"

And then Rose went close to her parents, closer than we'd ever seen those three be, and for a second they were all there together, studying this heart, and then another second went by, and they didn't seem to be studying the heart anymore. They seemed to be just standing near one another, feeling what that felt like now, and maybe remembering what it had once felt like at some point in their past. Alice pressed her lips with her two fingers and shook her head fast. "Ma," Rose said, softly. She put her hand on her mother's shoulder, and Hank put his hand over Rose's hand, and there they were for a little while, on Alice's shoulder. We were watching, forks poised in mid-air, knowing we were seeing a special spell. Alice nodded, her eyes squeezed shut. "Thank you, Rose," she said. "No words," I think I heard Rose whisper. Alice nodded again, and then we saw her back out, into the kitchen, her slow steps on the stair treads above our heads. Rose and Hank turned towards us, cleared their throats.

Hank touched the brim of his big cowboy hat. Rose had a bridle slung over her shoulder. *Jill's turn.* "You and me, kid," Hank said to Rose, his voice thin and almost hopeful. This was, it seemed to me, the one activity they shared together. "We've got some work to do," Hank said.

"No." Rose said. She took a long look at Hank and then she said, simply—

"Dad."

It seemed like an hour passed between the word *Dad* and what Hank did next, and who knows, maybe that's true.

Hank nodded then, once, decisively. "Okay, Rose," he said, as though he understood, and clearly he did. He took off his big broad-brimmed hat, hung it on a hook in the breakfast room, and then went out the door. And that was the last I ever saw of him close up, Hank hanging his hat on that hook and walking down the still damp steps one morning at the end of August. I'd be there four more days.

And Rose. Well, Rose, for the first time that whole summer, she ate breakfast with us. She pulled out a chair, laid the breaking bridle on the table. And that's when I saw that this was different than the other breaking bits; it was not studded. This bit was dainty, two silver tines linked with a rubber *0* in the middle, a teething ring. "Pass me the jam," Rose said to no one, and

Jenny passed the jam. "You know the expression there's more than one way to skin a cat?" Rose said. We nodded. "Well," said Rose. "That's not true, is it? There is really only *one* way to skin a cat, if one was ever so inclined, but when it comes to most other things, I'd say you usually have several options."

Now, Rose pulled the lid off the jam jar, held it up, sniffed. "Apricot," she announced. She slathered that baby bit with the apricot jam and then, once it was totally tacky, she sprinkled it with sugar, the grains visibly white, and bright, in the golden gel. And then she brought us all down to the barn, holding the bridle out well in front of her.

Jill, the filly, was already there, sleepy in her stall. Rose didn't halter her or cross tie her or anything. Instead she entered the stall, still holding the bridle, closing the door behind her, and turning then to face us, her face and the filly's side by side. "Long time ago," Rose said, "people had their ways of doing things and those ways change except when we don't want them to. My daddy taught me one way to break a horse, but I learned others from those hippie horse girls I never much liked." Rose laughed. "I can't say who's right and who's wrong in terms of making a trustworthy horse," she said. "We've always done things one way at our farm here, and no horse here has ever hurt or even thrown a girl so . . . ," Rose trailed off. "That's *significant*," she said and nodded crisply, and the filly nodded crisply too and we laughed.

"But in the end, the more tricks a trainer has in her grab bag, the better off she'll be. I learned the sticky-bit trick . . ." She cast her eyes upward, counted to herself. ". . . Eight years ago?" Rose said. "Eight years already?" Her brow furrowed. She swiped her eyes, and then inspected her hand for streaks. "I'm forty years old," Rose said. "That's right. 1974. So I'll be nearing seventy when the year 2000 comes. And when you're forty . . . ," Rose said, looking at me and Em, the youngest. "When you two girls are forty, I'll be . . ." And we could see her counting down the years until a stunned, slapped look came across her face. She stopped speaking.

And when she started again, here's what she had to say: "Horses live a long, long time. Some can go forty years. But because they only need four hours of sleep *a week*, they get a lot of living in. Way more than we do." Now, Rose tickled Jill beneath her pruny chin. "Right, little girl?" Rose said.

And Jill, well Jill stepped forward, *towards* her taming. Rose held Jill's jaw with one hand and with the other she slipped that sugared bit right between the horse's lips. We saw the bit move back until it snapped into its spot, and Jill's eyes went bright with surprise. "Taste buds all over the back of a horse's tongue," Rose explained. "Good girl," Rose said. Then she turned towards us, shrugged.

"That's it," Rose finally said. "No drama now," she said. "Show's over."

"That's *it*?" Jenny said. "Jill's broken?"

Rose turned back towards Jill, who was savoring the sweetness. "She doesn't look broken to me," Rose said. She smiled. "We'll leave her for a little while. She'll get used to the gear. We'll work with her—over time. We can make it easier," Rose said. "Sure, we can be kinder. I know I—" And then she stopped.

I raised my hand.

"Slater," Rose said.

"Why haven't you been?" I said. And then added, quickly, "Kinder?"

Rose sighed, rolled her eyes. "You know, Slater," she said. "Do you gotta push every single goddamn limit you see? It gets tiring."

"Sorry," I said. I didn't know exactly what she meant.

"Okay, girls," Rose said. Her voice took on its familiar, authoritarian, irritable, regal tone. "Slater has one of her typical *profound* and *provocative* questions, and as your camp counselor and equestrian trainer, I'm gonna answer it. But listen to me, girls 'cause I'm gonna say this once and only once, and if you forget it, don't waste my time running to me when you should have listened up from the start instead of daydreaming about boys and bubblegum and god knows what else you think about in those adolescent eggheads of yours. You hear?" Rose said.

We heard.

Jill was still tasting her tameness.

"I said I'm gonna say it to you once, right now, and never again, so don't ask me to repeat myself, don't make me waste my breath, 'cause I don't have much breath left, according to my most recent calculations, so I'm saying this once, not twice, not thrice, just once and only once am I going to say I'm goddamn sorry."

We stood there, letting the words linger.

Rose herself seemed surprised by her last three words, her head cocked, as though, like us, listening to the linger. And then: "Would you all *stop* with your gawking and *get to work!*" Rose bellowed, and so we did. We scattered fast.

I'm sure it was the sugar. I could tell a long story about this, but I shouldn't now. Now the day is done, and that bugle is playing, like it did every evening at Flat Rock Farm, us twelve girls and the family standing in a ring around their flagpole while "Taps" played on their tape recorder set in the kitchen window. Day is done. Gone the sun. Strange, isn't it, that every evening the sun just slips away, soft as a slipper falling from a woman's foot. You can't ever hear it crash. Because it doesn't.

And last night—speed ahead thirty years now, Rose seventy-something and I know not where—last night I was lying in bed next to the daughter that is mine, helping her find her way to sleep. Sleep is not easy for Clara. My son plunges in with glee, the same way some kids plunge into pools. But Clara, well, she is like me, picking her way carefully down a set of stone stairs, slippery, the granite treads emerald with old moss and damp.

And so I lie next to my daughter, this growing girl, this girl growing away from me; night after night she lets me lie close—for how much longer?—me, hoping to ease that passage, trying to give her what I was not able to get, and we talk. I so *treasure* this time. Every night. I treasure. The darkness loosens our lips. Lying together, side by side, I think it makes us less afraid of the bit we both know is lodged in all of life. She's learned that one without me. Tell me, who is totally free? And who is not hurt by what holds them?

And Clara, who has been studying the solar system in school this autumn, asks, "Why, if the sun is keeping the planets in their orbit because of its gravitational pull, well then, why don't all the planets just get totally sucked straight into the sun?"

"Good question," I say. I stare up, into the darkness. Light spills from beneath her door, from the hall, where it is golden with glow. "Could it be because there are other solar systems beyond ours exerting an equal but opposite gravitational pull? Could it be that the force of our spinning through space counteracts the force of the sun's suck?" I don't know the answer. Neither, obviously, does she. We guess and guess and then, when we have nothing left to wager, we just lie there together in the dark, mother and daughter in a blue twin bed, a beautiful bed, French blue, two stars and a moon cut out of its planked headboard.

And then she finally falls asleep. It happens every night, the same way, the same fear, the same soft landing.

Rose sugared the bit on Friday, and on Saturday, the day before the Sunday that marked the end of camp, I fell.

My falling was neither orchestrated nor artful. We were in morning lessons. I was riding, of all horses, Hero, a large white pony with a heavy plodding gait. Rose set the cantilever bars for me at just three inches and instructed me to trot the pony over them. I'd done this before, several times, and it had none of the thrill of a real jump done at high speed and height. I was sleepy, sad. Camp was coming to a close. I felt the way one feels at the end of a long frightening movie so wholly absorbing that you lose yourself for hours in the matinee, and then it's over, and you are tossed back into time, and you emerge from the theatre, blinking, disoriented, your homework undone, your shoes too tight, everywhere the plain plodding plot of your life, and you understand that the real fear is here.

Something had softened in Rose. She set the cantilevered bars. I turned Hero towards them, pressed him into a desultory trot, my eye not on the jump but on the distance, where Hank was riding his rusted tractor high in the farthest field, going around and around.

And because of this—my wandering eye, my blank brain, because I failed to lean forward or convey to the horse—an exquisitely sensitive prey animal designed by eons of evolution to pick up even the slightest signal—any sense of urgency, the horse simply stopped just before the jump. I, however, forced to live by the laws of physics, which say that an object in motion remains in motion—well I kept going, flying over the jump and landing with a thud on the other side, in the sand.

The girls clapped and laughed. I stood up, brushed off. Hero had taken my leave as an opportunity to get in a quick graze, munching at the thin vegetation that struggled up through the fill. I looked at the horse. The horse looked at me, a chomped-off daisy dangling from his mouth. He quickly slurped it up, swallowed. That's it.

That's *it*? A sudden stop, a tiny toss. Painless. Yes. The real fear is here. When the show is over. When you fall not down but out. I shoved my hands in my jeans and looked at my horse, chewing his greens and florals. I looked at Rose, chewing her lip. She smiled sadly at me. I think she saw what I saw, or maybe she saw *that* I saw—a million things. A billion years. The single shred called your life. How it's so impossibly small in this trail ride through time and yet so stuffed with all your significances. How you are forced to grow, to go, crooked or straight, east or west, just go, go, go, leaving versions of yourself behind as sketches you can't complete. I couldn't have said it then but I knew, in the bone-way one does, that at the core of any life is the truth of its tiny hugeness, yourself more serial than singular, so who you were then is not who you are now or will be in the future; it was obvious. My horse was bored and digesting daisies. Four years ago I didn't love horses and four years hence I probably would no longer. Perhaps scarier than falling down is falling out. Of love. I would lose my love. And when I took that tumble, what would be there, beneath me? What hoof would I hold? What would make my world move with such pounding beauty? Who could know? One could only hope for the presence of passion or, alternatively, for the balance one needs to bear its absence.

High in the hill above me stood Hank, staring at stalks.

4: Time Passes

What I have wanted in my life is a form in which to cast my fears. Horses were that form. I now suggest, having wandered back into my past, that on their backs a girl practices paradox, balances paradox, bears paradox, which we must be able to do if we are to live with authenticity, in a world where everything wavers. It is not about sex or even love. It is about, I think, learning to find the ground by giving it up, casting aside the clenched classifications of a culture terrified of thinking beyond the binary. I am giving you, here, my best guesses, each guess grown from the loam of personal memory, and no more. And yet more, because are not horses living proof that, despite what science says, our nervous systems are not, in fact, in fear, locked into fight or flight? Horses remind us that humans can choose to respond to terror in flexible ways, *wait* and *watch* primary amongst them. Remember Amy, my daughter's riding instructor? Remember how, when she whistled, the horses would surge across the field, the pounding we felt beneath our feet and the keen desire to step back from the fence, to flee? "Wait and watch," Amy would say, and so we did, and we felt our fear turn over. *Ungripping*, when your patriarchal world has trained you to do the opposite.

And more. I think that girls see their corporeal contradictions in the tethered mare or stallion—so strong, so strung, pure prey, hard hooves, once wild while drawn, inextricably, to things manmade, those muscles.

In the end, there is no single summation or simple sketch that can capture the bond between a girl and her horse. There is, for sure, no science to what I'm saying here. I speak from my experience only but, then, also from what I saw, year after year, my sample size just twelve, plus Rose. She's reading what I'm writing here, smiling over my shoulder, living, now, in a place of motes and stars. She approves of my hypotheses. She's pleased with me at last. She agrees that when a girl goes to her horses she is not in a craze but, I'd wager—we wager—in a state of grace, able to at last admit what we wish most of all not to know: that we have to find a way of falling before we can claim our little lives.

I loved horses and rode horses until I turned fourteen, at which point I stopped, not because, as Freud might say, I found my way to men. I didn't. In some ways, I think I never have. What I found, around that time, was a whole new family I went to live with, my new room in this new place tucked beneath the eaves of a house so old it slanted sideways, the pine floors pitted and amber. It was in that new old room, in this new old home, that I found, stashed in a crawl space, a bent book about a lighthouse and the passing of time, a book that had a canter so airy yet pounding you had to hold on hard lest you lose your way in the sea of this story. The words and their way awoke in me a desire to master the many gaits of language. I wanted to turn it, trot it, tether it to the page, and yet also let it spill, this constant playing with paradox. Eventually, as I grew up, I left horses behind. Words became my mount, sentences my stable, the entire enterprise anchoring me even as, still today, it drives me too fast, too long, too much, eclipsing days, weeks, months, everything around me in a haze.

Except my children. In their faces I see centaurs, centuries, the comings and goings of many people from here to there to here. Sometimes my children's eyes go back so far I see, in the tiny point of light at the end of their infinite tunnel, a person dancing there. And sometimes I see, in their eyes or in my reflected face, a place before we were, and then before the before, and then before the before the before, and once I went so far back I came to a place where I was not, and when I returned I knelt down, and, like my mother once had, I kissed the ground called *home*.

There is so much to do in this new home, in this new country, just forty miles from the city where we still live on school days. I am certainly under no illusions that out here in the country I'll beat back time and find the girl I once was, pure in her passion for horses. That girl is gone for good, and when we finally move here full time, when we finally get our horses, when I finally ride again, it will be a different me on my mount, long past that point of intense interest. I hope I like it, at least. That my daughter loves it is enough. We are moving here for her, for horses, but for more than that too. We are moving here so we can know this ancient earth without its cities and its cement, this planet born from a big bang, proof perpetual that something comes from nothing, and also proof, perpetual, that nothing is the state to which it all returns.

The fact is, every animal eventually goes extinct. The average life cycle of a species is five million years. There is not a single species on this earth that has been here for forever, and as for us, according to the clock, it looks like our time is just about up. We're five million years old, more or less, and beyond that, scientists believe we're at the cusp of an ecological disaster. Thus, we are moving to the country—to the horses, the goats and pigs and cows and coyotes and crabapples—because how will our children choose to try to save the earth if they do not even know it?

If our time is up, I hope the horse's isn't. Long ago, during the Pleistocene period, horses survived a mass extinction caused by a radical glaciation, an ice age so severe that when it was over, 95 percent of life on earth had vanished, forever. The equine's superior adaptability and sparse caloric needs, combined with its enormous speed may have contributed to its survival then and, I hope, again, in our most uncertain future.

If humans were to die out, or in some other fashion to leave the earth forever, who would hold the histories? Who would speak about the first people who struggled to straddle wild equines thousands of years ago, in the Ukraine steppes, when civilization was barely born? Who would tell about how horses changed our world so entirely that time and space shifted while trade blossomed, bringing with it wars, bullets, blood; the glorious chariots and then the plain old plows, the day's work, the working days, the hauled loads, the forests falling, the black blinders, the crops cracking, the heavy harrows and the bright red barns and the hay-smelling stalls where, boxed up, boxed in, our horses rested before the next difficult dawn.

Just yesterday I read a report in a respectable science journal about new research suggesting flowers sing to one another. If indeed this on-it's-face-absurd claim is true, or even worthy of serious consideration, then perhaps we can allow ourselves to imagine that in some way we are entirely unable to fathom horses know how to whisper their history down their own long lines. And what would these whispers be? A story, of course, a tale about a once wild life shrugged off for the love of man, and then woman, both of whom seemed mythic from a distance but up close turned out to be silly little hoofless creatures with eyes so small they could not see the sky was falling; hairless creatures with blinders so, so total they would not, could not grasp a basic critical fact: they were not giants but rather *on* a giant, at its beck and behest.

And if horses survive the next great extinction some say we're tunneling towards, might they maybe do more than merely remember us? I'd like to think that long after we've left the world, horses will, in the myth I'm making, know how to cross the line and enter wherever we are once our bodies are gone. I like to think they will carry our spirits on their broad backs, across galaxies and through solar systems, so that, at last, we can see the orb where we once lived, for five million years or more. Finally freed from us, the planet will pulse with pure pigment colors, with all manner of life, the seas stocked with fish so wild and fresh they look like lamps beneath the wavy water, the trees splayed sky high, every landscape as if wrought with a watercolor brush, pinks bleeding into blues bleeding into the thalo greens of leaves.

Who could not hope—without us to muck things up—that the planet will find some beautiful balance again? And who could not hope still harder that even though we're gone, some sort of partial return will be possible? At least in the myth I'm making. Straddling their backs we ride through space, our forms transparent, our bones—if at all—white wisps.

Who, in the end, can accept that? Who can pry themselves loose from a living ledge? Who can let themselves fall and then get up with grace, or a giggle? Did you know that once we leave the world we will be light as feathers, as flakes? Do you hear the horses now? Or now? Listen hard, Clara. Feel them with your feet. They are thundering towards us. They travel in packs. They are hard and healthy. Come, while we still have time. Hold out your hand and say, *Come now.* Say, *Amen.* Call the names of all the horses you've been lucky enough to love. Say, Here, here, *White Night, Pride's Starlight, Evening Mist, Rocked Steady, Oh Gosh! Fly Me to the Moon, Desert King, Hope 'N' Glory, Glory Be—*

It is time, ladies.

Let us all go galloping.

3

Old Homes

1: Kosher

They might as well have been from the Isle of Skye. Or Australia, the Antarctic, what have you. Her hair was long and very blond, her skin so pale I could see the blue throb of a vein in the nook of her neck. Behind her hung a child, similarly pale, as pale as powder, with two long braids expertly woven, tied off at the ends with red ribbons. The child lingered at her mother's legs. The summer sun glared on the stoop where I stood. I tried to peer behind the little girl, but the house was dark, the only light glinting off a gun hung on the wall.

It was high summer, midafternoon, the cicadas creaking and my vinyl suitcase absorbing sun like a sponge so when I lifted the handle to step inside the plastic seared my skin. I abruptly dropped the suitcase. From behind me I felt my father—*go now*—his hand at the small of my back. The woman motioned me in. The powder girl sniffed, swiped her nose, held up her hand, a long string of glisten webbing her thumb and first finger. *Go now*, he said.

And so I went.

I was shown to my room. The house was already crammed with children, none of them strays, like me, but several of them with questionable connections to one another: steps and halves, which made me think of a girl sliced down her center, half her mouth missing. I was neither step nor half but foster, sent from the state, which is maybe—though I doubt it—why I got the smallest room, under the eave at the right end of the house, a room so small if I spun in its center my outstretched hands brushed the walls, which themselves were busted and bulging with all manner of mysterious cracks. Generations of different people with different tastes had left those horse-haired walls piled high with paper flaking off here and there, revealing new patterns beneath old patterns beneath city scenes beneath boats on lakes and boys with balls. Built in 1774, the old arthritic house groaned and sighed at night, hunkering its sore summer-baked body more deeply into the dirt, and I'd lie there in that new old little bed and sometimes it seemed I was spinning so fast I'd have to steady myself on the warbling walls. Other times those walls seemed to speak to me, to beckon me, and I'd spend hours past midnight peeling off paper to see what lay beneath. I remember finding grapevines whose twisted paths I could trace with my finger, up and down and around, up and down and around, over and over again, a rhythmic, almost melodic movement of mind and body that reminded me of riding and eventually sent me to sleep. In the first summer month of my three-year stay with that family, my dreams seemed always sparse, my slumber all static, an occasional stick figure or single tree appearing over and over again. I'd wake most mornings parched, a bedside fan churning the boggy air, their tap water tasting tinny as I drained it down.

I became the Trevor family's foster child in August of 1978, at the age of fifteen, just when, as I'd predicted several years before, during that first summer at Flat Rock Farm, my passion for horses was passing, in its place mementos, like the pink and red ribbons I'd brought with me to the Trevors, stuffed into the bottom of my suitcase. The date and name of the show was ink-stamped on the oval, on its back, proof that the past had happened, that the people and things I'd loved could not be completely erased. What scared me was how fast faces faded from my mind. I'd sit on my bed in the Trevors' house and hold those ribbons hard, but my grip, it seemed, was gone, Rose a slashing shadow, my mother a sound without shape.

That was the summer a heat wave had descended upon the city and its suburbs, the lawns turning taupe, the gardens all beds of brown. Wherever you looked you saw a hot, whitened world. From a distance people appeared as though they were wavering, their bodies uncertain, as if they might never materialize. Air conditioners rattled in windows all up and down the street, but in the Trevors' house it was quiet and close, the circuitry too old to support so much wattage, the windows all open and the white curtains flapping like flags in the thick air.

Instead of central air or window units, the Trevors reclined on lounge chairs under their large grape arbor, bottles of wine in a bucket of ice, long-stemmed glasses on a low table before them. I watched Cranston, my foster father, lift a corked bottle by its dripping neck and with exaggerated elegance—*du vino pour la femme and les petites?*—pop the top and pour the liquid for Annie and himself, and then in still smaller amounts for all the children, encouraging us to savor the stuff before swallowing. "Go ahead," Cranston said to me when he saw how I was hesitant, and so I did, if only to obey. I stepped up to the table and held a giant goblet by its skinny stem. "Now take a sip," Cranston said, and so I did, a small sip, a sharp tang, my eyes tearing and my nose filling up with flavor. A second sip and my skin seemed to shed its outer layers so now I could feel beneath the heat the barest breezes stirring. After my third sip, Annie removed the glass from my hand and said, "Enough is enough," which was true, for the wine had moved up my spine and kept hitching my head higher.

Perhaps the wine was their secret, for Annie and Cranston, my foster parents, shrugged off the heat as though it were an unwanted piece of clothing, their skin fresh and dry even as the thermometer inched into the nineties, the humidity turning the air to jam. At sundown the family would steam mussels on the porch, prying them open and sucking the innards down, tossing the hitched shells into the bushes. "Compost," Cranston announced each time he lobbed his leftovers, but I had no idea what he meant. Where

I was from, we didn't eat shellfish—it wasn't kosher—so when Cranston offered me a mussel, I felt I had to say no. Still, I watched them all closely. I saw the opened shells, the oily glimmer of the packed fish inside. I saw how they tipped back their heads and, using the shell like a spoon, sucked down the steamed meat, a little trigger bobbing in their throats when they swallowed.

Annie and Cranston, along with their five children, were connoisseurs of a certain kind of lifestyle for which there is no easy word. To say they knew the art of relaxation would be far too simple a summation. Annie's kitchen was packed with cookbooks and she'd labor over them for hours, but always humming as she worked, a small smile on her face as she read the recipes and then altered them to suit her taste, the big wooden spoon lifted to her lips, a thoughtful pause as she stared into some distance I could not name, and then a sudden swerve as she added more chives or a dash of dark pepper. "Try some," she'd say, wanting to draw me in, and obediently I'd try, and obediently I'd stare, my head cocked as though in thought. "Well," Annie would finally ask. "What do you think it needs?" I could never answer. Where I was from, meals were not for fun. A portion dropped on the floor might bring a bruise. You put your fork to your food and lifted with all the care you could muster. No one cocked their heads and mused about spice while the kitchen window clouded from some steam. "What do you think it needs?" Annie would repeat, perhaps confused by my silence and I'd stammer, "Salt?" every time.

I don't think there's a reason for everything, but if I did I might say God—not some system or the state—but God matched me with the Trevors because they were everything I was not. Or maybe it would be more accurate to say their household was everything mine was not. I was Jewish. The Trevors were blue-blooded Brahmins. I'd grown up celebrating the Shabbat on Friday evenings, lighting candles and singing the Schma, my mother with a covering over her head, which was bowed in unusual deference, her hands for once not fisted. The Trevors knew nothing about Friday nights, instead serving their Sabbath on Sunday, at the odd hour of

3 p.m., so by evening you were done with the whole thing and had nothing to do but watch the red disc of that summer sun flare behind the trees you could see from the window.

As a Kosher girl I didn't eat shellfish, but the Sabbath pork I was willing to try, stabbing it with my fork and sawing sideways, the whole family watching me as I lifted a small slab to my mouth, took it in with my teeth, chewed for what seemed four hundred minutes, like chicken, a little, and unlike anything I knew, a lot, so after I'd swallowed I shrugged and, then, seeing their disappointed faces I said, "Tasty."

"Really?" asked Annie. "You liked it?"

"I liked it," I said.

"She hated it," said Kyle, one of their sons and my newly acquired foster brother. Kyle was sixteen and so blond he was almost white.

"I did not hate it," I said, but suddenly I wanted to cry.

"It's nothing to get upset about," Cranston said. "There's always PB and J."

"Who's upset?" I said, but my voice gave me away. It got snagged on something and then there were tears. Why? What for? I wasn't sure. Later on, alone in my room, I thought about this clan, their wine, their pork, the way they loved to lounge beneath the leafy shade of their own vines. I thought about how their antique house stood out on a street of small square boxes and tidy lawns, the gardens all preplanned except for theirs, packed with run-away perennials and spires higher than my head. Cranston, a history buff, insisted that all the children under his roof memorize the names of the kings of England from the fourteenth century on, a pedagogical plan no one paid much mind to. Still, at night the entire family read together, two parents, six kids—counting me—everyone sitting around the dinner table with a book, no noise except for the turning of a page or a small sigh or some muted expression of delight or dismay. I'd bring a book down right along with everyone else, but my words seemed always senseless, scrambled , and I had the feeling I was up above, attached to no one or nothing, circling a place without pain, this home so singular and basically serene, I couldn't see how to settle.

Pain is a point, a direction, a signal; its presence assures one's existence in the world. You are alive because you hurt, or, similarly, you are alive because you hurt others. In my mother's house, pain was a language that overrode all other kinds of communiqués. Thus I learned to live with a heightened awareness that put my every sensory organ on alert. I listened to the sound of footfalls coming closer, now going away; lying awake at night, I heard her making her way down the hall, a shadow gliding over my sheet. I was nourished on danger, and rage too, a heady brew that brings the world to its brilliant boiling point for hours of every day; and you come to need it that way. You lose the casual manner of living, how many make their way through, tasting a little of this, a little of that, the music on low, the page turning slowly, some sustaining story emerging. I knew nothing of this sort of sanity. Thus the Trevors were aliens to me, and I could not adjust to their territory. It was so much more than pork on Sunday or mussels packed in a striated shell. It was a style of living on land that I had never seen before—wacky, happy, harmless. It left me empty and disoriented, longing for my long-lost poison. I missed my mother, yes. I missed more her atmosphere, all arrows and opera, with a little bit of blood here and there.

2: Holes

The house was old and had many holes. Not all the windows had screens. Once that summer a starling flew into Annie and Cranston's bedroom, went round and round in circles near the ceiling and then abruptly flew out, leaving his bird dirt here and there on the floor. The family had a dog named Bruno and a tabby cat named Mince, who gave us eight mewling kittens at the end of June. We found a chipmunk living in the cupboard and mice sometimes streaked across the floor, disappearing behind baseboards or under beds. The heat broke with a crack, and rain came crashing down and after that the air was as fresh as something scrubbed, the day shining at its edges. Then the temperature soared again. From my window in the morning I could see steam rising off the red roofs tented up and down the streets, and the streets were strange to me, and stayed strange, because I resisted exploration. A few times, in the evenings after dinner, I agreed to walk with Kyle the short distance into town and we bought ice cream cones from a store called Barbar Jean's, but mostly I stayed inside, citing the heat as my excuse. The truth was I'd never liked newness. I was the type of kid who would read the same book over and over again, who compulsively chewed the inside of my cheek in the precise same spot, who, even at fifteen years of age, still had to close the closet door once the lights were out for fear of the beasts in there. Walking with Kyle in the torpid early evening we passed the old abandoned house four doors down, the yard there sandy, filled with feral cats and crooked crab grass. The cats were so starved I could see each individual rib and as the day darkened their eyes stood out like stars, some circling, others staying still.

Living mostly within, I read my books and, when no one was at home, explored the Trevors' house, which in both its spirit and its setup bore no resemblance to the one I'd come from, a contemporary my mother kept maniacally clean, even her wallpaper washable. My father—a passive man with none of my mother's verve or nerve—my father had always claimed that my mother had changed once her babies were born, that before her pregnancies she'd been carefree, and I have a picture that suggests he was correct. In it my mother is young, not much more than twenty, and she wears a paisley kerchief tied beneath her chin, some stray curls blowing in a swift sea breeze as behind her a massive ocean moves. Her mouth a festive red, she purses her painted lips in a coy kiss-me pose as somewhere in time the camera clicks and captures this second self. Once the babies came, my father always explained, so too did her unhappiness, her rages growing right along with me, her once playful smile crimped into a curve beneath which stewed a sadness for something I could never salve, in her or in myself. Social Services got involved a few summers after horse camp, when, without distraction or passion, forbidden by my mother to continue the only out I knew—riding—I began to cut myself, the red rents some primitive sort of signal as hurt and help entwined in my mind.

I missed her, even though. It was she I thought of—and tried to conjure—as I explored the Trevors' old home, opening their medicine cabinets, palming their pills, unscrewing the tops of mysterious glass bottles with alien scents inside. I tried on Annie and Cranston's reading glasses, hooking the rims behind my ears, my held-up hand suddenly huge and pink and misty, not mine. What was? Once, climbing high into the Trevors' attic, I found a dwarf-sized door that opened into a closet, inside canes hanging on hooks and scrawled on the dingy wall mysterious signatures—*Harry Mumford, Faith Mason, Robert Smutter, Earl Greylot*—people who had come before me. Over the old beehive oven hung that gun, a rifle really, a relic from the Civil War and part of Cranston's antiques collection that included pink and black butterflies preserved under glass, copper chamber pots gone green round their rims, and dusty medical books picturing midgets and giants, those pages so old they flaked away in my fingers.

Houses never rest; I knew that, but this was a house especially full of chatter. I could hear the mice, the mosquitos, the cats crying, the signatures scrawling, and then sometimes from within the walls the sound of large mammals making their way; I heard as they tumbled above me, their play so raucous that bits of my ceiling sifted down, and I heard as they walked right by my bed, nothing between us but cracked plaster, paint, and paper. "Racoons," Annie said when I asked her. "They live in the walls here." She held out a spoon. "Give me a taste test," she said.

Every night now they came, walking in the wall beside my bed, so close to my ear I thought I could hear them breathe. I started to scratch at that space, trying to widen a tiny puncture already present. Plaster snowed onto my sheets. I found an X-acto knife in the desk in my room and, after checking to see that my door was closed, I used its precise point to trace a small porthole. Flexing my first finger, I gave the wall a push, surprised at how cleanly it all gave way. The hole I'd made was quarter sized and perfect for peering.

I turned out my light. I peered in. From far down the wall I heard the tell-tale lumbering of a single coon. He came closer and closer still, and then I could smell him, pungent and moist, and then I could hear him chuffing as he ambled, closer and closer still, my heart picking up, and suddenly, for the first time, I felt like I lived here, like I was pinned to this place that was silent with sleep except for me, still staring as his smell grew stronger and then, quite suddenly it seemed, he came around some corner and I was eye to eye with a beast.

The eye I saw had a wet shine, with a dark ink drop of a pupil. The pupil seemed suspended in liquid, and when the coon blinked I saw its lashes, thick and tar-black. "How goes it?" I asked and because he didn't care to answer or perhaps had other business to do, the animal suddenly vanished, and I found myself staring at space.

Every night I waited at my porthole for communion with the coon. And every night the animal and I did nothing but simply sit and stare at one another. Still, it seemed to fulfill some need for both of us and then, abruptly, it was over. I would look away, look back and the beast would be gone, or the beast would blink several times in rapid succession and then, without further ado, ramble off. Whenever it happened that way I felt somehow stung, or sniped, and in response I reached for the X-acto knife, closing it in my grip. It was always late, midnight or plenty past. I sometimes tried to picture how this house would look from the street, every window black but mine, the one way off to the right, a cube of marigold. The coon had left. Alone, my hand closed round the stem of the knife, leaning in close to the hole and then bringing the blade up. Sometimes just then my eye caught sight of the moon outside; it was huge that June, swollen, indecent, and so close it seemed I could cup it. It was the exact same moon that hung over my real home, no more than twenty miles from here but seeming so much farther. I pictured a person awake there just as I was awake here, seeing that light in the sky and wondering if I was too. My mother? No. My father? He'd gone to Egypt. My siblings? Scattered in different schools. This moon was mine alone. And knowing that, and thinking that, I'd lean close to the hole I'd made in the wall and sculpt it larger, cutting crescents out of it until, one night, a pointed nose emerged from my aperture, leathery but wet, two dark dots for nostrils and then a tiny tongue. Slowly, I offered my upturned palm and the snout pushed further out, eagerly taking in my myriad scents, so many it seemed I had, because the snout just went on sniffing, salt and sand and who knows what else lay in the layers of me. This went on for I'm not sure how long, because when I woke up the coon was gone and I'd apparently slept slumped against the wall with my hand held out like an offering.

And so it was that night by night I made the hole larger and night by night the coon presented more of himself to me. I'd say the coon had maybe come a quarter of the way out of the wall when Annie discovered my project. She was cleaning and found the busted plaster by my bedside and when she leaned in closer to look she saw the treat tidbits I'd started to use, all lined up on the wooden beam that ran just inside the wall. That night she and Cranston took me aside and with my bedroom door closed asked me what on earth I was doing. Because I had no fib readily available I simply told them the truth, wondering if this would be the sort of behavior for which unrelated children were kicked out, kicked back—and would I want that? Suddenly I wasn't so sure. I told them the whole story, how I was courting a coon, my many midnight visits.

When I was finished—a long silence. I could hear my heart. It was hammering high up. I thought of the things I'd found here in this severed space, the coons of course, the reading around a table, taste tests, and pink pork; it all seemed strange, still, and what I'd lost was so much larger but nevertheless, and having come this far, would I want to leave? The silence had stretch, went on and on. I'd ruined one of their walls.

Now Cranston walked across the floor, knelt by the bed, and examined my punched-out place. Annie stood, looking serious.

At last Cranston spoke. His back was to me as he fingered the rim of the hole. "Boy or girl," he asked.

"What?" I said.

"Your midnight meetings," he said. "Is the raccoon in question a boy or a girl?"

"Boy," I said, suddenly sure.

"Why do you think that?" Annie asked, her face still solemn, but I thought I saw the small flicker of a smile.

"It's how he smells," I said, and then suddenly they were laughing. Cranston went up on his feet and Annie's shoulders were shaking as she swiped away a tear, and I said, "What? What?"

"Kids," Cranston called, striding across the floor, opening my bedroom door and leaning over the bannister, "kids! Come look at the coon hole Lauren has made."

All the kids came and I described for everyone going eye to eye with the beast, and even the boys were impressed. "I'll tell you what," Cranston said, looking at me.

"What?" I said.

"Let's make this hole a little larger and tonight we'll pull him all the way out and make him ours."

"Can we really do that?" I asked.

"We can try," Cranston said and then he took my X-acto knife from where it lay on the desk, knelt on my bumpy bed, and began to widen what I'd already made, working his way up and down and around, up and down and around, his hole larger and darker than anything I'd dared to do. When he was done I went forward and put my whole hand through and then kept going, feeling with my fingers the dusty innards of this place, the spiral spiderwebs and broad beams, everything crisscrossed and crazy back there, not easy to interpret.

"You want to try?" Cranston asked.

Yes. I wanted to try.

Because coons are nocturnal, we had to have darkness. Come midnight, and with the lights off, we all crowded around the cutout by my bed. Cranston handed me his bait, bits of bacon and blue cheese. I lay it all carefully on the ledge and then we sat back to wait. A light summer shower started and I could hear it ticking against the windows, but other than that, and for the first time since courting my coons, the house seemed completely at rest. The rain stopped, and in its wake came a deep nighttime kind of quiet, outside clouds scudding across a polished sky, wind teasing the trees, but inside, in this house, we heard not a single stirring, not a tiny footfall, not the merest squeak. It was as though all the animals that lived here caught wind of what we were up to and had fled, en masse, the mice followed by the coons followed by the bats and the beetles and the ants. "I think they're gone," I said.

At last Cranston, sitting in a chair by my desk, rose without a word, left the room, and came back with a broom that he held high and swished against my ceiling shouting, "Wake up critters. It's meal time."

Nothing.

"Let's sing," suggested Annie.

"Sing?" said Cranston.

"You never know," said Annie.

"I'm not singing," said Kyle.

"I'd sing," I said, because at home we sang, on Friday nights, we sang the blessing over the bread and the wine, we sang together, and even though god never answered, the singing itself seemed something.

"Michael, row your boat ashore," Annie began, and I joined in, and Cranston sighed, put down the broom, and Emma, the youngest started up and pretty soon, drunk on the darkness and the general silliness of the situation we were all yodeling away, pretending to paddle or trimming the sails, our pantomimes so intent that for a few moments we forgot all about our coon so it shocked me when I turned around to see a dark darting snout and two petite paws gripping the edge of the aperture. I elbowed Cranston who then coasted across the room and grabbed the coon by its ample scruff, pulling a shockingly small body into the air. The song stopped, all of us frozen in various poses of pantomime while the coon swayed, waved its tiny mitted paws, and then started to scream.

Like crying, screaming, I'd always thought, was a uniquely hominoid form of distress. The coon suggested otherwise. With its mouth open and its tongue trembling, the animal screamed and screamed, its sound eerily familiar as it struggled under Cranston's insistent grip. Tears sprang to my eyes. I hadn't meant them to but there they were, and Cranston said, "Shush, little baby," and curled the animal into the crook of his arm. It was just so small, so much smaller than what I'd expected, clearly an infant and barely even that. Cranston rocked it. The coon quieted. "I'd say," Cranston announced, ferreting in the fur below its stomach, "I'd say our catch is a girl."

For a second all was silent while we took in the news. Then the coon started up again, shrieks of pure anguish as it flailed for its freedom, desperately twisting this way and that while Cranston held on hard, his expression suddenly grim. "Shush, shush," he said, rocking fast now, speaking fast now—nervous now—I could tell. Even in the darkness I could see the sweat on his neck. When I looked back at the hole by my bed it seemed for the first time downright menacing, its edges all jagged and ripped, pouring dust and darkness. I don't know how long we stood there, Cranston desperately trying to quiet the coon, the rest of us with our hands hanging uselessly by our sides; it could have been an hour before the animal's voice gave out and the crying turned to croaks turned to quiet.

"Jesus," said Annie, her eyes wide.

Exhausted, the animal suddenly settled. Cranston kept rocking. The coon's eyes began to close and faster than I could say *night now* the animal was suddenly asleep.

No one moved. From far away I heard a siren, and then a series of chimes. My clock glowed, the second hand silently sailing. The animal yet out a yelp and we all went stiff with startle, but then its breathing became rhythmic again. My feet tired, I went to sit on my bed. Slowly Cranston walked over to me, knelt by my side and, as carefully as he could, transferred the still-slumbering mammal into my arms. "She's all yours" Cranston said to me. "She's in a brand new home. Now help her find her way."

3: Some Slender String

That night, the raccoon stayed in a large cage in my room. She made strange noises—chirps and chatters, squeals and yips, calls, perhaps, to her cohorts on the other side of the wall, and indeed I heard what seemed like answers, strange scratches, long yodels, nervous pacings back and forth above me. Finally the dawn came, the sky fringed with pink and the sun bright as a coin in a spill of rising red. Gradually the hazy trees assumed their familiar shapes, and the tidy lawns of the neighbors came into view, hoses wrapped around reels and tiny tricycles tipped on their sides.

Soon the family would awaken and crowd around the raccoon, wondering what she could do. I wanted to be the first to see and so, as quietly as possible, I freed the latch on the cage. After crawling out, however, the animal refused to move. She stood in the center of my room, hunched on her hind legs, her front paws dangling down, kangaroo style, looking left and right as if assessing her surroundings, all traces of her terror gone, just gone, replaced with, it seemed to me, a systematic sort of study she carried out with staring—at the walls, at the floor beneath her feet, at the spackled ceiling, at a loose sock she batted with her paw while quietly cocking her head. It amazed me, how fast grief could go, how quickly, in certain sorts of beings anyway, curiosity took the place of terror. I watched her watch, my stare following hers, here a desk, there a book on the floor, these objects defined, it seemed to me, not by the fact of their foreignness but by what they might hold or have, her curiosity keen and clear and far from me, a girl who yearned for the familiar even when all its edges were sharp. "Here, here," I whispered, kneeling down, holding out my hand, yet another unknown object she leaned forward for.

I instantly admired that raccoon, even if I anthropomorphized her, and I'm sure I did, but not to the point that I failed to note her differences, everywhere, all the time. I admired the raccoon first for her curiosity and second for her affection, which I was about to see, how she could go from being completely at sea to securely anchored in what just happened to be this noun called me. Of course I could not have said so with such certainty at the time. These thoughts and reactions were in no way worded all those years ago, when I was perhaps too young to know my metaphors. What I did know, however, was how new this old house was, for her and for me, and whereas I'd wept for weeks, she for no more than a moment. Why wouldn't that amaze me, a fifteen-year-old human who shared with this mammal almost all the same chromosomes, our brains eerily alike, save a few uniquely hominoid garnishes that guaranteed my grief would be wetter and longer and packed with a past she couldn't carry.

"Come," I said, but the coon—alternatively absorbed in staring and sniffing and batting—paid me no mind. And because, watching her, I suddenly felt a wild, yes, wild elation, I opened the door to my room and, bowing like a butler while gesturing towards the hall, I offered her full run of the house. No thanks. At last, then, I simply stepped around her with no plan or strategy in mind, and it was then that I discovered how fast her ties formed, because here, in a few mere moments and with no language exchanged, that animal took to following me with what seemed like total faith, scampering after me as I made my way down the stairs, at my heels as I traveled towards the kitchen. As an experiment I circled the dining room table ten times and ten times she went with me. It was as though the raccoon were hitched to me by some slender string, which is why I finally turned the tumblers and unlocked the front door, stepping out into the dawn. The street, usually busy, was dead this time of day; I crossed, the coon still with me, and, after climbing the opposite curb, we both turned to see, from a distance, the house where, like it or not, we lived.

We called her Amelia Earhart, Amelia for short, although looking back now I cannot recall the reason for the name. What I can recall is how much she changed my stay with that family, how impressed I was by her seemingly immediate adaptation to her new circumstances, how she attached to me so easily and then found the fridge, learning to open it with her agile paws, pulling out bunches of dark grapes and blocks of wrapped cheese. Unlike me, Amelia would eat anything and, taking my cues from her, I began to do the same, one warm night mixing my meat with my milk, another night sucking the mussel straight from its peeling shell, so who was following who here, and did it really matter? I loved to pat her backwards, the flat fur bunching up into bristles and then smoothed into sleekness again. Her gold mask was always spiky to the touch but her paws were soft, split into four velvety segments, it seemed they worked better than human hands, tossing small balls, closing round your thumb with a pulsing dexterity.

The summer stayed hot. Amelia, however, was always on the move, couldn't be caged, rarely seemed to sleep, her sounds making their way into my dreaming, my night-mind now full of impossible animals: humans with tails, fish with feet. Occasionally I'd startle awake to find her hunched at the end of my bed, looking straight at me, something so insistent in her gaze one could almost think she was trying to pass me a message. Sometimes, unable to fall back asleep, I'd toss aside my single sweaty sheet and, with Amelia next to me, I learned my new nocturnal neighborhood, the houses doused in darkness as we walked here and there, back and forth, setting our stamp in soil, leaving behind us a trail of where we had been, proof I'd done my discovery.

We'd return at dawn or well before, slipping into a silent house, her fur wet with dew. Any insomnia we both had was cured by these long dark walks, or perhaps her nature was incontrovertible and, despite living with humans, she could only sleep when the sun came up. From almost the first second she became mine I wondered what of her I could change and what would stay the same. How far could a being bend and at what point did a flex become broken? I was still a child and thus I believed, somewhere inside, that she had these questions too, because I thought I saw them in her intelligent eyes that inched down slowly as light filled my room and she dreamt like a dog, her paws paddling while she chased invisible prey. She slept each morning away and, as if propelled by an invisible clock, reliably woke by four, stretching responsibly as though she'd taken a course on the importance of it all, taking care to bend each limb before finally finding her feet. We fed her fish or meats from a can and once she was done we'd venture forth a second time, her urge to explore becoming mine, or could it possibly have been my heretofore hidden urge hers, but either way, both by day and by night, my new neighborhood now revealed itself to me as, with the help of a six-pound mammal, I made the grids and crossroads my own.

Even today, thirty some odd years later, I recall the names of those streets I found with Amelia, perhaps because of Amelia, but I recall more what it was like to learn them—Oakvale Road, where the Carneys lived, and Dale Way, where almost every house had an above-ground swimming pool hidden by high fencing. I recall telling Annie with a studied sort of nonchalance, "Oh, I was up on Dale Way today," as though this were a major accomplishment. Maybe it was. That girl back then and this woman now—both hated and hate change, preferring to cling to the creaky rather than to stretch into space.

I don't know what drew so many to us when we walked. Or perhaps I do. People like to watch the wild, but we like it even more when nature and culture collide. There I was, a fully formed human, my tongue trained for language, my hands for napkins and knives. And there Amelia was, at my heels or perched upon my shoulder, an animal pulled from a parallel universe and living proof that two separate spheres could happily intersect. Back then, as now, I had a fascination with cosmology, and I remember I was reading a book about how, after the big bang, not one universe but billions formed side by side like bubbles sitting on a string. According to that book's author we were living in a vast world right next to neighbors in a dimension we simply couldn't see, and so it was the same for our neighbors, blind to the existences on either side of them, and yet still somehow we sense them. We try to imagine our way into ants and aliens and come up struck by the barrier called skin.

That small plain raccoon had none of the grandeur of grand questions even as the fact of her following me tickled people pink because it suggested, I think, proof of what was possible, down here, up there, and all around. And thus, when people saw us exploring the streets, parading up and down, Amelia's tail atwitch, as curious as we were proud—for, Look what we had found! Look what we had formed!—everyone came running out of their houses, hurrying down their walks, old women holding curlers in their hair, mothers with mixing bowls, men, their tails untucked. "What have you here? What animal is that?" they all wanted to know. The children surged forward, held back by nannies while Amelia chattered deeply, luxuriantly, standing high on her hind feet and turning in showy circles. Except for the immediate neighbors, no one knew where I came from and no one cared to ask; the final point perhaps was this: cosmology aside, I went from being an invisible person to "The Girl with the Raccoon," and by midsummer it seemed everyone in my new town had heard of me. I was practically popular.

One day, out walking, I came to a squat house on the edge of town, down by the railroad tracks where the hip-high grasses were. Bindweed grew wild here, great white wheels of it strewn everywhere through the field, the long stems tangling at my feet. I picked armloads of the flowers, feeling their fleshiness and admiring their centers, the tiny pistils packed with pollen.

I didn't see the man, at first. I wasn't sure if I was walking on his property, although I thought not for he had a tidy lawn that ended abruptly where the tangle of flowers began, the two separated by a clear seam.

The man was standing on the small porch of the small house painted a dark green or maybe a grey. He was smoking a cigarette but flicked it away after only a moment or two. "You live around here?" he asked, one eye on me and the other on Amelia who was sitting on my shoulder, preening. The man had silver hair combed in a side part, and he scowled at Amelia, unimpressed with her presence.

"Birch Street," I said. "321."

"321 Birch Street?" the man said, tilting his head in thought. "Isn't that where Cranston and Annie Trevor live?"

"That's right," I said.

The man stared at me. "You're not one of theirs," he said. "Are you?"

"Yes," I said, and then, confused I added, "I mean no."

The man raised one eyebrow and then slowly, his stare still solidly on me, he reached into his shirt pocket and slid out a second cigarette, placing it between his lips before snapping a match into flame.

"Yes and no?" he repeated, and then said nothing, letting the silence amplify the absurdity of my answer.

"I mean," I said, but in fact I didn't know what I meant, or how to explain what it was to be both in and out of a family, to belong but on the cusp. The man opened his mouth and smoke emptied into the air. It was like my systems shut down. All I could do was shrug.

"Linda," the man called, still staring straight at me. "Hey, Linda. We've got a girl with a raccoon out here."

Linda—she must have been his wife—came to the door, wiping her hands on a washcloth. "Good god," she said.

"Name's Amelia," I said.

"Your name is Amelia," the woman asked, "or is that what you call your raccoon?"

"Raccoon," I said. "I call the raccoon Amelia." As if on cue Amelia scuttled down my arm and leapt to the ground.

"And your name is?" Linda asked.

"Lauren," I said, and then added after a beat, "Slater."

"Lauren Slater here is telling me that she's living with Annie and Cranston and their bunch up on Birch Street," the man said, and then he scratched the bald dome of his head as though this were the most confusing thing in the world.

The woman peered at me over the porch railing, and then, suddenly, a soft smile. "You must be their new au pair," she said. She turned to her husband. "Annie Trevor told me not even a year ago, when we ran into each other at DeMoulas, how she was thinking of bringing in a girl from overseas."

And then suddenly it all came clear, how to tell this story. "That's right," I said, and I smiled up at the couple. "I'm from Ireland. I came to see your country."

The man looked visibly relieved. He pulled on his cigarette and said, "I'd offer you one, but here in our country we have laws about that."

"Not a problem," I said and then, suddenly, the man said, leaning forward, his voice dropping down, half whisper, half hiss: "You know, you don't have much of an accent for a girl from Ireland."

"American schools," I said, thinking quickly. "My parents sent us kids."

The man rocked back in his heels and I could practically hear him chewing on what I said, trying to decide whether to believe me or—

"You from the city," he said, "or are you—"

"Country," I said, before he could finish his sentence. Suddenly I was filled with exhilaration. Whatever I said I saw, emerald fields dotted with bright red barns, gold cubes of hay stacked in the sunlight, laundry on a line, the wind perfect. "At the base of some of the biggest mountains around," I added, and then there were mountains too, rumpled across the skyline, their tops lost in mist, mine. I told them how in my homeland I walked in forests with huge fronds, berries bright against stalks. And as I talked I learned, right then and there, the freedoms I could claim. Cut loose from a clear category, I could construct my own—at least it seemed that way to me—even as I felt my world warble the way it does when living a lie, no matter how swift or small. "We had horses," I said, my voice suddenly small, the reversal rapid, all my gladness gone, the flowers flabby in my arms.

"Horses," the man said. He looked entranced now, the woman askance. "That's quite something," she said, "living out there in the fields and forests like that. I imagine this here must all seem incredibly tame to you."

I looked around me. Trash blew in the breeze. The railroad tresses were rotted, the tracks bars of black. All of a sudden I was seized with a panic it took me a second to make sense of. Amelia was gone, had wandered off while I talked, the grasses behind me so high all I could see were their feathered tips. "Amelia Airheart!" I called, and then I waited for her sound in the stalks, nothing. "Amelia," I called again, my hands cupped around my mouth, a sick feeling inside me. "I've gotta go," I said, and even though not much more than a second had passed I'd already cemented my lie to her loss, which meant she wouldn't be back. When I finally found her at the fringe of the field, chewing on a stick, I grabbed hold of her fur—hard.

4: The Cupboard

In real life, the Trevors lived in a town in southern Maine, on a semi-busy street, in that old, old rambling house set on a grassy plot with two one-hundred-year-old fruit trees that flowered first and then bore peaches so soft that they bruised before falling from the branches. Bees feasted on the rotting pulp. In the evenings, once the bees were gone, I followed Amelia to the trees and watched her eat the goop left on the ground while I wandered around, picking up peach stones and studying their surfaces with my thumb. Cut free from my family of origin and a home gone gothic with dread, those peach pits interested me simply because I could see them.

And I saw other things as well, as though my actual eyes were changing, my vision, trained for terror, for trauma, for large sweeping scales, now narrowing in on plain everyday objects and experiences previously hidden from me. The peach pits. Dust furred on the rim of a cup. The pleasures of picnicking, which Amelia introduced me to, down by a pond stocked with carp. Annie provided us with the basket, but I'd insist on packing it, slowly sifting through their cupboards, holding up the glass woman full of salt and the glass man full of pepper, sniffing the cinnamon stored in a perforated tin. In my mother's home we weren't allowed to loll about in the pantry, so this too was new for me, and strange, and strangely delightful, canned cherries floating in fluid—*May I have one? Help yourself*—Annie watching as I, raccoon-like, fished about with my fingers, pulling two up by their black stems, dropping my head back and popping them in my mouth. I found the nutmeg, the dried packets of milk, the caramel sauces, and split peas packed in air-tight canisters that made a sucking sound when I opened them. Their fridge yielded up bibbed lettuce, tomatoes on the vine, wedges of chocolate cake, and wheels of cheese coated in a thick white wax. Piece by piece I'd decide what to bring, usually mozzarella—a favorite of Amelia's—plus enormous quantities of grapes, the fat purple kind, with juice as dark as iodine inside.

Basket packed, we'd walk off into the woods, laying a towel down by the pond, Amelia immediately crouching at its edge, ready to fish for her supper. Although the pond was stocked she always waited a good long time, looking, I assumed, for the perfect catch, while I lay there watching the sun cross the sky. Something uncoiled in me in those woods with Amelia, something long held hard and tight, a plaque of protection; I lay it down for a while and learned what life was like lived at a slower, lower level. I thought of Amelia fishing, or the Trevors all reading around a table at night, or Cranston polishing his antique pots, patient and quiet, the rag dark with dirt as he worked sometimes for hours in pursuit of something small. I still missed that high-stakes, home-grown fright; I'd be lying to say otherwise. But by poking a hole in the Trevors' wall, it seemed I'd opened up a separate space inside of me as well, a space I could sense, and almost see, like a cupboard waiting within me, and inside that cupboard: A cane. A comb. A stone. Sometimes I'd open the cupboard door to find an old woman sewing; other times I'd see grass that went back and back and dim in the distance a piebald pony grazing. I never knew what I'd find in there, or why; it's only now, years and years later that I see what united these objects was their quotidian character, the plain and quiet kind of plenty you miss when walking on a wire.

When Amelia came to us she was wild, but within twenty-four hours it seemed to me she'd consented to tameness. I had no way of knowing that this was untrue. I didn't understand that when Amelia followed me everywhere she was acting out of instinct, not fondness. Years later I would read the work of ethologist Konrad Lorenz, who made famous the fact that orphaned wild ducklings would cathect to the first person they saw when they struggled free from their shells, that person's face indelibly imprinted on the infant animal's most malleable brain. I'd see in Lorenz's book photos of him walking like the Pied Piper, a long line of geese waddling behind him. Lorenz also discovered that if, upon birth, the wild geese first saw a boot in motion or a spoon in motion, they would imprint upon it with the same ferocious loyalty, longing only to be near the inanimate object, somehow sucking from it succor and safety, reflexively, without thought or plan.

Amelia, in other words, was not following me because she was tame and almost certainly not because she loved me; she followed me because some dumb inner drive urged her to do so, the drive itself as wild as wings or water. I didn't feel in the least let down by this later-in-life discovery. What counted was not how I was loved. People often cite their pets as sources of "unconditional love," but surely they must know, at some level, that Fido likely sees in them a food source, first and foremost. Does this diminish the encounter? Not at all. We adore our pets not because they love us, but because they prove to us, day after day after day, that we love them with a purity not possible in human-to-human encounters. Our animals prove to us how capacious the human heart can be, and in doing so they give us, over and over, a great gift.

5: Going Wild

Amelia, not a human, not by a long shot, began to grow, and with a wild alacrity. Her baby teeth disappeared, sliding from their slots, and in their place came fangs of polished white. Her claws, previously clear, grew cloudy and dark and so sharp she left pits in the pine of the Trevors' antique floors when she walked over them. Her fur changed too, not in color but in hue, the bristles tipped with gold and blue. Yes, Amelia grew. She grew and she grew and she grew and then August came and with it a series of changes that seemed sudden and severe. My raccoon expanded so swiftly in August that one day, and all of a sudden it seemed, she was too wide to perch on my shoulder. Soon after that her behaviors became odd and unpredictable. At times she would snarl at something I could not see: a scent, perhaps, her wet nose raised and quivering, catching imperceptible currents, her world loaded with lavender, hot tar, wet leaf, rotted loam, bone. She started to tear apart our trash, clawing open the big bellies of bags, raiding the compost, dragging dead things over the stoop, once a rabbit no bigger than my fist, its ears ripped. Neighbors began complaining of trashcans tipped, their garbage ransacked, their cats, they claimed, attacked. I tried to keep Amelia in at night but she paced the house, up and down, around and around, stopping to stare longingly out the window and then, cued by something we could never see, she'd go berserk, clawing at glass, cocking her head and then clawing again, and again, her cries so high and hard that eventually I'd let her go. I'd open the door and watch her romp off into the darkness, heading diagonally across the lawn, through the shrubs, up over the Raymonds' chain-link fence, dropping down soundlessly onto the ground, going each and every time towards that old abandoned house, just four doors down, drawn there, over and over again, passing her nocturnal hours beneath its broken roof, or around its grounds; I wasn't sure. Perhaps she had a beau there, or a group, or a gang, or maybe, there, she could fight with all the feral cats she wanted and no one cared. Deep in the middle of the night we sometimes heard the fights, shrieks and snarls and shatters. Every morning, the streets were strewn with trash and neighbors started leaving us protest notes.

I'd go there, come morning. I'd go to the abandoned house. I'd stand at the edge of the busted steps and whistle two highs and one low, our special signal, and every time, within seconds it seemed, Amelia would climb through a hole in the wrecked outer wall, slide down the siding, and amble towards me, blood on her whiskers, dried drops here and there. I don't know why I never recoiled. Despite her outbursts, her pacing and scratching at glass, her ripping apart our trash, she never hurt us, never came close. Towards the whole Trevor family, she was nothing but unendingly affectionate, and I wonder if her sweetness seemed all the more so when set against her sometimes savage displays. Back home, I'd pour her milk in a yellow saucer and she'd delicately lap it up, chortle for more, and then climb into my lap, turning twice before wrapping into a coil and settling down to sleep.

"Soon," said Cranston, "she'll be too big to handle."

"She's already," said Annie, "too big to handle."

"She shouldn't live here," said Cranston. "It's not right."

"She doesn't live here," I said. "She sleeps at the haunted house."

"She's here every day," Annie said.

"All day," Cranston said.

"Inside," Annie said.

"It's inappropriate," Cranston said.

"Dangerous," Annie said.

If not now, they said. Then soon.

I went on a mission then. I needed to prove to people that it was possible to make a wild animal safe. I pedaled to the library in town where I found half a shelf dedicated to the topic of taming and training beasts. In 1852, I read, Sir Walter Rothschild, a British nobleman, had had a fleet of zebras shipped to him from Africa. Convinced he could tame them, he built a beautiful state-of-the-art barn and then hitched several of the equines to an impressive carriage whereupon, after cracking his long crop, he was taken for a ride through the cobblestoned streets of London, people stopping to stare as the carriage ricocheted past them. Dusting dirt off his trousers, Rothschild worked with his zebras day in and day out, surviving, I'm sure, grievous bites and backside bruises. Although Rothschild did eventually convince his zebras to haul some heavy loads, all in all the breed resisted his efforts, too severely stubborn for the whip or the bit. Still, many others tried after him, the zebra, because of its close connection to the horse, being an obvious beast-of-burden candidate.

The dog was the first domesticated animal, and the hamster probably the last, but in between, rodent and canine people, since the earliest civilizations, have been trying to domesticate dozens and dozens of animals: the cheetah, the kangaroo, the brown bear, the hyena, to name just a few.

As Jared Diamond tells us, of all 148 large mammalian species who inhabit this earth, only fifteen—sheep, goat, cow, pig, horse, Arabian camel, Bactrian camel, llama, alpaca, donkey, reindeer, water buffalo, yak, Bali cattle, and mithan—have proven amenable to domestication or the taming that precedes it. Zebras have that nasty temper and have probably sunk their teeth into more male hindquarters than we would care to count. Elephants, those gentle giants, mature too slowly, while deer and antelope panic in a pen. In general, only a handful of mammals are really fit for the farm or the human household; as for the rest, their encrypted temperaments render them perennially dangerous or just plain unsuitable, beyond the grasp of human hands.

I was just fifteen when I imbibed this sobering information, old enough to understand it but young enough to decide to discard it. Inside the library I made my way down the alphabet, riffling through the collection of books until I finally found what I was looking for. I read about a Portuguese prince who had successfully tamed a tiger and Pygmies who had, with great delight, taken wild pandas as pets.

In the days and weeks that followed I stayed on the lookout for similar stories, sampling libraries in surrounding towns, telling Annie and Cranston my research proved them wrong, while Annie and Cranston, caught between my deep need on the one hand and their common sense on the other, looked with escalating worry from Amelia to me, me to Amelia, day by day her contours coming clearer as her size, and her temper, increased. My aim: to make my raccoon into an animal other than what she was, this despite all the information I'd received. Who, after all, had taken me to meet my neighbors, or called me around corners I might have otherwise just dodged? I had come to understand that adventure and adrenaline were not necessarily the same. Mostly I can credit Amelia, an animal who had no words, with helping me talk to the Trevors, so that first we became friends and then something else, one evening Annie reaching across some space to touch the back of my head, asking, softly, "Where'd you get this cut?" A few days later I went with her to a stylist, all three of us looking at books showing bobs and shags, bangs and layers, Annie sweeping my matted hair back, this way and that, considering me carefully in the mirror, as a mother might, and I woke up to a series of wants. I went down with a throat so swollen breathing became difficult, and Cranston brought me to the hospital in the middle of the night, his hand testing me for a fever, and my wants went wayward, turned into inevitable needs. Soon after that, lying across my bed beneath the eave one afternoon, the window open and autumn in the air, I realized that somehow, somewhere along the line, this room had come to feel like mine, and something in me settled, and then days later spilled when my social worker called and asked me about my placement. *Placement*, rhymes with basement, and I recalled, with a dull thud, a buried, bottom-line fact: everything about this family was fleeting for me. Unlike the zebra and the cheetah, I ached to be domesticated, tied and tethered to a single spot, but in fact I was radically free. Unlike a child by blood or adopted by law, the Trevors could, and eventually would, release me, and that fact seasoned my stay with anger and appreciation both.

The seasons changed; summer turned to fall turned to winter. One afternoon in the fading light of a December day, when all the trees in town were strung with tiny teardrop lights, I found on the kitchen counter a check from the state—the monthly payment for keeping me. I studied it for a long while, turned it over and over in my hands, and then, before I could stop myself, I crumpled it up and threw it in the basket by Annie's desk. "Did you do this?" Annie later asked me, holding up the creased check.

"No" I said, too quickly. And then added, leaning closer, "What is it?"

"Nothing," Annie said, pulling the paper away and folding it in half. She slipped the check into her pants pocket and walked upstairs.

Raccoons normally hibernate, but that winter Amelia had no need. We were still her steady food source, and every morning, even in the thickest of snows, she'd exit the abandoned house four doors down and show up on our stoop, covered with cobwebs, waiting for her milk and table scraps, which she'd eat and then settle down to sleep before the hearth until late afternoon, when she wakened in an always playful mood. She loved to bat around balls, climb up the curtains, taunt the dog, and bathe in the bathtub, her fur when wet showing its oily sheen. Her antics endeared her to anyone and everyone and must have had something to do with why Annie and Cranston, despite their stated misgivings, continued to allow her in, day after day, all day, despite the threat of injuries large and small. She'd grown now almost to my knees and, at some point that winter, she started to snap her jaw and growl if anyone touched her while she ate. One December morning, thinking she was done, I accidentally stroked her head and she sunk her teeth into my wrist, the blood falling fast on the snow. I tried to hide the wound but anyone could see it; Annie wrapped it up tight muttering "Jesus" under her breath.

That night, Annie and Cranston took me aside. "It's over," they said. "She could get rabies," they said. "We're sorry," they said, and I wept tears that snaked down my face and collected in the corners of my mouth. I wondered if she'd starve without us, if somehow, by taking her into the human realm, we'd torn or tainted the basic instincts she'd need to survive in the wild. It turns out the answer is yes, although back then, I'd no way of knowing for sure. But the fact is that when we take the wild out of the wild we often confuse, or corrupt, the animal's ability to navigate its natural habitat. Had I known that then would I have acted otherwise? I can't say for sure. I felt the lure that must be as ancient as it is intense, the drive to shed your skin; the need to know the utter other who looks back at us with eyes in which we see what we once were, and still are in corners culture forbids us to investigate. I remembered how we took her from the wall, how the hole looked after she'd emerged, a punched-out place gushing dust and darkness.

The next morning, when I woke, the Trevors told me I could not call her from her nighttime shelter in the old abandoned house. Annie took the yellow saucer that had, for all these months, held her morning milk and set it on a pantry shelf. I figured Amelia would be back begging soon enough, standing on the stoop, high on her hind legs, and what would we do then? I wasn't sure. I smelled smoke. I smelled it far away, as if coming from another world, a past place, maybe from my mind, because no one else smelled anything. "You can't smell that?" I asked Kyle, Emma, Annie, Cranston, and they each said no, and it snowed and the night went into a deep, silent freeze, fangs of icicles hanging from the drip edge off the roof.

I fell asleep then. We all fell asleep on a frozen night deep in December, Cranston feeding the wood stove kindling and papers from the pile on the side of the stone hearth. The stove had a glass window in it, and you could sit and watch the spastic flames leap and lick, and if you turned out the lights their orange intensified until they looked liquid. I fell asleep in front of that fire, wrapped in a grey blanket, and when I woke up the night had thickened to the point where all objects were eradicated, the wood stove out but the smell of smoke stronger than ever, a tang on the tongue, in the air. I instinctively turned towards a window, looking for light, for life, and that's when I saw it, not here but there, four houses down, the old abandoned house blazing away and now the sound of sirens, the flames visible and unreal, their edges so defined against the darkness they looked like Halloween cutouts, orange paper pasted on a black background. Amelia was in there. No, maybe not. Sparks showered and radios crackled commands as well-aimed water shattered whatever windows there were. We all put our parkas on over our pajamas and went outside to watch, the air so thick with smoke I could smell it on my skin after everything was over.

I awoke late the next morning, a Saturday, 11 a.m., my mouth gummed up, my lips flaking flesh, the skin beneath a perfect intact pink. The whole house was sunk in silence, strange for this time of day, and because of this silence, and the smell of char still clearly in the air, and Amelia not here, and who knew where, dread spread through me. Our windows were crystalled with cold, smashed stars limiting my view. My bedroom door screeched when I opened it, the sound so sharp in the silence my insides jumped. When I peered in the master bedroom I saw Annie and Cranston immobile on top of their sheets, their sprawled bodies still and white in the flashing sunlight. Sometimes this happens to me, a thought, a vision, both gory and absurd. I couldn't see their breathing; the whole house was dead, I was totally alone, surrounded by rot. "Annie," I yelled, and when she failed to move I went forward, poking my finger into the soft spot at the side of the human head, where the pulse prods on, if we're lucky. "Annie," I yelled again, and suddenly, from the other side of the bed Cranston stirred, his movements massive and jerky as he bolted upright, his hand blindly grasping for his glasses on the table beside him. "What is it, what is it?" he asked, his voice at once gruff and childish, fringed with fear, a sound that made me sad. "What is it?" he asked again, unaware I was there, staring as he struggled up from sleep. I saw him reach up and rub his eyes; the glasses clattered to the floor as, for a reason I don't understand, I ran from the room.

Gradually, as if struggling out from under a hundred-year spell, the house started to stir. I heard Cranston groan as he stood upright, and then from various doors the other children emerged, tying their terrycloth bathrobes or shuffling in shaggy slippers. At half past the hour of noon, despite the Trevor's prohibition, I took the yellow saucer from the shelf where Annie had stored it and, after filling it with milk, set it on the stoop to see if she'd come by. By late afternoon the dread I felt had settled firmly in the pit of my stomach. Stepping outside, I made my way towards the burned-out building where yellow tape flapped in the breeze. I walked easily across the line, looking here and there, whistling the notes, two high, one low, no show. I saw broken bits of glass and chunks of charred wood and, right out in the open, just sitting in the snow, a single blackened staircase I climbed to the top of, looking out over the dismal land. Clouds rolled in, low and full. From up there on the staircase I scanned the land for bodies: cats, corpses, her, but there was only debris. When I came down sleet started, flying sideways into my face. I didn't put my hand up; I just let the frozen granules melt against my skin, slide downwards, wetting my scarf.

For the next seven days I set the yellow saucer out for her, and the Trevors, seeing my sadness or maybe knowing it wouldn't matter, let me do it, but Amelia didn't return. I went, then, back and back to the ruins, whistling my whistle, the cold air clarifying the notes. Perhaps, I thought, the fire had not taken her. Perhaps the sirens had scared her away. When I held out my arm I saw her marks on the satiny skin of its underside, scratches from claws, a cleft where she'd taken some flesh. Perhaps she knew she'd outgrown us. Perhaps somewhere in that bean-sized brain she'd always seen how it would happen. Amelia, I now knew, had never been mine, which didn't mean I didn't love her, but she could never belong to me same as I could never belong to them. What these long-term loans meant in terms of love I was not so sure, but that love was a component, I saw that.

In my mind, when Amelia left, my stay with the Trevors was over. In fact that's not true. I lived with them for three and a half more years, going from sophomore to junior to finally senior, busy with tests and homework and theatre and sports, applying to college, during this time losing contact completely with my family of origin, my mother claiming I was wild and beyond help, her proclamation, uttered so many times during the years I was under her roof that I often wondered if it was true, if I carried some criminal smell, some snarl that rendered me permanently unfit for human culture, the Trevors assuring me I was fine, but I've never known for sure. Not even now do I know. There are facts, there are feelings, and then there is memory, and in my memory Amelia went out like an ember, and the next thing I knew I grew and I grew and I grew, with each added inch that much more to be managed, to be burned, and so quickly, how it happens. Fires. I hate the sound and sulphur smell of a striking match. I hate how the flames are jerky and irrational. People talk of taming fire as though it, too, is an animal we've leashed, but fire is a force altogether other; it has no heart, no hide, no evolution. The universe is full of such timeless powers and when we face them—person, primate, horse, hare—we are all wild; we all respond with the same untamed terror that tells me how much the species share, when you get right down in the dirt. When the wind turns tornado or the heat too high.

Three and a half years after Amelia disappeared, I did too, packing my bags for college and leaving early one morning, when the house was still slumbering, so I could avoid the good-byes. I arrived in the freshman quad of my new university by 7 a.m., the first one there in a series of cinderblock dorms with metal beds and see-through curtains on the shower stalls. Soon enough my Swedish roommate appeared and then the orientation started, all of us freshmen divided into groups and led around, campus building by building, the bulletin boards layered with fliers for political protests, for housemates, for help. Classes began and with them late nights at the library, the days blurring by, I so stunned by the newness that I recall little from this period but a feeling of automation and the occasional breakthrough of a loneliness so pure I wanted to whinny, to make some sound or find some shape to pour it into. I didn't, of course, because I couldn't, and because I, at age eighteen, knew enough not to break down in public places, which meant I wasn't wild, right? I tried hard, dressed according to code, did what I could to prove her wrong. And then came the day, three weeks into it all, when I, an official adult now, old enough to vote but in reality still a kid, trying to pick my major, well, then came the day when I took my tiny key and, opening my silver post office box in the university's mail room, found the formal typed letter from social services explaining that I'd aged out of custody, out of the foster-care system. Despite the fact that I'd already known that, reading the official letter sent me spinning. I heard a snap, in my head, or in some space, and then the feeling of free fall even as I stood, still, frozen in the bustling busy mail room, clutching a letter that meant everything and nothing. After all, we are always alone, in some fundamental sense. And yet who amongst our species does not yearn for the yoke that tethers you, if only in fantasy? Of all the mammals we have domesticated, we have forgotten to count ourselves, the human being, Homo sapiens, shaped by the cultures we've created, hooked up to harnesses, we flail to be free as we feel their weight with real relief, because how else would we know we are here, amongst others? *Amongst others.* I read the letter again and again and a field appeared around me, growing and growing until at last its edges curled from my sight and, then with nothing left to do, I walked across campus, my cinderblock room a real relief, a roof, if only for a while.

I could have done things differently, and I cannot explain why I chose what I did. I threw out the letter from social services, crumpling it up and tearing it in two, as if that might somehow solve things. But its words—"aged out of custody; no longer in custody"—stayed with me, a ringing in my ears, and rather than call the Trevors for succor, I chose instead to avoid them, brashly trying to make my way on a campus seething with beer steins and wines, political uproars and classes on Caravaggio, the angry artist who painted himself holding his severed head in his hands. Freed from custody, undomesticated, with no turf I could really claim, I threw myself into whatever currents came my way, too busy to see the lack of this solution. That autumn was brilliant, though, the trees all ruby and gold, leaves floating in puddles that iced overnight, trapping them there, pointed and perfect. I smoked clove cigarettes, unfiltered, my previously clean lungs burning with each aromatic inhale, my head in a whirl as I chased the burn with beer. Somehow, between studies and cigarettes and parties where I chatted with everyone and talked to no one, time scrolled on and out, and the trees lost their leaves and a bone-cold December came with a burst of blizzard. In my dreams the animals arrived, all those we'd tried and failed to tame, and then they ran free towards a speckled sky I fell through.

I was so busy with all this—falling and fleeing and studying and sleeping—denying half my life while whooping it up in the other half, I failed to see the trap I'd set for myself. Christmas vacation was coming, and with it a mandate that every student vacate the dorms for the month. Where oh where would I go? Students packed up and left with bulging bags, driving their own cars home or picked up by parents, until finally the campus got very quiet while the temperature plunged and stray flakes fell from a sky so clear I could see, it seemed, the edges of every star.

I stowed away two nights alone in an emptied-out dorm, but the heat was too low and when I woke in the mornings my breath hung before my face, a scrim. I didn't even have a dime to make a phone call. In the "freed from custody" letter it indicated that the Trevors had been CCed; but they hadn't called me. On the third day, I tossed some clothes in a suitcase and loaded my busted-up car with books and bedding, and then I went back, past midnight, doing whatever I could, I think, to make the reunion difficult, wanting them to take me in no matter how hard, how wild I was.

And then their house was before me, as old and as new as it had been that day, four years before, when my father had said, *Go now.* Sitting in my car in their driveway, the engine ticking as it cooled, the moonlight bright on their white chimney, I contemplated ringing the bell and wondered what they would do when, still half asleep, they saw me.

I knocked first, very softly, and when no one answered, louder and louder, and when still no one answered a senseless panic descended and I forgot about the bell, instead banging on their door like a mad girl or woman, whatever I was, at age eighteen. I banged and banged and called their names like they were all I had in the world, which wasn't true. They were not. I had my arms and legs, a head, a heart, a whole self to wedge into the ground and from which to make my proclamations, but I hadn't grasped that yet. Instead I rained my fists down on their door and called them through snot and tears, and I was so immersed in this odd tantrum that I failed to hear their footsteps or the turning of the locks and it wasn't until the door was open and their slippers suddenly appeared before my downcast eyes, it wasn't until then that I realized: I'd been heard.

Animals can switch states very quickly. I'd seen Amelia go from a full growl to a sweet simper on the turn of a dime. As soon as I saw those slippers, everything bad went away—my tears and the snot from my snoot and my frenzied fists—it all got calm quite fast. "Hi," I said, as though it were a normal mid-morning and not 3 a.m., and then I swiped the wetness from my face with the heel of my hand. "Cold out there," I said. "Brings tears to the eyes."

Annie and Cranston were, well, surprised to see me. They stood on their threshold, which had also once been my threshold, and stared at me for a few seconds, seconds that felt full of weight, because what would happen next? How could I explain this? "I know it's late," I said, "and—"

And then, before I could say another word, Cranston grabbed me by the collar and hauled me in. "Jesus effing Christ," he said, and I flinched and then he hugged me, hard. "Where the hell have you been?" he said. And then he stepped back, Annie and Cranston both stepped back and took a good long look at me, and then Cranston said, "So, yer a college freshman. Have you learned all the kings of England yet?"

I reached up to rub the back of my neck, because it hurt where he had hauled me, and into my mind then came the image of Amelia, how he hauled her from the wall and made her ours, if only for a while. "I don't do Kings and I don't do England," I said. "I'm majoring in anthropology." And then, just to bug him I said, "But wasn't Cromwell number six?"

"You can't be serious," said Cranston, and just at that moment Annie flicked on the switch so light flooded the hallway and there were their familiar faces, with all the same grooves and lines. Past them and up the stairs I could see their sleepy kids peering from behind a line of doors, and Emma, now ten, lifted her hand in a salute. "Lauren Jean Slater," Annie said, enunciating my name in all its difference from theirs, "may I ask why you picked this time to return?"

"Oh Annie," said Cranston. "Don't be such a. She's a freshman in college. She has no judgment. She's probably stoned out of her mind."

"Are you stoned?" asked Annie.

"Do I look stoned?" I asked.

"You've got a little bit of red-eye there, but," said Cranston, and then he lowered his voice and leaned in close to me, "I know tears when I see them." Of course his statement brought a fresh flood, my eyes pouring with no restraint, and my nose too.

Annie fished a tissue from her bathrobe pocket. "What is going on here?" she asked.

"I've come back," I said, and then I shrugged with my palms turned upwards. "Do you have a bed?"

Sometimes you say something stupid and the instant it's out of your mouth, you know. Other times, a perfectly innocuous-seeming phrase can cause a clenching you can't quite understand. I said, "Do you have a bed?" and suddenly the half-jocular conversation fell flat on its face and, in their faces, a clear shift, a sudden darkening, even though the hall blazed bright in the night.

Annie and Cranston looked at each other, and I saw some unspoken understanding pass between them. "Actually," said Annie after a moment had passed, "the room you used is . . ."

"Annie here," said Cranston, a bit too jovially, "yer old friend Annie here decided to turn your old room into a sewing station."

Annie gave Cranston a fierce stare. "No one turned your room into a sewing station," said Annie, still staring at Cranston. "We do, however," she said, turning back to me now, "use it sometimes for sewing."

"Not a problem," I said.

"Not a problem at all," said Annie just a tad too tightly, and then she turned to face Cranston again and said, "See?"

"I see," said Cranston, "that this is not a problem. I also see that its half past three in the morning and we all should get some sleep."

And then, for the first time in four months or so I was back in their house. I lugged my stuff up the stairs, turning right at the top, left by the bathroom, the route engraved in my brain, the door exactly the same, scuffed up and scarred, the knob polished onyx, I turned it and stepped inside.

The walls, those old horse-hair-plastered walls piled high with paper I'd traced through many of my nights, those walls had been stripped, scrubbed, and painted a sage green. The pine plank floor had been sanded, the previously pitted boards gleaming a golden hue. My desk, or, well, their desk, was gone, and in its place a sewing machine hinged to a table on which folded fabric was stacked. What bothered me most was the box, in the closet, holding the few things I'd left behind, stored out of sight and an obvious inconvenience. When I closed the closet door and turned around, I saw Annie and Cranston in the doorframe, looking askew, Cranston clasping and unclasping his hands, his palms making a soft sucking sound. "We made a few changes," said Annie.

"Not a problem," I said yet again, something achy in my voice, "I'll just put my stuff under the bed—"

"You know," said Cranston, trying to go jocular once more, "Benjamin Franklin slept on two boards on the floor, and he swore it built strong character."

I looked at him, and then I looked back at the room, scanning it quickly, its changes a jolt and a jab, so much so different that it took me more than a moment to realize that there was no bed in the room anymore; where it had been, a barrister's bookcase filled with who knows what.

"If you had called," said Annie, her voice trailing off.

"If I had called then what?" I said, my voice suddenly gruff and low. "Then you would have reconsidered your decorating scheme?"

"Lauren," said Annie, "for four months you didn't—"

"Neither did you," I shouted, and then, like a child, I kicked at the floorboards, pleased to see the dark scuff I'd made; it wouldn't be easy to erase.

"Listen, ladies," said Cranston, holding up his hands like a police officer. "Can we have this powwow in the morning?"

His eyes indeed looked tired, Annie's too, and I said, "Sure. Of course. Who needs a powwow anyway? I'll be fine on the floor."

Annie disappeared then and I heard her rummaging in the linen closet. She came back carrying a stack of blankets and pillows, and I held out my arms and she placed the linens in them, the gesture frankly formal, so formal I felt like bowing, just a bit. "Thank you," I said, and I meant it. After all, it was past three in the morning, the night was cold, and I had no place to go. Somewhere in this conversation I'd realized that, whether I liked it or not, I'd better behave.

The Egyptians tried and tried to change gazelles but they could not. Amelia, on the other hand, proved it was utterly untrue about a leopard always having his same spots. She'd demonstrated amply that an animal, if only for some time, could adapt to utterly strange situations with alacritous finesse. Where, then, did that leave me? Precisely where I was, as it turns out, standing in a room, under a roof, with two people who would never be my parents, no matter what my histrionics; this was not my house. If Linnaeus came back to life and decided to categorize human groups down to their smallest boxes, I would not be placed here, and that, my dear, was that.

But because humans have two hands, there is always another hand, and on this other hand were other incontrovertible facts that did not contradict the boxed-up truth but turned it slightly sideways, so it looked different under different light. The fact of the matter is that wolves will adopt baby dogs and suckle them as if they are their own; all across the animal kingdom are examples of this cross-pollination, pigs taking in lambs, goats nurturing geese; it happens. In the Bible, the guest is an honored being, a foreigner you break bread with and, by doing so, you hugely enrich your dinner. We all knew, that night of the no-bed, that I was a guest who had, for a short period of time, been something like their little lamb, minus the wool and sweetness. That night, for the rest of that night, I stayed on the floor, the moon framed like a decal in the square of the window. I didn't sleep very well. Sometime just before dawn I got up and wandered the house, just like I used to do, when I'd been their foster child. In the bathroom I opened the medicine cabinet, poured out some pills, going so far as to put one on the pad of my tongue, tasting the tang as it started to melt, and then spitting it fast back into the bottle and closing the cap. I climbed the stairs to the attic and opened the dwarf-sized door to the old dingy closet, the canes still hung on the same hooks, just as they'd been for all these years, and the signatures still scrawled beneath them: *Harry Mumford, Faith Mason, Robert Smutter, Earl Greylot.* Taking a stub of a pencil from my pocket I knelt in the dingy darkness and pressed my own name into the surprisingly soft wall, *Lauren Jean Slater,* just passing through or part of the family, either way, I had been here.

The following morning, my head staticky from so little sleep, I went to make myself some breakfast, opening up the fridge and then realizing, hand on the dome of an egg, that there'd be no state paycheck to cover any of this. "Can I offer you money?" I said, and Annie said, "Don't be silly," but I knew I wasn't being silly. "How'd you sleep, L. S.?" Cranston hollered, his humor feeling forced, and I said, "Great!" the faux exclamation point dangling there in the air for us all to consider, palpable, practically visible; I shrugged. "I'm a little stiff I admit," I said, and Annie turned to Cranston and said, "Don't we have a cot somewhere here?"

"Don't worry, really," I said. "There's no need for a cot."

"See how tough we raised 'er?" Cranston hollered again, for some reason the strained situation causing him to talk like a cowboy; I smiled at him; he smiled back, a little sadly, and that was that. All of a sudden there was nothing left to say. Now that my official tenure had ended, and with it all of our obvious assigned roles, we weren't sure who we were to one another anymore, or how we might proceed, which made everyone extra polite.

I figured I'd stay for a couple of days and then move on. They had a full house, all the steps and halves around for the holidays. I nursed my hurt and then gradually it faded. Or rather I pushed it back somewhere, let it occupy a smaller space. And in its place, what the Trevors were best at—fine wine and a lot of lounging by the fire, Cranston reading various histories aloud to us, stopping to spread some tapenade on a crusty roll with a butter knife and then biting in, stray flakes flying all over him, the dog licking him clean. I remembered in front of that fire how scared I'd been when I first came here, years and years ago, how my ears were full of the sounds of my own home—footsteps coming closer, the crash of a glass, someone's scream, my body coiled tight as if for a fight. Somehow here, in this house, with the hugely generous help of a certain surrogate family, along with one small but also beyond-big creature borne from its beams and innards, I'd learned a series of different sounds, a different kind of posture for a body always rigid with fright. The next morning was clear and beautiful, one of those winter days when the sun sparkles in the sky and the trees look tremendously black against their hard blue background. I put on my boots and went out into the yard by myself. Snow had fallen over the night and the Trevors' yard was a perfect wedge of white, and as I tromped through it I saw signs, tracks, skitters, and then the markings of what had to have been a coon, the particular paw prints in the fragile crust of white. I followed those tracks for a while, let them lead me where they would, until before I knew it I was back in the woods, by the frozen pond where we'd picnicked, that hot still summer, the basket full of cheese and grapes. "Amelia," I called, my voice echoing back to me, bouncing off branches and tree trunks. I stood for a long time and no coon appeared, although the tracks were clearly cut. I could come back here tomorrow and keep following these tracks, day after day, willing what would not be, or I could, instead, stay still, and let her nest in my memory, which was—would have to be—its own sort of house; I would do it. I would make a place within me and so keep close to me the animals and people I had loved. And what from my life would I put here, in this place of my own making—my very own house!—which I now saw could be spacious and white with turrets and many circling stairs. My mother's keys, carp in the pond we'd fished from, a cupboard full of beans and books and blankets, many maps, my toothbrush, all the kings of England; a room beneath an eave on the right side of a certain dwelling, her fur and how it felt when it was wet and when it wasn't, how she came from a hole in the wall, tiny and terrified, the sound of her singing, the look of her swinging, *Go now*, he said, and yes, on and on it would go, this house—of *mine*—was so fine, so grand, sitting there before me in the snow.

4

The Swan with a Broken Beak

I took a job as a vet tech one of the years between college and
graduate school. Most of my adventures concerned your common
housecats and dogs, but I did by chance one day meet a girl who
saved a swan on a Sunday afternoon during the time when I was
on duty. The swan was at the lake, a large body of water behind
the hospital where I worked. Some nights I'd go to that lake and
contemplate my unhappiness. This was a time in my life when
words wouldn't come, and when the span between what I was—a
vet tech—and what I wanted to be—a writer—seemed impossibly
wide or impenetrably deep, I'd go to that lake and look out across
it, searching for the other side.

And then the swan arrived. The girl found her on a warm
spring day in the middle of April, while she was walking the lip
of the lake, the willows blistered with nubs and the sun-warmed
water tepid to the touch. A lot of people were out and about because the winter had been long, and the sound of melting snow—it
must have been everywhere—trickling and kerplinking, made the
world seem magical. And this is how, I think, the girl must have
felt—as though in a fairyland—the lake, the sudden warmth of the
weather, the rich mud, the tall grasses, the rustling weeds, and then
appearing around a bend in the lake bed—a series of swans, one
proud matriarch with her curved head held aloft, her beak bright
as an orchid on a soft white stem, and her babies, also white, their

webbed orange feet peddling furiously in the clear water, turning up froth. I see the girl see. I see her kneel down and scoop a
stale crust of bread from her pocket. The swan family bobbed on
the wavelets and swam closer to shore. They came so close the girl
could see the dark dots of the mother's beak—cygnet nostrils—
where the air came and went. She could see water beading on
the backs of the baby birds. She tossed out crumbs and the swans
dipped their beaks in the lake, ladled up the crusts, ate quietly.

Most people know there exists in life at least two planes upon
which we play our seemingly simultaneous parts. There is the appar-
ent and then there is the down-under, where whole other plots and
purposes evolve, and these plots can seem utterly surprising when
they rupture the smooth surface on which we thought we stood.

Down under then, one feet, two feet, trawling along the lake's
muddy bottom, was a snapper. I've seen snappers before. They
have domed shells, wizened heads, beady eyes, and generally in-
dolent attitudes. Their mouths work as if on hinges, and their jaws
have the power of a door slammed shut in a sudden summer storm.
Above, in the daylight, the lovely swans were drifting. Below, in
the lake's lamp-light, the snapping turtle inched along.

He must have seen the peddling feet, the orange meat. The
snapper nosed up out of the water, just enough so on the shore the
girl could see the tip of his head, the scrawl marking his mouth
now closed, and then in one swift second that mouth flashed open
and closed around a baby swan's dunked head with a clear crunching sound, and there was a struggle.

She was horrified, the girl. At least later she told me she was
horrified as she stood there frozen, watching the infant cygnet
with its head lodged deep in the turtle's gulping throat, the turtle
twisting this way and that, trying to snap its meat from the bone
that held it fast and firm, as the petticoat of feathers swirled, and
down flew, and blood bubbled up on the surface of the lake and
then something also in her own throat, something stuck and struggling. And no one else seemed to see. It happened in a snap, a flash.

The girl bent down, reached for a rock, and, winding her arm
back as far as she could, she set a sharp stone flying so high and
hard it bonked the snapper on his slick scalp, so he saw stars, we're

sure, his mouth flapping open in surprise. And in that split second of surprise the baby swan slipped free while the disgruntled turtle regained his senses and stroked away from the scene with a few filaments of bird flesh for a snack. The swan pushed her wrecked head above the water, blood pouring from the beak bitten off.

There was so much blood it just kept coming, more blood than it seemed the body of a baby could possibly hold. And now people saw. They saw the girl standing there—she had started screaming— and they saw the ruined swan with its beak torn in two, swimming slowly to shore, leaving a trail of red and feathers in its wake.

The girl's mother, who had heard the screams, came running, and she picked up the swan in one hand, the girl in the other and brought them both—along with the story I've just told—to the veterinary hospital where I was working during that difficult time in my life, my supervisor an eccentric man named Dr. Brumberg, who cursed his colleagues as corrupt, claiming they cared little for animals and much for money. Dr. Brumberg had wounded monkeys shipped to him from Brazil, and he had the hide of a bat hung on one office wall, its webbed wings pinned in place.

It was later on in the day when the girl and the mother brought in the bloody swan. Dr. Brumberg and I named her Ivory. Her white seemed all the whiter because of the blood streaked body.

Ivory, surely, would die. How, after all, can you save an animal whose beak has been torn from its face? How is the bird to eat, to drink, to laugh, which birds surely do, just listen. Listen in the morning, before the cars have started, when all the trees are full.

And then, on top of the physical problems, there were the political ones. A swan? How can a swan be political? During my year as a vet tech I learned there are extensive laws in place preventing *most* vets or anyone associated with them from treating wildlife, especially endangered species. Dr. Brumberg had told me how once, in Florida, he'd seen a wounded dolphin thrashing in the water, near to drowning. He'd pulled the dolphin to safety, only later to find himself penalized with a heavy fine, because dolphins are endangered.

A swan, of course, is not endangered, except when it is, as it was then. That was, however, only one of the barriers to care. More immediately pressing: cash. The perpetual question was cash.

Unlike a vet, a human doctor faced with a dying poor person in an emergency room would never risk his job because he treated the non-paying patient. State and federal funds exist for just such situations. I saw Dr. Brumberg though, several times, in trouble with his supervisors for treating animals—strays who desperately needed care but who had no payer tied to their tale. This is probably one reason why some studies have found that veterinarians are amongst the most unhappy of professionals, why they rank high in problems, with alcohol and suicide attempts. They are regularly faced with the impossible conundrum: save your job and violate your ethical mandate; honor your ethical mandate and risk losing your livelihood. It was, at least when I worked in the field, a wearying, repetitive problem that reared its head every time someone showed up with a sick stray or a child brought in a chipmunk.

Here then, was a white swan stained red and sticky with blood. If Dr. Brumberg treated the animal, his hospital would receive no funds. In fact, his hospital would lose funds, because there would be no way to ever replace the expended resources—the time, the medicine, the technology. But if he didn't treat the animal it would hurt his heart, violate his morals, and, as he often told me, he'd grow sick in a way no human could ever heal.

But now, with the swan before us, we didn't have time to think through all this. See—a baby bird! See—so much blood! What one does in such situations is simply act, both fluidly and thoughtlessly. The primary danger was one of infection. Dr. Brumberg started stitching; he put the baby on IV antibiotics. I helped thread a butterfly needle through the froth of feathers. Then another line for water. We found a box; we found bedding; then another line for pain.

I stepped back. Hours and hours had passed and I had no idea of how. When I looked up, night had fallen, fast.

I left the hospital later on that night and drove home, the roads doused in darkness and just a few stars scattered overhead. The moon was thin but bright, a curved bird beak set against the sky.

I wondered about the girl who had brought the swan in. The image of the swan molested by the turtle would probably stay with her for life, a little slice of horror. That is one way memories are made.

All around me, as I was driving, the woods lining the sides of the road were thrumming with life, seen and unseen. Behind the trees, miles into the green New England forests, there were deer and even coyotes; there were tawny chipmunks and moles in their underground tunnels. Farther out there were bears, big and brown, some slumbering in protracted hibernations, others up, swatting at prey with their huge mitted paws, their claws so sharp they could rip the face from a person in a single swipe. Fierce. Frightening. Beautiful. All creatures great and small, they surround us, for sure. And more shocking than their various pelts and tails and instincts is the very fact that they are here, that the planet is so populated by such a myriad of forms, that beneath our feet live millions of microbes and that in the rich gritty soil of our gardens are ecosystems spawned by slippery worms and snails in whorled shells. We talk about appreciating animals as though they were adjuncts, accessories to our lives. But we forget, or fail to ever learn—animals are our lives. If we were to lose the microbes thrumming in the dust you vacuum up each day, the planet would deflate like a big balloon. Even back then, before global warming was so much as a green glow on the horizon, I could—everyone could—see the intricate, impossibly possible connections between disparate forms of life. Dr. Brumberg saw. Save a swan and you save yourself.

I did not sleep well that night. These were times when often sleep eluded me, with the result that my dreams dried up. Sometimes I would stay awake the whole night through, listening to the church bells clang by the hour, listening to my clock tick by the minute, my mind empty of sleep's greatest gift—those strange hybrid dreams where sounds come in color and colors seem to sing.

I tried to write about the swan, but my wording was weighted, awkward, and sentences slipped past me before I could secure them in my snapping flapping maw. In the mirror in the hall of my house I looked beastly to myself, greedy for something I could not name. I tossed and turned in bed. Although not yet summer, the mosquitoes seemed rampant, nibbling on my neck. When I finally fell into a fitful slumber it was early in the morning, and I swear I'd been under no more than seconds when an anguished cry cut through my dreaming and jolted me up right. What was it? Nothing. Silence and bugs. I was about to lie back down when the sound came again, this time more piercing than the last, the cry of an animal in anguish somewhere in the woods that fringed the yard, and this time the sound didn't stop. It was stranger than anything I'd heard before. It was a cry, unearthly, in agony; it was a shriek of pain and protest, and it just went on and on, piercing the night. I tried but failed to imagine what could cause such distress, such unrelenting pain. I had the sense then that I sometimes did when I slipped beneath the surface and saw the horror of the ordinary, the cruelness in the quotidian. Eventually, maybe after an hour, or two, the cries ceased.

As soon as it was light enough I got out of bed, slipped my feet into my slippers, and plodded out across the dawn-moist yard to find the source of such sound. I thought there would be a carcass there, somewhere near my rented house, something quartered with its innards spilling out. But I found nothing. I searched the sky for vultures, but the sky was just a gentle blue, a barely blue, no sign yet of the sun. There was great pain but no particular place of emanation; I saw that then. One could not pin pain down. It would come and come from every direction, from any direction, and you could try to treat it, try to send some soothing, and you might get lucky and succeed. But pain was the one animal that could never be captured, trained or domesticated. It was a wild beast for sure, and it lived by laws we could not ever learn.

For these reasons—the sleeplessness, the beastly sound, the bugs nibbling at my neck—for these reasons I figured that I would find the baby swan dead in her enclosure at work. It would not have surprised me if she had failed to survive the night, what with half her head gone and a tube in her neck. I got to work early that day, turned the key in the door, entered the hospital's hallways.

Dr. Brumberg, indeed no other vets, had arrived yet. Dogs dreamt in their cages. A cat sat on its carpeted perch, her maple-colored eyes huge and glowing. I could hear my footsteps as I walked the long hall and then opened the door to the baby bird's room. Inside: silence. The smell of scat and straw. "Ivory?" I called out. I clucked. No response. Slowly, I made my way over to where she was, looked over the edge of the box and saw her there, dead or sleeping, I wasn't sure which.

"Ivory, Ivory," I called and then I put my hand on her tiny, toy-sized body and felt the waxy warmth of the white feathers. Elation moved through me, slowly, like heat, it spread from my hands up my arms into my neck and up through my eyes until it seemed light was coming out of my eyes. This is what it means to beam. You find the baby bird alive. You feel the waxy warmth of feathers. You watch as the cygnet wakes up, one swollen lid slowly opening to reveal the dark ink drop of the pupil floating.

"Lauren, Lauren," someone called.

Dr. Brumberg's supervisor, and mine by extension as well. Dr. Proctor. He owned the practice. His picture hung in the hall. "Lauren," he called, beckoning me from where he stood in the shadow of his open door.

I met him in his office. "The swan has survived the night," I said.

He was a good man, Dr. Proctor, but here's the problem: not good enough.

"We can't keep the bird here," he said.

He told me to turn her out.

"But I can't do that," I said. "I'm just a tech."

"Precisely why you can," Dr. Proctor said. "And will," he added.

"She's not my patient," I tried again. "She's Dr. Brumberg's—"

"Turn her out," Dr. Proctor repeated.

"But she'll die," I said, and then I had tears in my eyes and was squeezing my toes. *Don't cry. Die. Don't cry. Die.*

"And if she lives, Lauren," Dr. Proctor said, "what do you think will happen to your swan if she lives?"

"The swan wants to live," I said. "It's clear. She has the will to live."

"No," Dr. Proctor said. "She has the *instinct* to live. But here's the problem with instinct. It is devoid of intelligence. You save that swan and you are consigning her to a life of misery, a life where she will be unable to survive on her own, unable to catch food, unable to mate. Do you call that ethical? Whose pain are you really trying to treat?"

The world is full of intelligent Homo sapiens who even as they propel a heinous argument make excellent points. How is that we humans are capable of thinking excellently about actions so dishonorable? Is this where we cross the line from rational to rationalizing creatures? True, if you looked at the situation from the perspective of pure logic, Proctor's points were worth tucking under one's big beret. Might it be better to have no life than a life so mangled it dispirits and despairs? One can endlessly balance the odds, tweak the scale, move this weight here and that there, but in the very end, the scale itself is the problem. I believe there are whole systems of celestial logics we have yet to unravel, and that there are ethical mandates that come from a place beyond what we can easily figure. Sometimes I think I know what it means to be human. You have to care. Side with life. It's terribly, terribly simple.

Vets don't treat wildlife for three reasons: money and law and some sort of ethics based on some sort of limited logic that says it is sometimes better to "let nature take its course." How silly. Is medical intervention outside of nature? Is anything, ever, outside of nature? You show me something that does not arise from nature while I wait. And wait.

In the meantime, there are things to tend to and care for. First and foremost, Ivory needed to eat. She had been almost twenty-four hours now without food or water. I tried feeding her crushed grass, fish sticks, but the beak didn't work and food would not find its way to her mouth. Dr. Brumberg arrived soon after. He inserted a tube straight into the small swan stomach and got her nutrients to her that way.

And it worked. Ivory grew bigger and plumper, filling out measurably, day after day. Her pain subsided, and Ivory began to waddle around her cage, dragging her wings behind her. Feathers floated up in the sunlit air. I sometimes scratched her long, looped neck, and like a dog or a cat she leaned into the feeling, taking pleasure, her eyes half closing as she drifted into swan-sleep. Other times, Dr. Brumberg would have me fill a tub with cool water and place her in it, and she would paddle her feet fast, circling around and around, her eyes bright and dancing. She never made a sound—she was a mute swan, because a bird needs a beak to sing. But I could tell, when Ivory heard the sound of water rumbling in the tub, I could tell she was singing in her mind, singing with her eyes. She would telescope her head up over the enclosure and look for the source of the water. She would hop into my hands with eagerness, knowing it was time for a bath. I would cradle her, carry her into the bathroom, set her gently down on her aquatic playground. Sometimes she twirled in place, like a ballerina spinning on tiptoe, she would twirl and twirl, making a whirlpool of the water, her eyes closed, as though she were remembering some other place.

In one of my favorite Greek myths that was read to me as a child, Zeus, infuriated with Leda, who spurned his advances, turned into a magnificent white swan with a huge wingspan and, flapping down from his regal perch in a pear tree, wooed Leda in disguise. In this version, Leda falls in love with the swan and marries him, living with him happily ever after, not ever knowing that her spouse is the man she rejected.

It wasn't until years later, in college, that I read another rendition of this myth. In this version, Zeus is enraged that Leda has rejected him as a lover. In retaliation, he turns into a swan, swims down the river on whose banks Leda is sunning, and clucks so sweetly to her that she awakens and wades into the water, drawn by the beauty of this beast. And once she is in the water, the placid river turns wild, the currents swift and strong, trapping her while Zeus sheds his swanness and rapes her as a male.

We, as humans, have so many, many stories in which animals play parts, but it is only when you actually come to care for animals that you see how these stories, powerful though they may be, bear basically zero relationship to the actual animal kingdom. In our animal stories the only animal we learn about is man, but when you come close to animals you see the true strangeness of the beasts who share our planet. Swans are extraordinary but not at all in the way our literature suggests. They are extraordinary because of their unique biology, which has created for them a way to manufacture, in a gland, a special oil they then, when preening, spread across their feathers, this substance more waterproof than anything a human could ever devise.

They are extraordinary because their brains are about the size of a kiwi, grey paste stuffed in their slender heads, and yet within that small scoop of grey matter they are able to memorize migratory routes thousands of miles long, and they never need a map. They are capable of mating for life, something we, as humans, have tried but largely failed to accomplish.

Dr. Proctor gave Dr. Brumberg and me a deadline. We could keep the swan at our facility for three more weeks, but at the end of that time, when the clock chimed, the bird was to go back to the lake, ready or not.

Dr. Brumberg and I had to think now, think hard and fast. Perhaps I or he could find a facility that would take the swan. Surely if we set Ivory back upon the lake from which she came we would be consigning her to death, either a fast merciful death in the jaws of some snapping prey or a slow miserable death due to starvation and fear. At work the next day I called a few habitats, asking them if they would be interested in housing a swan with no beak on a permanent basis, but this is like asking a barn to accept the care and maintenance of a lame mare—what's in it for them? We thought about zoos, but zoos in this country are largely built for the pleasure of the people who pass through them—what fun to see the tiger snoozing in the sun or to see the spider-tailed monkeys swinging from their branches. Who wants to pay twelve bucks to see a badly mangled soundless swan, an ugly duckling with no chance at transformation? Where were our wands when we needed them?

Transformation. I had seen that word somewhere not long ago. Where? On a billboard? *Transformation*. Oh yes, that's right. I had seen it on the cover of a magazine in our waiting room, a fashion magazine, the sort of thing that holds no interest for me.

Now, however, I had an interest. I went to the office waiting room and found the publication—*Vogue*, the slick cover showing a breezy model in a diamond dress with her hand on her hip and her eyes in provocative slits. The headline: "Transformation: Plastic Surgery in Ten Minutes or Less."

I flipped to the article. It was about facelifts, chemical peels, and supposedly other low cost fix-its for aging. According to the article, one in four women in the United States now have some sort of cosmetic procedure, as do one in eight men. The number of people having cosmetic procedures has risen by 68 percent in the past decade. It's de rigueur.

Veterinary care has become expensive in part because it uses much of the same technology as human medicine. CAT scans, MRI machines, complicated blood tests, delicate eye surgeries, replacement hips, even replacement hearts; slowly all of these options have become available for animal patients as well as human patients, although few pet owners have pockets deep enough to actually pay. Even dentistry has entered veterinary care, and it wouldn't surprise me if in a few years one can get veneers for Fido. There is one area of care, however, that has not really caught on in animal land—plastic surgery.

What about a case where an animal loses a limb, or is badly torn apart; is there not a role for plastic surgery in veterinary care in these cases? Dr. Brumberg and I discussed this. He was not afraid of seeming stupid. On speaker phone, so I could listen in, he called a plastic surgeon at Yale Medical Center.

"This is Dr. Brumberg," he said. "I have a patient I need to refer to you."

"Okay," said Dr. Feldman. He waited for Brumberg to tell him more. He did not know, had no way of knowing, that Dr. Brumberg was a vet and the patient in question was nonhuman.

"There has been a traumatic injury to the . . . the face area," Dr. Brumberg said, "and portions will need to be rebuilt."

This was a surgeon known for his work on faces.

"Age?" asked the doctor.

"Oh," Dr. Brumberg said, "very young. Very, very young." He paused, glanced over at me; I shrugged. "Just about," Dr. Brumberg said (he later explained to me that swans live fifteen years roughly and he based his calculations on that), "just about four years."

"Four years," the surgeon said. "What happened?"

"She was swimming," Dr. Brumberg said. I could see he was smiling slightly. "Bitten by a turtle."

"Do four-year-olds swim?" asked the doctor.

"Look," Dr. Brumberg said then, and sighed. I swear I could see the air go out of his sail. "I'm a vet over at New Haven Animal Hospital. The patient in question is a swan. I have a baby swan whose beak was bitten off, and I need a plastic surgeon to make her a new beak so she can survive."

"A swan," Dr. Feldman repeated. Even over speakerphone I could feel his shock. "A swan . . . ," he repeated.

"Yes," Dr. Brumberg said. "Very sweet animal with no chance of making it unless she gets a b—"

"You are," Feldman interrupted, "you are a vet and you are asking me, a plastic surgeon, to do a procedure on a swan. You are," he cleared his throat, "you are essentially asking me to do a nose job on a bird."

"Well," Dr. Brumberg said. "Well, yes. That's exactly what I'm asking. And as free care, of course," he said. "Because the swan does not have Medicaid."

"I see," said the surgeon. I could almost hear him smile, and somehow, at some point, a little bit more levity entered the conversation. "And may I ask?" the surgeon said, "may I ask whether or not the patient in question has a preference for what sort of prosthetic beak we might build? In nose jobs," he said, "patients have very clear preferences. Upturned, downturned, narrow, tilted, et cetera. Oftentimes," he said, "patients have a certain celebrity in mind, upon whom they wish their nose to be modeled. Is there, in this case—"

"We have no celebrity in mind," Dr. Brumberg said, and he seemed on the verge of being elated and then—

"Donald Duck, I suppose," said the surgeon.

Dr. Brumberg's face fell.

"No, not Donald Duck," Dr. Brumberg said in a soft voice. "The patient, after all, is not a duck."

"Right," said Dr. Feldman. "Precisely." And suddenly then the surgeon's tone changed, veered swiftly and sharply into iciness. "Dr. Brumberg," he said. "The patient is not a duck. Nor is the patient a person. Are you out of your goddamn mind thinking I'm going to do a plastic surgery procedure on a . . . on a . . ." He seemed at a loss for words.

"A swan," Dr. Brumberg said gently. "It's a swan. We call her Ivory."

But he didn't ever hear her name. He had hung up.

Dr. Brumberg called, then, a dentist. Yes, by the way, he was out of his goddamn mind, which is sometimes exactly what you need to step out of, if you are to find a solution.

Dr. Brumberg called a friend of his, a Dr. Eric Soth, who was a dentist. Dr. Soth, also, was out of his goddamn mind. Dr. Brumberg told me how they had been good friends at Berkeley. Brumberg had come to college with a snake, and Soth had come to college with a kilt and a pair of bagpipes. At night, in their dorm room, so the story goes, Soth would get dressed in his kilt and play the bagpipes while the snake danced on Brumberg's desk.

Dr. Brumberg explained the situation to Eric Soth. The very next day Soth drove from his office to ours, saw the baby bird, and said to both of us, "Guys, this is possible."

Eric Soth showed us how he planned to do it. Retainers and other orthodontic materials are made out of a pinkish, inner-lip-colored resin that the doctor pours in a bowl as powder and then liquefies with water, making a kind of clayish substance that he then molds to the patient's teeth. You may have had this done to you before, the cold metal clamp filled with the waxy pink stuff, jammed up against the roof of your mouth while you wait for it to harden just enough to hold an impression of your bite. This impression is then left to dry under a heat lamp and the dentist uses it to fashion whatever mouth gear you need.

Eric Soth's idea was to do something similar for our swan. Because she had lost her beak, there was no impression of the original beak that he could make. But there was a ragged beak stump left, and, very gently, the dentist made a mold of it—the beak's base—and then, using measurements derived from pictures, fashioned a full beak out of the same stuff your retainer is made of.

In fact, it took a long time. The process of fashioning a prosthetic beak took days and days. Soth was a meticulous craftsman. He created the acrylic beak to resemble a real swan beak as closely as possible, using tiny hinges to allow it to open and shut.

Now, the core questions—how would we attach it and would it actually work?

Ivory is the first and only swan to have a prosthetic beak, but that is really the least of it. She is the first, and perhaps the only swan to have benefited from plastic surgery and, by doing so, to demonstrate that the "luxury" medical procedures human use can in fact have critical relevance to animals who truly need the procedures. More than that, she is the first and only swan to have illuminated so starkly, so clearly, the truth about her species—the vulnerability, the sociability, the capacity to connect with humans—and by doing so to bust through the myths that have kept swans caged in misconceptions. They are elegant animals, yes, but they are also sweet, love to play, understand language (Ivory knew the words *tub* and *water*). Still more important, Ivory helped me to find and articulate a certain ethical stance: all questions of logic, of risks and benefits, cannot stand up to this simple mandate that drives my life today, as a psychologist treating humans in a clinic not so different from that twenty-four-hour crisis veterinary hospital where I worked so long ago. The humans I treat have no money to pay; they are all Ivories, badly bungled, empty of purse. Care should not cost; air should not cost; they are both basic animal rights and thus the economic burden should be placed on all of us, collectively.

I am happy to be able to say that Ivory had her new beak within the three-week deadline set by Dr. Proctor, and because the beak worked, because it opened and shut and allowed Ivory to take food on her own, she grew fat to the point of independence. However, independence would never mean life as a regular swan for Ivory; she would never return to the lake from which she came. On the day of Ivory's discharge I called the mother of the girl who brought her in and said, "Come now. Come see the swan."

So they came. I wanted them to. Dr. Brumberg and I treated animals but all pain was our concern. If that day of the snapping turtle had made a memory for this girl—a memory of horror—then we wanted to help make its alternate. A memory of joy? No. A mangled swan with an acrylic beak is not a joyful sight. But it is a hopeful sight, a sight that suggests there are always possible solutions to seemingly intractable problems.

So the girl came down and was amazed to see the baby bird who was now, twenty days later, no longer a baby but a full-fledged teen with an enormous appetite and a sense of her own beauty. Ivory, it turns out, was a large bird, as white as snow, the pink of the prosthetic beak all the pinker when set against the blizzard of her body. The girl touched the beak, watched the tiny golden hinges work. "Wow," she said.

At the end of that day, after the visit, we moved Ivory to a wildlife habitat in Maine where she could spend her long life in safety and in peace, in the midst of humans and also other birds. The director's name was Ginny. Dr. Brumberg and I drove Ivory there and left her in the hands of Ginny and walked away, something sad in me, something I could not say. We walked away. We had had her for less than thirty days, but in that time so much had happened, so much growth, for one, and then so much fear, for another, those nighttime sounds, the creature I never found, and then the one that I did. From Ivory I had learned what I believe to be right about medical care—it should come at no cost to the consumer, and because of Ivory I frequently recall the necessity of faith in any healing endeavor. Poor Dr. Feldman, the eminent plastic surgeon. He could not see it. He lacked either the imagination or the sheer chutzpah that allows caring to happen. And why not,

Dr. Feldman? I'd like to ask. Why not a nose job for a swan, a beak for a boy, if that is what is needed? You must, sometimes, be a little out of your mind.

Not long after Ivory had gone to her rehab center, Ginny called us to tell us that she was using her beak to eat, to kiss, and, yes, to sing. The girl had begun to sing, soft but real songs nonetheless, a gentle mournful music that you can hear only if you listen very quietly. Dr. Brumberg and I went back to visit Ivory several months later; we went to hear her songs, and we did, and the soft music was like a river running over rocks or a fast falling rain. It went on and on, her beak just slightly ajar and her lids at half mast, she swam and sang, and though we knew nothing of what she meant—the struggles against the turtle, or just smelt and scat, no matter— the melodies clearly had meaning, because the other birds listened, all cocking their tiny heads.

Anyway, this was all years and years ago, when I was younger, and perhaps more easily charmed. Maybe now, twenty years older, and that much harder, I have more of the Proctor and less of the Brumberg in me; I hope not. I hope I'd still support the quixotic risk taker over the bureaucratic conservative, but one does not know where one's values lies until one is pushed up against a living ledge. For me, Ivory was that ledge. I have not seen her in years and years. But I do keep tabs on her, and last I heard she was still alive, an old lady now herself, but very elegant and still as playful as ever. According to Ginny she still likes to be scratched like a cat, and she uses her not-new-anymore beak to snack on smelt and bluefish, and she enjoys all her meals. She enjoys paddling in the small habitat pond. She enjoys mothering the foundling birds brought to the habitat; she has never had babies of her own, but she has come to know what it means to care. When the injured birds are brought in, Ivory, an old timer, takes them quite literally under her enormous white wing, sings softly, and then pecks them gently with her gold hinged beak, a kind of kissing.

My status as human being practically ensures that I'll never know what Ivory's singing really means. As intimate as I was with her body, I'll never cross that last bridge that would give me access to her mind. Are the songs warbles for a mate? For food? For the pure pleasure of the sound and the mechanics of its making? It seems endlessly odd to me that we can be so close to animals, physically, emotionally, and yet never will we see through their ancient eyes; never once will their day be ours.

As for me, Ivory was a brief hiatus in what was otherwise a difficult year of drudgery, working as a vet tech, cleaning the cages of cats and dogs. Like I said, at the ends of my days I'd try to write, but, unlike Ivory, no melodies came to me; no stories to sing. And sometimes in the night I'd wake to hear that terrible scream from the woods again, it would go on and on, raising the hairs at the nape of my neck, and if I blocked my ears, it was still there, and so I saw the forest was within me, along with its simian sound.

I would hum then, I would hum Ivory's songs, and whenever I did she appeared in the air, as if straight out of a giant book; beautiful, huge and white, her beak gone golden: I'd say *Sing to me, muse*, and she'd sing to me and she'd sing to me and she'd sing to me until the screams in the forest receded and dawn was limning the sky. "Don't leave," I'd say, but the swan always did, once her singing was over, and I was sound asleep.

5

The Sixty Thousand–Dollar Dog

1: Pressure

My dog, Lila, is forty pounds packed with muscle and grit. Her hide is as rough as the rind of a cantaloupe, covered with course hair that is nevertheless somehow soft to the touch. She is a dumb dog in the sense that all dogs are dumb, driven by genes and status, she will willingly fight any mammal that threatens her alpha position, and she delights in bones, big greasy bones she can crunch in her curved canines, and then swallow, splinters and all.

My husband disparages Lila, and, to his credit, there is much there to disparage. She lacks the capacity for critical thought. She has deposited in our yard an estimated four hundred pounds of feces during her ten-year tenure with us. Her urine has bleached our green grass so the lawn is now a bright yellow-lime, the same shade as the world seen through a pair of poorly tinted sunglasses, at once glaring and false. Lila farts and howls. Lila sheds and drools. Lila costs us more per year to maintain than does the oil to heat our home. There is her food; her vaccinations; her grooming; the four times yearly palpating of her anal glands; her heartworm medications; her chew toys; her city leash; her second, country retractable leash; her dog bed; the emergency veterinary visits when she gets ill; the sheer *time* it takes to walk her (my husband estimates my rate at fifty dollars per hour). Picture him, my husband, at night, the children tucked in bed, punching the keys on his calculator. Picture Lila, unsuspecting (and this is why she charms us, is it not?), draped across his feet, dreaming of deer and rivers as he figures the cost of her existence meshed with ours. It is cold outside. The air cracks like a pane of glass and sends its shards straight up our noses. He presses = and announces the price he claims is right. *Sixty thousand.* The cost of Lila's life. I look out the window. The lawn she's bleached is covered with a fine film of snow and the sky above is as dark as a blackboard, scrawled with stars and beyond them—what? *Six trillion suns.* Ancient radiation that still sizzles in our air. Scientists now claim there is more than one universe, but precisely how many more? No one knows. *Some things cannot be calculated.* I won't tell my husband this. I love my husband. I love Lila too.

Why I love Lila is not clear. The facts, after all, are the facts. There are, by some estimates, 2 million tons of dog feces deposited annually on American sidewalks and in American parks and lawns. The volume of the collective canine liquid output in this country has been estimated at 4 billion gallons. Dogs are the carriers of more than sixty-five diseases they can pass to their human counterparts. Some of the more well-known ones are rabies, tuberculosis, and Rocky Mountain spotted fever. Six hundred and fifty four people died last year in the United States from dog bites, and over thirty thousand were injured enough to require a visit to the emergency room. Seems a no brainer, right? Knowing these facts, you would have to be as dumb as a dog to have a dog in your home.

Now, another small fact. I don't have one dog. I have two. And if I had a bigger home, I would have three. Maybe even four. Or more. My idea of heaven on earth is to have as many dogs as I do socks, or spoons. All the facts in the world cannot change the final fact in this matter, which is that dogs and I—we get along.

I don't know why this is. Nor do I know why I so adore dogs while my husband fairly despises them. I have a hunch, though not up to investigation. Still, here it is. Dogs evolved from wolves. The modern-day human evolved from the Cro-Magnon man. A long time ago, so long that even all the dog scat stretched into a single smelly string could not go that far, a few wolf pups crept into a few Cro-Magnon caves and kept some scared families company in a night dense with danger. These wolf pups howled warning when a wildebeest was near. Their multilayered coats emitted continuous waves of warmth. Faster than us on their feet, they became indispensable hunting aides, twisting up in the air and bringing down the deer, teeth sunk into the blood-speckled neck of an animal we feasted on, sharing scraps, breaking bread with these canids whose evolution is all tied up with ours. Eventually, these progenitor pups, perpetually in our presence, grew domesticated, and thus the dawning of the dog. This, understand, is the short, short, *short* version of what was probably in reality a synergistic push and pull, a unique kind of coevolution that kept on keeping on over spans of thousands and thousands of years.

Sometimes, if I lie very still in the flat part of our field and if, as I do so, I stare up at the spattered sky, I think I can feel those years tumbling me over and down, over and down and back. My guess? I must have descended from those early wolf-welcoming Cro-Magnons, those hairy hunters with the genetic predisposition that allowed them to open doors they didn't know they had. I must have descended from a line of people who liked the stink of the wild, smelling it on their palms pressed up to their faces; who knew long before Crick unraveled the chromosome that there was not much difference between our genome and theirs. And these people, perhaps they were lonely and needed the feel of fur in order to salve the skin-stinging openness of the Pliocene plains. Most of all I believe we believed, even back then—a wordless, wild belief—that humans only become *beings* in relation to the animals with whom we share this planet; the differences defines us and the similarities remind us of some essential primitive cry we keep a clamp on.

The bottom line? Maybe Homo can only be Sapien (wise) when he respects the radical others who populate our blue ball, when he considers their sentient suffering and their planes of knowledge. Literary critic Donna Haraway puts it well when she writes in her book *The Companion Species Manifesto*, "Dogs, in their historical complexity, matter here. Dogs are not an alibi for other themes; dogs are fleshy material-semiotic presences in the body of techno-science. Dogs are not surrogates for theory; they are not here just to think with. They are here to live with. Partners in the crime of human evolution, they are in the garden from the get-go." This is all a lot of hog wash, or poodle poop, according to my husband. Jacques Derrida wrote about feeling shame when he saw the face of an animal in part because that face reflected back to him his moral failings as a man amongst men who had trampled the planet past the point of recognition, almost. My husband is a gentle man who cares about this planet. He says sorry to a tree before he cuts it down. He dutifully recycles, patiently sorting our scumbled trash, putting tin in the blue bin, plastics in the pink. He grows exotic mushrooms in our backyard's shadiest spot, fragrant plants with gilled undersides and suede-soft caps of gray. But when it comes to dogs, my husband feels next to nothing. He has, I think, a kind of canid autism, almost utterly unable to engage in the social play between people and their pooches. His actions and attitude lead me to wonder if his long line is entirely different from mine. While I must be descended from those hairy hunters with genetic pre-dispositions that encouraged them to welcome wolf, my husband, well, he must come from a tribe the genetic constitution of which lead them to either overtly reject the canine or simply fail to hear his knock at their door. Some theorists believe that the reason why the Neanderthals became extinct is because they never took to the pups sniffing the perimeters of their property and thus lost out on all the riches that the human/canine relationship had to of-fer. As the Cro-Magnon flourished, the Neanderthals—living in an iced-over Europe, in a land of perpetual twilit snow—dwindled down; cold, hunger, scarcity the name of their game. What this may mean: all those "not dog" people, the ones who push away the paws and straighten their skirts after being sniffed, well, they may have one foot in the chromosomally compromised Neander-thal pool, while, on the other hand, those of us who sneak food to Fido, roam with Rover, or insist that the Pekinese is put on the bed each night, well, we may be displaying not idiocy or short-sighted sentimentality, as our critics would call it, but a sign of our supe-rior genetic lineage. It's possible. But I don't want to tell my hus-band this. I'd hate to hurt his feelings.

Despite our different attitudes towards dogs in particular, pets in general (we also have a cat, two hamsters, and I'm planning on hens and horses when we move full time to the country) have not been a subject of sore dispute in our home until recently. In the past, my husband and I have had brief spats about Lila and her brother, Musashi, but nothing that led to a deep and abiding impasse. Now, however, circumstances are starting to change. When I got the dogs they were puppies, and so were we. Twelve years later, I have begun to read the obituaries in the paper. I worry about osteoporosis, and I experience occasional sciatica. My eyesight is going, the distance still crisp but all that comes close to me fuzzy. Furred. Words warp and melt, slipping sideways on the page. The other day, while admiring my hydrangea in the garden, I could not recall its name. *Hydrangea. Hydrangea. Hydrangea.* Now I walk around repeating the names of plants to myself, as if words will keep my world intact. *Hydrangea. Aster. Sedum. Astilbe.*

My husband, a deeply private person, has his own assortment of worries, aches, and pains. Two years or so ago his arms started to hurt, a flaming deep in the muscles. The pain had made him smaller, solitary, sitting in his study, his wrists gleaming with Bengay. Before he left his job, unable to use a keyboard, he worked sixty, seventy hours a week and got his exercise while commuting in his car, steering with his left hand and lifting a five-pound weight with his right. Then he'd switch sides. He claimed that kept him in cardiovascular shape. I view this claim as the distortions of a desperate man. Forty-five, forty-six, forty-seven. Unemployed, now; cornered and chronic. He has a beautiful bald spot on his head, a perfect cream-colored circle haloed by red hair. He knows enough not to try a comb-over. Our children see his bald spot as a toy. Our son races his cars around and around its circumference. Our daughter draws on it: Two eyes. A heart. Enough, he says. Enough. As for our dogs, our aging reflects theirs, or theirs ours. Musashi, the elder of our canines, appears blessed with youthful genes, his only sign a whitening of the whiskers. But Lila, like me, is going gray all over, her urine mysteriously tinged with pus and blood, her hips eroding, clumps of fur falling from her hide, her skin beneath raw red and scaly.

Until recently, I viewed Lila's decline like my own, an un-happy inconvenience auguring a foreboding future that was still a ways off. Then, a few months ago (it was spring then, a beauti-ful blue and yellow May day) I came downstairs to find my feisty dog crouched by the front door, her eyes squinted shut, her breath coming fast and hot. I called to her. She struggled towards me, then sunk sideways. When she refused the ice cream I offered her (Oreo cookie, her favorite), I knew it was something serious. I rushed her to the twenty-four-hour veterinary hospital located ten miles from our house. *Why*, I thought, as I waited at a series of in-terminable red lights, my dog now panting in pain, *why are there no ambulances for animals?* While an ambulance for animals may strike some as absurd, it is likely no more ridiculous than a pet ER would have seemed to the general public one hundred years ago.

In the earliest days of veterinary medicine, back in the 1800s, there were no hospitals for pets. There were far fewer pets to treat. That's because animals were everywhere, although their primary purpose was for labor, not love. This doesn't mean that there was no love. There has always been love, to greater or lesser degrees. What's changed, more recently, is, perhaps, the intensity of the love along with our ability, and concomitant willingness, to treat our animals with the same, or similar, technological prowess that we would want for ourselves, or nearly so. Thus, gone are the days when veterinary care occurred in the barnyard, often by failed far-riers looking to earn a living. The tools of the trade back then were brutal, flailing horses held down as cigar-chomping "surgeons" hacked off the blue bags of a stallion's testicles.

The twentieth century saw many technical and scientific ad-vances—the combustible gas-powered engine, vaccines for polio, and pasteurization for milk, to name a few—and there's no ques-tion that veterinary medicine was amongst them. As barnyard ani-mals disappeared more and more from mainstream American life, so too did the barnyard vet, his primitive tools replaced with anti-septic power-driven appliances that characterize so much of mod-ern medicine, his sheep and goats and chickens now shampooed lap dogs and fine-boned huskies with bead-blue eyes and soap-white coats. And whereas, in the nineteenth century, "vets" had minimal education, if any at all, they now are required to slog through years of training more intense than an ordinary doctor's as they memorized the anatomy of everything from elephants to octopi. Thus, the burgeoning of high-tech animal hospitals all across this country reflects both the fierce attachments contemporary people have for their pets, as well as the increased numbers of highly trained veterinarians who come not only with a medical degree but often with one or several subspecialties under their belts. These are veterinary doctors who can reengineer gimpy legs, who can cut out a tendrilling tumor with near total precision, who can concoct chemotherapies in different doses and degrees depending on species and the specifics of the cancer in question. These are doctors who push titanium pins into bones and put pacemakers in hearts that look very much like ours. The price for these specialized services? Let's just say—a lot. We'll get to that. For the moment, think of people emptying their pockets. Pets prove our economic theories all wrong. Pets have almost zero monetary value, and yet we willingly invest in them, again and again. Unlike children, they can't care for us in our dotage, or better yet, carry on our chromosomal torch. Basic economic theory says that people spend money to earn it—the core concept in investment—but when it comes to our pets the opposite is true. We spend money to lose it, again and again, in love.

The hospital I arrived at that day with my dog is emblematic of the vast shape-shifting changes in veterinary medicine and animal owners that have occurred over the past few hundred years. It's a piece of prime real estate located amidst a row of biotechnology companies on a tony road just off the highway. I carried my panting puppy in through the pneumatic doors. A Bernese mountain dog lying sideways on a stretcher was whisked past me by two masked attendants. On the wall behind the reception desk hung poster-sized photographs of the veterinarians: no barnyard surgeons here. Each one was coiffed and poised, and below the framed photos were gold plaques inscribed with their specialties: neurology, oncology, pediatrics, psychology. The Bernese mountain dog was stalled outside the OR doors. He lay still on his side, his front paws politely, precisely, crossed. His yellow eyes met mine. I had the distinct feeling he was from a fairytale, a prince put under a spell, his carcass canine, his mind man.

A doctor ushered me into a small examination room. With thumb and forefinger she pried apart Lila's clamped lids and I could see it then, how her normally amber eyes were filled with milk, glinting a dull bluish color, all opaque. Her eyes were oozing, and when I touched the fluid dampening her fur it felt gluey.

The doctor called in the staff ophthalmologist, who came trailing some sort of machine, the probe of which she pressed right up against Lila's pupil in a way that made me wince. "Seventy-five," the ophthalmologist said. The two doctors looked at each other grimly. Lila had gone still, stunned or dead I could not tell. They peeled back her other eye and again, pressed the probe right to its center. "Eighty-three" the ophthalmologist announced. They turned to me. "Your dog has glaucoma," the ophthalmologist said. "The pressure in her eyes has risen well beyond normal."

Glaucoma. I had heard of that before. It did not seem so bad. I was wrong. In people glaucoma is manageable. In dogs it is devastating, in part because it is so much more painful. The pounding pressure winches the canine's much smaller skull, causing a migraine well beyond what humans can conceive. Lila lay rigid with agony, her snout and fur hot to the touch. "The pressure has gone so high," the ophthalmologist said, "it has crushed both optic nerves. Lila is permanently blind."

I left Lila at the hospital that day and for two days following. I left distraught; my puppy was in pain. On my way out, the receptionist presented me with the first half of my bill: $1,400. This made me more distraught. I looked again. *My* eyes, after all, were working. Fourteen hundred dollars for the ER visit, the emergency ophthalmology consult, the forty-eight-hour boarding fee. The projected costs were on the second page. The only one I recall is the $1,800 charge for the CAT scan that might be necessary. "Does everyone pay these charges?" I asked. "What happens if people don't have the money?"

"That hardly ever happens," the receptionist said. "People find a way to pay."

No one knows exactly when pets were invented. That they were invented is not a subject in much dispute. Though animals have populated the planet long before hominoids made their mark, pets are a product of human culture. And, like all cultural products, their meaning has evolved as fads and fashion change.

In Victorian times, only one in fifty families in the United States owned a dog or a cat. Now, in 2011, roughly 62 percent of families own a pet and there are three times as many pet owners as there were in the 1980s. Sociologists hypothesize this is due to rising divorce rates and the "Bowling Alone" phenomenon so well described by Robert Putnam in his book that discusses the collapse of communities in a country where civic engagement—membership in clubs and leagues, for instance—is on the decline while mistrust of government steadily rises. Pets, people think, are filling a vacancy, our devotion to them coming from deficit.

I disagree. Might our increasing willingness to not only own but finance our companion animals come from something finer? As the planet erodes, and as our role as its destroyer becomes harder and harder to deny, might we not be considering, for the first time, the idea that the human species is far from sacred? Might we, in losing the sense of our own sanctity, be better able to see our kinship with species not ours? I don't know. What I do know is that in several states, along with some provinces in Canada, the term "pet" has become disagreeable to enough people that the word has been virtually banned and in its place this phrase—"animal guardian." I do know, according to a 2007 British study funded by Purina, that 75 percent of respondents claimed to spend more money on their pets' health than on their own. After Hurricane Katrina, when hundreds of thousands of people were forced to abandon their pets because emergency helicopter transfer refused to allow the animals on board or emergency shelters banned animals from entering, Representative Tom Lantos introduced the Pet Evacuation and Transportation Standards Act, which requires any state

seeking FEMA assistance in an emergency to accommodate companion animals in their evacuation plans. And if you think those
plans circle mostly around cats and dogs, think again. Pet-owning
Americans have snakes, gerbils, black-bear hamsters, furry ferrets,
pot-bellied pigs, and, perhaps oddest of all, fish. Fish? Yes, apparently we've become fonder and fonder over the years of plain old
carp, or koi, with more Americans owning them than dogs and
cats. Thus there are now, in this country, more than two thousand fish vet specialists who perform CAT scans, X-rays, and even
MRIs on our aquatic friends and, yes, people are willing to pay,
people like David Smothers whose koi, called Ladyfish, was struck
by lightning as she swam in her pond during a violent electri-
cal storm in the summer of 2001. According to a *Nova* episode,
a vet fish specialist did a series of CAT scans and ascertained that
her back was broken. Said Smothers, "The fish was certainly going to die. There was no doubt about that." The fish vet specialist
brought Smothers's koi into both neurosurgery and orthopedic surgery, where other fish vet specialists were able to stabilize her spine
using screws and wires, plus some epoxy.

I drove home. My dog was neither dying nor dead, but the fact
of her pain was painful, and then what would her life become
once the pain subsided? A blind dog. A dog who had lived an entire decade with the benefit of sight, her vision suddenly yanked
away from her, and no words to explain what was happening. It
was late in the day now, the clouds like cataracts spreading. Inside,
my daughter was riding her scooter in our hallway. "Lila has gone
blind," I said to her. I started to cry. I told my husband later, when
he returned from work. I did not mention the veterinary bill. Instead, I called the bank, cashed in a CD, paid the penalty.

Two days later, I drove back to the hospital. The final bill was
$3,338. I figured this was a one-time cost that my liquidated CD
could cover. They brought Lila to me. She did not come out on
a leash. She came out carried, and when they set her in my lap I
could see, immediately, that a dog can be devastated. The medications had brought the pressure down, so her eyes were open, but

they were thickened, blank, like pale-blue opaque sea glass, glassy, reflective but not receptive. In her eyes I could see my face, but she could not see mine. "Lila, Lila," I whispered. She moved her whole head in the direction of my voice but gave not the tiniest tail wag, not the slightest ear prick. I started to weep again.

Back at home, I set Lila on the floor of our living room, but even here, amidst familiar scents, she would not move. Musashi, our other dog and her sibling, bounded forward in his typical greeting style but something, some smell, some sense, stopped him short. He skidded to a bunched halt and then cautiously extended his snout to sniff his companion of eleven years—where had she been all these days? Lila stayed stone still. Musashi backed away and then clattered, fast, up the steps. "Lila, Lila," I called, my daughter called, even my husband called, but the dog was too terrified, or despairing, to move. At last I picked her up, carried her to our bed. I slept with her for one week straight, my face buried in her fur, her pee soaking the sheets, her eyes weeping pus and drops.

I ordered a book about blind dogs and when it came—express shipment—I read that older alpha dogs do not adjust well to the sudden, inexplicable shift of total blindness. I stroked Lila's skull, moved my fingers through her dense fur, sent my husband to the pharmacy to fill the prescriptions. My husband—with his own mysterious arm ailment aching away his days—had been kicked out of the marital bed and was daily scraping up with a putty knife the hardened scat Lila left on the floors. "Four hundred dollars," he said when he returned, holding the paper bag. "Four hundred dollars for a one-month's supply of this stuff."

Now this was hard to believe. The tubes were doll sized and when you squeezed, a glistening bead of gel oozed to the tip of the nozzle. How could grease cost so much? What choice did we have? While the medications would not restore a single stripe of sight to Lila's world, they would prevent the pain of pressure crushing her head.

"Maybe," my husband said, "we should put Lila down."

"Put Lila down," I repeated mechanically. "Put her down."

"She's had eleven good years," my husband said. "Look at her now."

Yes, look at her now. Lying in a puddle of pee on what was our marital bed.

I called the ophthalmologist. "Should we put her down?" I asked.

I expected equivocation, but instead she said, "God no! A blind dog can do quite well once it adapts. Dogs rely primarily on their sense of smell. It's not like a human."

"Lila's depressed," I said. "She won't move."

"Put her on her leash," the doctor said. "Take her out. Have expectations. Refuse to baby her. I've seen blind dogs forge rapids, climb mountains. If you teach them toughness, they'll be tough."

I brought Lila outside. I made a Hansel and Gretel path through the woods by our home, using beef instead of breadcrumbs. That got her going. She found the shreds of roast, tasted baked blood, and remembered the meaning of life.

Slowly, over the weeks, Lila began to make her way. I watched my husband watch her. His own unnamed pain was slowly shrinking his world; by day he sought a diagnosis and then night after night he sat in his study with just one little light. And now here was Lila, with no little lights, forging forward, and he watched. A month passed. We needed more medication.

It was June then. School ended. My daughter's day camp was three thousand dollars, one of the hoity-toity arts camps I'd signed her up for as a way of alleviating the guilt I felt for not being able to afford private school. Now, however, I had to choose between Clara's camp and Lila's eyes. My husband insisted the issue was clear. We should choose Clara's camp. To me it was not so clear. If Clara did not go the fancy camp, she could still enjoy her summer. If Lila did not get her medications, she would not only not enjoy her summer; she would pass it in agony. And agony is a serious problem for any sentient being.

A dilemma such as this one is relatively new in the history of pet owning. Sixty years ago, the average pet owner could expect to spend somewhere in the ballpark of $200 for care during the entire lifespan of his or her pet. Now the average lifetime cost of the

American pet ranges from $10,000 to $20,000, and this isn't simply due to inflation. It's due to the fact that veterinary care, starting sometime in the 1980s, began to change dramatically as its technological capacities expanded. Prior to the 1980s, animal care meant yearly vaccinations, an occasional splint for a broken bone, and the price of euthanasia if necessary. Compare that to today, as veterinary students are now training in specialties and subspecialties and subspecialties of those subspecialties, and can therefore offer Fido, should he need it, a kidney transplant, cancer chemotherapy, back surgery, titanium hip-joint replacement, radiation treatment, neurological correction—you name it. Add to this the fact that from 1987 to 2000 the life spans of dogs and cats increased by more than one-third due to improved nutrition and vaccinations. Prior to 1987, my Lila may very well have died from crappy kibble before reaching old age and its complications, like glaucoma, and thus I would have been spared the difficult game of weighing the relative value of my daughter's education versus my dog's comfort.

The whole experience of struggling with the relative worth of dog and daughter led me to seek out other like-minded people who had made what many might consider outlandish, even outrageous decisions as regards their animals. My husband felt (felt at first, but soon this, like so much else about his connection to our blind beast would transform in the face of his pain) that I was being led like a blind donkey on the string of sentimentality and that if I took a hard-headed view of things, I would see that spending four hundred dollars a month on a decade-old dog was wrong—wrong for our family, wrong for our marriage, wrong for the world. Because that's what I was doing. I took on as many extra work assignments as I could. According to my husband, everyone would be much better served were I to donate the monthly medication payments to the starving countries on the continent of Africa, to the Green Party, to victims of lymphoma. His beliefs are echoed by Dr. Bruce Alexander, professor of psychology at Simon Fraser University in Canada who told me, "If Americans were to take all the money they spend on kibble yearly—an amount that's surely in the millions, if not the billions—it would be enough to feed countless people starving in Africa. It would be enough to fund multiple orphanages in Asia for the foreseeable future. " In other words, dog lovers are baby killers. Shame on us.

Shame on Darrell Hallett and his wife, Nina, a Seattle couple who, in 2005, spent $45,000 to get their dog a stem-cell transplant for lymphoma. Shame on Agnieszka Onichimiuk, who, according to the *Wall Street Journal*, spent $7,000 to remove a tumor from her dog Jake's eyelid. Shame on all the people who are spending roughly $10,000 *a year* to house their aged pets in Japan's newest, and only, long-term-care facility for geriatric animals, a posh place where one can be assured their feline or canine companion is living, and dying, with more dignity than millions of human octogenarians and nonagenarians in the surrounding area.

It is of course *not* difficult to find many naysayers when it comes to spending funds as large as these on *pets*. The idea that such expenses may be valid, while gaining ground, is still well below sea level. And that disdain crosses cultures, and is probably more prevalent in non-Western cultures, the people of which, in general, tend to believe that doting on one's pet is a sign of Western excess. Thus, the Saudi Arabians have, as of September 8, 2006, banned the sales of all dogs and cats in their country. This decree, which applies to the city of Jiddah and the holy city of Mecca, states, "Some youths have been buying them and parading them in public." Wrote one Aleetha al-Jihini in a letter to *Al Madina* newspaper, "One bad habit spreading among our youth is the acquisition of dogs and showing them off in the streets and mall . . . this is blind emulation of the infidels."

I know I am an infidel, in more ways that I care to mention. I have made too many mistakes in my life and have too often been propelled out of greed or, more problematic for me, fear, so that I clutch rather than touch, ruining whatever it is I seek to claim. I can discuss my deficits, but I am not yet ready to admit to the particular one of which we are speaking, even as I state it as a possibility. Could it not be equally possible, though, that valuing nonhuman animals as much as, if not even *more than*, our own kind, is a sign of a higher kind of consciousness composed of the very sort of sentience and humility we may need if we are to clean up the mess we've made on Earth? It stands to reason that, if we made the mess out of deep disregard for the ecosystem that sustains us, we are only likely to change course and correct once that deep and damaging disregard turns into real respect, or even love.

Such a sweeping change of heart, and values, is unlikely amongst our species, despite the fact that, though the Judeo-Christian religion condones the dominion of mankind over all the other animals, science cannot sustain such a view. What, I have to ask, in the Darwinian theory of evolution, posits human beings are at the top of the heap? If one believes in evolution then one must accept the fact that the "tree of life" is laterally designed, branches branching branches branching branches, no one unwinding design "better" than any other.

That people tend to believe their kind have value above and beyond nonhuman animals is an assumption for which there is not a lot of convincing evidence, an assumption that may have served our species well, up to a point, up to this particular point, facing, as we are, ever-rising amounts of greenhouse gases, scientists now saying that we have done irreversible damage to the Arctic's ecosystems and that, within just a few years, CO_2 will be at 450 parts per million, at which point we'll be past the tipping point and well on our way to a world vastly imbalanced and possibly not viable, with weather so labile crops will fail, droughts will crack the parched surface of the earth, while the tundra steeps in its own wet rot, releasing, as it does, ever more methane into our already densely saturated atmosphere.

Even though some, maybe most, don't think of the disaster looming just over the line, I believe we sense it in our brains and in our bones; we smell it in the congestion of our coughing cars, in the foul smog that casts its pall above some cities, and in the eerie yet lovely sight of pink blooms set on a snow-crusted branch, early spring, time and time again.

I wonder if the willingness of more and more Homo sapiens to put their animal's welfare on par with, or even above, that of themselves and their kin, is a sign of a slow sea change caused in part by our dawning awareness of global warming, its possible role in disasters we as a human community have lately faced, along with a sense of our foreshortened future. Are we not, in some sense, feeling our smallness, shedding, like any good mammal, the gleaming coat of our supposed superiority as we face, over and over again, evidence of our extreme mistakes? How can we believe we have god-given dominion over all the other animals on this planet in light of our spillage and spoilage, the seas slicked with oil, blackened birds washed ashore, not once, not twice, but in one way or another, over and over again. A long, long time ago Copernicus suggested that human beings were not at the center of our solar system, and by doing so he shook the souls we say we have to their ethereal roots. There is, as of yet, no single scientist who has done for our relationships to life forms on earth what Copernicus did to our relationship to the stars in the sky. That doesn't mean, however, that there have not been some especially resonant voices, one of the earliest ones belonging to philosopher Jeremy Bentham who wrote, in 1796, in his *Introduction to the Principles of Morals and Legislation*:

> The day may come when the rest of the animal creation may acquire those rights which never could have been witholden from them but by the hand of tyranny. The French have already discovered that the blackness of the skin is no reason why a human being should be abandoned without redress to the caprice of a tormentor. It may come one day to be recognized that the number of the legs, the villosity of the skin, or the termination of the os sacrum, are reasons equally insufficient for abandoning a sensitive being to the same fate. What else is it that should trace the insuperable line? Is it the faculty of reason, or perhaps the faculty for discourse? But a full-grown horse or dog is beyond comparison a more rational, as well as a more conversable animal, than an infant of a day, or a week, or even a month, old. But suppose they were otherwise, what would it avail? The question is not, Can they *reason*? nor, Can they *talk*? but, Can they *suffer*?

More recently philosophers such as Tom Regan and Peter Singer have argued against what they call "speciesism," the tendency to assign value or give consideration based on a being's species membership. In speciesism, physical differences are given moral weight. For Singer, as for Bentham, the issue is almost always one of sentience and suffering. In his book *Practical Ethics* Singer writes:

Racists violate the principle of equality by giving greater weight to the interests of members of their own race when there is a clash between their interests and the interests of those of another race. The white racists who supported slavery typically did not give the suffering of Africans as much weight as they gave to the suffering of Europeans. Similarly speciesists give greater weight to the interests of members of their own species when there is a clash between their interests and the interests of those of other species. Human speciesists do not accept that pain is as bad when it is felt by pigs or mice as when it is felt by humans.

In Singer's world, sentience and suffering are the key concepts, and they lead to what some might say are outrageous claims. For instance, if one had to inflict pain on either a brain-dead infant or, let's say, a normal mature dog, in Singer's world (as in my own) one would choose (regrettably but inevitably) the brain-dead infant, because the human brain-dead infant cannot suffer in the same capacity as can the dog. Speaking of which, dogs are often used in animal experimentation, and animal experimentation is often defended by claims that critical cures for humans are being developed, and how could one deny, let's say, a baby, its cure for, say, leukemia, on the one hand, while saving some mutt on the other? Singer might argue by pointing out that not too long ago blacks were called "mutts" and much worse. Now that we have made the mental switch that allows people to see blacks as human beings, however, it would be outrageous were we to suggest that we perform painful experiments on "people of color" in the hope of saving some white child, even though we have no choice but to admit that not so very long ago we saw slaves as "animals" and used them for whatever we needed, with no thought to their suffering. "But," claims the average middle-class American at the dawn of the new millennium, "but would you let hundreds, thousands, millions die if a single animal experiment could save them?" Singer's retort, from his book *Animal Liberation*:

> The way to reply to this hypothetical question is to pose another: Would the experimenters be prepared to carry out their experiment on a human orphan under six months old if that were the only way to save thousands of lives?

If the experimenters would not be prepared to use a human infant then their readiness to use nonhuman animals reveals an unjustifiable form of discrimination on the basis of species, since adult apes, monkey, dogs, cats, rats, and other animals are more aware of what is happening to them, more self-directing, and, so far as we can tell, at least as sensitive to pain as a human infant. (I have specified that the human infant be an orphan, to avoid the complications of the feelings of parents. Specifying the case in this way is, if anything, overgenerous to those defending the use of nonhuman animals in experiments, since mammals intended for experimental use are usually separated from their mothers at an early age. . . .)

So far as we know, human infants possess no morally relevant characteristic to a higher degree than adult nonhuman animals.

It boggles the brains of some to consider their dog as equal to their daughter, and, indeed, from our embedded human consciousness, it isn't so. But when we rise above our immanence, we see, we *can* see, a very different picture. When we consider who and what we are, not from our own eyes but from the perhaps point of view (if I may say so) of "the Universe" or, to be more specific, of evolution and its awesome but blind engine, another sort of story emerges. Up here, on high, the galaxies streaming past us, we can see that evolution is arbitrary, and its array of vast and amazing forms is simply the result of adaptation to whatever environmental conditions happen to prevail. We were created, in other words, not because we possess some special powers over and above the other species with whom we inhabit this earth, but because, just like every other species who inhabits this earth, we have been able to make our mutations work in and for the world as we have found it.

These facts sting the human heart, and one might well argue that the sting itself is evidence of our superiority, because dogs, after all, don't fret about their relative place in a manmade hierarchy, but then again, do they? They don't. One can spend weeks, months, years, playing philosophical ping-pong on these points, but, in a story about animals, it seems especially fair to just cut to the chase. Here we are, then, in dew-drenched Oregon, rain sparkling on the leaves of all the trees. Roger Fouts, a primate specialist, has a lab where the walls are windows looking out onto the saturated land, where chimps play on ropes he's hung from big, bent branches of old-growth oaks and alders.

"It is a fundamental misperception," Fouts says to me, "to think human life has more value than any other life form. I raise chimpanzees. Here's how to think of it. Picture you holding your mother's hand, and then your mother holding your grandmother's hand, your grandmother holding your great-grandmother's hand, your great-grandmother holding your great-great-grandmother's hand. At some point in your family line, whether you like it or not, one of your great-great-great-grandparents would be holding the hand of a chimpanzee."

I like to hold my dogs' paws. Their paws are rough, scaly, the skin cracked like quaked earth, the nails smooth and curved in their sharpness. A dog's nails can be difficult to cut because, unlike humans, they have veins in them, and if you snip too low, a bead of blood wells up and the animal winces in a way that is hard to hear. I did this to Lila once, cut too close to the base, cut the blue-violet vein that threads the nacreous nail of this beautiful beast I call mine. I call her mine not because I own her but because I love her. I call her mine as I call mine my children, my husband, my self. She is mine for as long as she is Lila, which amounts to no more than a nanosecond in the scheme of things, and when that second passes, she, like us all, will undergo the phenomenal changing of categories that we call death. But until she does, I will care for her with everything I have. I will struggle to divide up my limited resources in the best way I can. I will admire her daily, as I do to all those I love, and why? That is the question I have not answered here, the question my husband always asks.

Just a few weeks into her blindness, we no longer argue about the cost of her medications, not because we've reached consensus but because we know what the other will say, and so there is no need. Thus, my husband no longer asks if it is *right* to so love a dog as he knows my answer already. "Yes, it is right," or, "One has yet to offer me any scientific proof that animals mean less than we do, so it is certainly not wrong."

My husband's question for me now, when he can question, when he is not pulled into some private place of pain, unable, like

Lila, to feel his way past the curved contours of a world made small by suffering, his question for me now, as he sits in his study, is simply *why?* After all, Lila farts and howls, drools and poops, her yearly excrement (he is calculating again, picture him, late at night, midsummer, the air heavy and wet, blind Lila savoring rawhide smeared with peanut butter) weighing in at four hundred pounds of crap. And yours? I retort. How much does your shit weigh? As for mine—a lot.

His question, however, is good. Why? I don't know. What I *do* know is that when I look into Lila's now-blind eyes I see amazing things. I see the wildness of the wolf; I see humans finding fire, the Pliocene plains, millions of molecules, the softest snout; I see an animal walk out of the water: a single cell split; I see the engine of evolution, and if I listen closely I think I can hear it too, a low continuous hum—*that is the world I hear*—a sound that doesn't stop, I must believe, even if, or when, we do.

2: Fixed

Although he is usually a kind man, a man, we now know, who lets his children race their tiny cars around the road ring called his bald spot, my husband nevertheless insists, as he always has, that an animal's worth is roughly equivalent to its edibility. If you can carve, slice, boil, or bake the beast, then it is generally welcome in our home, packaged and frozen or live and wild; but if the animal presents no potential for consumption of the gastrointestinal sort, then in my husband's mind the life form is an excess weight on the world, an evolutionary glitch that serves no purpose except to clutter our already jam-packed planet. Recently I've begun to think his attitude has something to do with the fact that, as a child, he watched his scientist mother drain the blood from rabbits regularly sacrificed for experiments, the soft carcasses tossed away in a floppy heap. As a seven-year-old child, I had a white rabbit, an enormous overgrown rabbit with pale pink eyes and a quashed nose that continuously quivered in response to the scents around her. I named my rabbit Boul de Neige, which means "snowball" in French, and this rabbit became a companion more important to me than any human at the time. Boul de Neige rode in my bike basket when I pedaled or in the baby carriage when I was in a maternal mood, a bonnet on her head and a blanket over her hunched form. Boul de Neige learned to take a collar and a leash, and hopped alongside me on the sidewalks of the Golden Ghetto, and although it seems impossible to believe now, she also learned a few commands, like "Sit!" and "Come!" which she did, bounding to me when I called from across our lawn, her ears streaming backwards like braids, her huge floppy paws uplifted so I could see their undersides as she galloped, thick and soft as slippers. Boul de Neige got to know her name, and when tired, she lay her fragile bony head in my lap, and I would stroke her skull and feel what a rabbit felt like; the head hard underneath the fluff of white fur, the seams where the plates had fused. Long after Boul de Neige died, I saw a picture of a rabbit's brain hanging in a hall at Harvard; it was so tiny, truly a pea on a slender stem, barely big enough for dreams, never mind love. And yet, the rabbit had loved me, loved me largely and well. Over the years, as I grew up, I came to understand that this was not the point. Whether animals can love, or grieve, or hope, is far less important than the fact that they elicit these emotions in us. What I learned from Boul de Neige was that *I* can love, and grieve, and hope, and so it was that I grew into my humanity, traveling the tunnels dug for me by some small, dumb beast. I am an animal lover. I say this in no small way. I don't mean I enjoy animals, or find them entertaining, or cute. Nor do I mean that I care for animals as accessories, a peripheral part of a well-lived life. What I mean is that animals—especially mammals, and not especially insects—enchant me and inhabit me. I feel as strong a connection to the cat in the cornfield or the white malamute in the park as I do to the members of my own species, defined as we are by tools and looms, smoke and steel, highways and homes and coffins. I understand that I speak from a position of privilege. I understand that if I were a struggling farmer whose chickens were always swallowed by coyotes, or a villager in Africa, hunted regularly by hungry lions, I might feel quite differently on the subject; I perhaps would be singing, as they say, a new tune. I am thankful for the simplicity of this song. I am also aware that its simplicity is in its surface.

Underneath lurk a million dilemmas. Is my attachment to animals a sign of some pathology, a flawed capacity for human intimacy? What is the difference between love and sentimentality? What would it mean if I actually care as much for the family dogs as I do for my husband, or, worse, my . . . children? Do I perhaps lack the very humanity I just claimed was mine? Am I a wolf dressed up as a lover, a mother? As I write this I can hear, downstairs, the dogs as they awaken. Their collars jangle; their claws click on the floor. The younger dog is blind. She has glaucoma. It's been four years now since she lost her sight completely, and much has come from the dark swamp of her unseeing, things for my husband and also for me, things we never expected. The blind dog's name is Lila Tov, which means good night in Hebrew. I hope, for her unseeing sake, that this is so.

If you are a middle-aged woman living in a suburb or a city in the United States of America, than chances are good that your chosen animal of adoration will be a dog. I met my husband before I met my dogs, Lila and Musashi, and my husband's soothing ways gave me no reason to think he was one of those speciesists, so aptly named by Peter Singer, boxed in by his own human brain. Benjamin, an engineer by trade and a chemist by avocation, used to tell me tales about *amanita muscaria*, which is a fancy way of saying mushrooms. I met him in the wet, humid summer of 1990, the summer Nelson Mandela came to Boston and preached peace and everywhere the domed caps of mushrooms were popping up in the rain-fed fields. We found enormous ears of mushrooms growing along the rotting trunks of fallen trees, and we found minuscule mushrooms huddled at the base of a stockade fence, and he picked one, tweezing it free with his fingers and putting it in my palm. "In Russia," Benjamin told me, "mushrooms are signs of good luck. The Siberians used to believe that at night mushrooms become reindeer."

It was easy to fall in love with Benjamin; he made the world seem elfin with his curious assortment of facts about plants and animals and star-shaped molecules he made from marshmallows and toothpicks so we could eat estrogen and air. He was, as I've said, a kind man.

And yet, if that is so, than why is it so difficult for me now to recollect the forms his caring took? What makes a man gentle? Why are some beings so easy to love, while others feel so serrated? And if love is easy—as in the love one woman has for her copper-colored dogs—is it love she in fact feels or something simpler, like affection? What I question is the question: Why the need to define love in the first place? I suppose it proves that I am human. A long time ago Linnaeus created categories within categories within categories—kingdom, phylum, class, order, family, genus, species—and that is how he housed the beings with whom we share our planet. We do not know of any other animal except the human who is so in need of boxes, so desperate for the four curt corners that can be rendered beautifully, as in in the painting I saw the other day, a glowing pink box against a deep-blue background, the lid slightly lifted and the emanating light suggesting that anything might be inside: birds, stars, clocks, pearls; the box gives birth to the whole of our human world. From the box, paradoxically, comes the infinite warp we walk in.

Where was I? Digressions, I suppose, are also uniquely human. Can you imagine a cat digressing from his mouse? Gentle. My husband was gentle when we first met, although the particularities—the proof—escapes me now. Benjamin chose the winter solstice as our wedding day; December 21, dark by 4 p.m., the trees jeweled with ice. I loved our wedding. We had a chuppa and fat white flowers in bouquets tied with blue ribbons of silk. When the guests left, Benjamin and I drove together in his tiny dinged-up car—a car he still owns today, fifteen years later—to a hotel, where we feasted on leftover root vegetables and drank cheap champagne foaming with fizz. We made love, more out of obligation than desire; but still, it was sweet. Four weeks later, while walking up a hill, my legs went oddly weak. The angle of ascent seemed suddenly unreasonably steep. I began gasping for breath. Collapsed on the curb, head in my hands, I knew I was pregnant. At home, the plastic test wand showed the palest plus, tentative but definite at the same time. We aborted that baby—too soon; it was just too soon. I remember lying afterwards in the white room, still stoned on anesthesia, repeating to myself over and over again "ontogeny does not recapitulate phylogeny; ontogeny does not recapitulate phylogeny."

What this means: There was a time in the 1800s when people believed (and many still do) that as the human embryo developed, it followed the same path as the evolutionary history of the entire species, taking on as it grew the successive forms of remote ancestral organisms. According to Ernst Haeckel, the German zoologist who proposed this idea in 1866, the human embryo in its earliest stages mimics an aquatic creature of the sort that lived deep in this planet's past. Haeckel proposed that the human embryo's pharyngeal slits were equivalent to the gills of a fish. In the ontogeny-recapitulates-phylogeny theory, the human embryo eventually moves from fish form to amphibian form, and from amphibian form to the form of an early mammal until at last, after the nine months of gestation, the developing being, having personally passed through its own mini-evolutionary saga, emerges as fully human.

This notion, so intuitively appealing perhaps because it suggests the superior status of Homo sapiens, has been discredited by modern biologists. Apparently we do not begin as bird or duck or dog. We are a singular species, stubbornly, immutably human. As for me, I had lost a human baby, a supposedly superior being; I had given it up, or over. Outside my window a black-and-cream-colored cat perched on the ledge, its nose as pink as frosting, its whiskers silver spikes in the winter sunlight. The cat stared and stared at me, its own eyes full of soul, and some slight accusation. I turned away.

A few weeks after that terminated pregnancy, I announced to my newlywed Benjamin that I thought we should get an animal. As a girl I had read Gerald Durrell's *My Family and Other Animals*. In Durrell's world, birds perched on shoulders and spoke a language that was and was not human; if birds could talk, than who—or what—else could know our words? Might I wake up one night to the moon telling its celestial news? Might the rocks have speakable stories? Animals sit on the edge of possibility. They imply—no, prove—that there are worlds outside our world, or worlds within our world—but beyond our grasp—and this fact is fantastic, and all one needs in order to experience enchantment.

And it was for the love of enchantment that I wanted an animal other than my husband in the home we were now making. I didn't want a human infant—that much was clear to me—so what was I thinking about? "A monkey," I said one morning to Benjamin over coffee. "Why not get a monkey?"

"An iguana," he said to me. "If we're going to have a beast in this house, then it has to be a reptile."

"Cold blooded," I said. "Who wants cold blood?"

"Monkeys bite," he said. "They're not necessarily nice."

"We could get a dog," I said.

"Foul hounds," he said. "Dogs have no dignity."

"And people?" I said.

"The only animals I want in my home are those that can fit in a soup pot," my husband said. "A beast must be fit to eat." He smiled then, took a bite of his cinnamon toast.

I knew he was half joking, but I could also see, and for the first time, something wicked in Benjamin's smile. I could suddenly see he had a second smile, different from the first one, which was, until that point, the only one I knew. This second smile was both curve and flicker, sharp and sudden.

I won't record the rest of the conversation, because it would be a waste of words: the typical "how could you say so's" followed by the generic, prepackaged "calm down's," ending in a sudden silence that was brief, like a bubble, and then burst into something soft again. We were, after all, in love.

Later on, that night in bed, Benjamin told me more. I knew when we married that his boyhood had been filled with science and that dinner-table conversations were more likely to be about correlation coefficients than current events, but I hadn't known how his mother used to take him to her lab where he had watched her inject guinea pigs with hormones so their litters came out large and twisted. A fertility researcher, my husband's mother had showed him the pickled preserves of hairless pups born to rats dosed up on Fertinex and the strange remains of monkeys disfigured by progesterone. At age nine he had learned to shuck the hide from a rat and it all seemed sane to him. He told me how his mother had once brought home a wild fox pup, which they kept until its adolescence, and this canine cousin of the dog he described for me fondly, waking up one morning to new snowfall, seeing the animal in the yard, its red coat starkly bright against the fresh encompassing white. "But mostly," Benjamin said, "we used animals for experiments. Their purpose was to answer questions that concerned human beings."

"And did you ever question the method of questioning?" I asked.

"No," he said. "How can you question human health?"

"If it involves the suffering of a sentient being . . ."

""What would you rather have: a few dead dogs or penicillin?"

"That's a predictable argument," I said. Back then I had not yet found my way to Peter Singer, so I lacked the logic—a logic I could feel in my bones but could not bring to the level of language—to really undo his argument. Instead I said, "I can't believe your mother showed her nine-year-old how to—"

Benjamin cut me off. And from his tone I could feel we had slipped into a new space, without warning: there it was. Little did I know that this was both a space and an oncoming speech that would pepper my marriage until, one day, long past the point of a pain with no name, it ceased to do so.

"Let me offer you a few facts," Benjamin now said. Later, years later, he would start to use that calculator I came to know so well to accompany his monologues. But—no calculator now—this was the very first time I heard what he had to say. His voice took on an eerie formality, as though it came from a machine inside him. "Dogs carry more E. coli on their tongues than a human toilet bowl that hasn't been flushed."

He paused. I watched him. I had no way of knowing, back then, that this speech, which he delivered for the first time that morning, and early in our marriage, would be some sort of salvo he'd repeat for me year after year, in one way or another, the words a dividing line.

"Dogs are supposed protectors," he continued, "but the fact is they're more likely to bark at the mailman and sleep through a murder; they're *domesticated* into dumbness." (So he despised domestication. Where, exactly, did that leave us?) "They are," he pronounced, "a significant biological burden on human kind."

"What's up with you?" I said, and I heard a wrong tone creep into my own voice as well. "Were you traumatized by a poodle or what?"

"Yes," he said. "By a poodle." Then he smiled, the old Benjamin again, but not quite.

"Come on," I said. "When?"

"Not every event occurs in traditionally conceived continuum of time," he said.

"You sound dumber than a dog when you speak like that," I said. "I'm not sure you're aware that those words are all noise, no better than a bark."

"Okay," he said. "I've been traumatized by not one poodle but by all poodles. Poodles serve as the ultimate evidence of human idiocy. Dogs with perms: how useless is that?"

"Poodles happen to be very bright," I said. I reached to switch off the light. We lay in the darkness then, without words. The sconce in the hall was still on, and it cast sheets of shadow over the wall. I don't know how many minutes passed, but just as I was falling asleep I saw my husband's hands, swollen in the shadow. He was making shapes: peace signs, pinkies walking, wings and wings and wings.

It is a well-documented fact that children who abuse animals are at risk for becoming sociopaths later in life, and from my training as a psychologist I know that standard forensic assessment tools include questions about harming animals right alongside questions about what weapons the patient owns or how many people he has hurt. Of course neither my husband, nor his mother, nor the thousands of others who have a cold disregard for animals would be considered abusers, but it's also impossible to deny the possibility that they nevertheless may share some of those traits.

On the other hand, any biped could well argue, we all know about crazy ladies who keep households full of felines and who mutter odd terms of endearments to pets called Precious. I once knew a woman who had an incontinent dog named Betsy. She so adored this dog that she downloaded the animal's bark as her own personal ring tone on her cell phone. Surely this zoophilia is some sort of sickness as well as its opposite, zoogyny. Granted I have made up these terms, but they point to a nonfiction phenomenon—that much is for sure. Sir Isaac Newton was a mean, socially isolated hominid who spent much of his lonely life studying apples and stars by candlelight. His singular love was for his Pomeranian pooch, Diamond, who shared his dinner plate with him. Similarly, Alexander Pope had a Great Dane, Bounce, to whom he was so attached he would not walk without him. Bounce padded about Pope's mansion and drank from a golden dish.

Though I may have never been quite as extreme as these canine keepers, I nevertheless knew, then and now, that my love of animals was extreme—but whether that was extremely good or extremely bad—a sign of mental health or mental illness—I couldn't tell, and frankly, I still can't. And because, in the end, love overrides analysis anyway, I didn't much think about what I was doing when, a few days after our bedtime conversation, with my husband on a business trip to Nevada, I traveled forty-five minutes from Boston and came back home with not one but *two* puppies. I decided on the Shiba Inu breed because they are smart, agile, and slightly aloof, all qualities that reminded me of my husband. "The babies' names," said the breeder, "are Wrinkles and Tinkles." Tinkles, I assumed, was the girl.

I have never understood the term some women use to describe their feeling of wanting a child—"baby lust." The term disturbs me not only because it fuses maternity with what sounds practically pornographic but also, and perhaps more to the point, because I cannot imagine ever lusting after a being so recently drenched in the juices of a placenta. Human babies, for days, weeks, even months after they are born still stubbornly reflect their neonatal state; they have that tough, grizzled, weeping stub of an umbilicus; they have that waxy lanugo and are speckled with blood. Human babies are essentially fetuses ejected too early. Puppies, on the other hand, are born as babies and within a few days of their arrival are playful and soft. Puppies catch onto cuteness ASAP and, at the same time, when you look into their eyes, you can see how they once were wild. I loved our new puppies, whom I renamed Lila and Musashi, immediately. I loved them because they were cute and because, perhaps, I lacked the depth or discipline needed to love a human infant so unambivalently.

I had the puppies, Lila and Musashi, for two days on my own and then it was time for Benjamin to return. I picked him up at the airport. In the week or so he had been gone, his beard had grown, not exactly longer but wider, so his face seemed fat.

Benjamin got into the car, kissed me. There was his smell again (another reason for my kinship with the canine?), and I loved him all over again.

"There's a surprise for you when you get home," I said.

What, he wanted to know.

"Guess," I said.

"You got a dog," he said, without even pausing to think.

"Jesus," I said. I paused. "Musashi and Lila," I said.

"You named the dog Musashianlila?" he said. "Cool," he said. "Original."

"Musashi *and* Lila," I said. "'And,' as in an article of speech, a coordinating conjunction between two separate beings, as in, two dogs: one, Musashi; two, Lila." I talked this way for a reason. Benjamin loves me best when I can use numbers in my communications.

"Two dogs?" he said. "Two foul hounds. I knew you were going to do something like that."

"Are you mad?" I asked.

"I am," he said. "A little."

"Look," I said. "I know with 100 percent assuredness that you will fall in love with these puppies. They are the cu—they are not only very cute," I said, "but they are the perfect vehicles through which to reflect on our culture's attitude toward cuteness. I'm telling you," I said. "Owning a dog can be intellectual."

He didn't say anything.

"All right," I said. "Aside from giving them back, what can I do to make this up to you?"

"You can stop at the next store," he said.

"Why?" I said.

"As soon as I buy two soup pots," he said, "everything will fall into place."

Then he smiled, and I figured we'd be fine.

We got home from the airport. The two precious pooches were right there at the door, so small, so furry, their tiny tails jiggling so hard they looked like they might detach. "Benjamin, Musashi," I said, picking up the slightly larger male and giving Ben his penny-sized paw to shake. Benjamin, good sport that he is (sometimes), shook it and doffed an imaginary hat. "Nice to meet you, sir," he said. We repeated the same ritual with Lila, who was very much unlike her high-strung brother. Lila had a Cyndi Lauper personality. She was tough and flamboyant, a rock star of the dog world. She howled and crooned her ballads while Musashi, at the sound of anything that snapped or popped, crouched in a corner and shivered. Lila gave Ben a wet canine kiss that left a line of glisten on his face. Before the dogs we had been a happy couple in an uncomplicated way. It was therefore inevitable, I suppose, that something divisive would enter our lives, because marriage—like physics, literature, and carpentry—is almost always synonymous with complexity. The dogs came over us like a cloud, something impossibly soft and fuzzy. They arrived in our home in the winter of our first married year, during a freeze so deep the snow was solid enough to stomp on, and mornings were filled with the sounds of cars coughing and squealing as they slid on icy streets. The puppies, of course, were incontinent, for all intents and purposes. Housetraining required that I rise every three or so hours and head outside, into the pitch-black coldness, parka wrapped around my nightgown, feet shoved sockless into big rubber boots. Midnight, 3 a.m., no one around then but me and my pups, their urine steaming small holes through the snow, good boy, good girl. There were the required visits to the vet, the building of a fence, a carpenter who came to cut a square in our back door—a dog door they learned to use with the aid of chicken and cheese as rewards. There were several emergency overdoses, rushing Musashi to the veterinary hospital at dawn, the embarrassing explanation to the blonde female vet who always seemed severe and judgmental. "He, um, he, uh, he swallowed my medicine." "What *kind* of medicine?" In an age of polypharmacy, embarrassment nearly replaced my fear for the dog's survival. First it was Prozac; then it was Ativan for anxiety; then it was the mood stabilizer, lithium—Musashi sampled them all, the child-protection caps no impediment to him as he cracked the bottles with his teeth and chomped on pills he found strangely tasty. "I don't understand," said the vet at our third visit, "how he manages to get your medication*s*." I thought I heard her emphasize the plural. "I mean, they are in a drawer, aren't they?"

"Of course they are in a drawer," I said. "This dog can open drawers," which was true, but she clearly believed I was delusional. I finally solved the problem by hiding my drugs on a shelf so high that to this day I need a stepstool in order to medicate myself.

And it was all terrible and amusing and fun and hard work, but in the center of it all was a little hole, like those the dogs left when they pissed in the snow, a cold, steamy, smelly little hole in my heart because Benjamin participated in none of this with me. These were not our dogs. They were my dogs. He petted them; he occasionally tossed a ball or a bone, but when I asked him, "Do you love the dogs?" he always said, "No. I like them." Once, in a fit of blind maternity, I said to one of the pups, "Mama's here," and he looked at me with something like scorn and horror combined. "You're not their mother," he said.

"I am," I said. "These dogs are a part of our family, aren't they?"

"No," he said. "These dogs are our roommates."

In every marriage there are betrayals; the question is how soon they happen, how many, and of what sort. I remember quite clearly the first time I betrayed Benjamin. The puppies were growing fast, their fluff becoming fur, the round snouts taking on a sharper shape. At four months or so Lila's urine came out tinged with blood; an infection? No. She was going into heat. Our regular vet—a jolly Irish woman completely unlike the ER vet—told me it was time. Lila needed to be spayed. Musashi, who had testicles so tiny one couldn't really see them, nevertheless now needed to be neutered as well.

Of course it sounds terrible—*spayed*—a sharp hoe, shredded earth—and *neutered*—not as violent sounding but shameful nonetheless. Still, the reason for the procedures far outweighs the recoiling they naturally give rise to. I told Ben. He was eating oatmeal at our table, spoon at the ledge of his lips; he set down his spoon. *Clink.* "You're going to *remove* Musashi's testicles?" he said.

"Yes," I said.

I could tell by his tone we were in for trouble, entirely unanticipated, because I knew he didn't give a damn about the dogs, so I never imagined he might care in any way about one of their body parts.

"You can't remove a man's testicles," he said.

"He's not a man," I said. "He's a dog."

"You can't do that," Ben said. He seemed truly stumped, his eyes alarmed; this was a highly articulate person, a person with a love of debate who was suddenly silenced, stumbling over a panic as primitive as what a fish might feel flailing on a hook. I could not believe it. I could not believe my husband, for all his professed distance from dogs, was confusing his testicles with theirs, and I said so.

"I am *not* confused," Ben said.

"Seems to me like you are," I said. "You can't be a responsible pet owner and not neuter your dogs."

"That's just some right-wing mumbo jumbo," he said. "Remove an animal's testicles and you fuck up its hormones. You cripple it. The animal doesn't mature the right way."

"I thought you didn't care about animals," I said.

"I don't," he said. "I raise this objection on theory. You can't take testicles from a male. I won't have a neutered male in this house."

"I see," I said. My voice grew icy then. "You won't have a neutered male but a neutered female is fine. And you call yourself a feminist?"

"I object to the procedure in Lila as well," he said, but it was obvious from his voice: he was backpedaling.

"Anyway," I said. "Who are you to call neutering an animal mumbo jumbo? What do you know of the issue?"

There then followed a still more ridiculous discussion about how he needed to know nothing of the issue because he was a scientist with a knowledge of the importance of hormones in the growth of any mammal, while I countered about the devastating effects of pet overpopulation, an argument that spiraled up and up like cigarette smoke, polluting the air until, at last, he said, "Don't neuter Musashi. I am asking you not to do it."

I knew, then, that I was dealing with an irrational man. And worse, a man who would protect his kind, but was fine as concerned the fate of the female. Lila would be sliced open like a freshly baked cake, her core cut out, the tiny bean-sized sac of the uterus, the ovaries even now stuffed with their millions of eggs, and then sewn up, her healing hard.

I said okay; I would not fix Musashi. The next day, Lila had her surgery, came home in a cage and didn't move for days. The vet, it seems, was rough; on her shaved belly we could see an oozing railroad of a wound that ran from her anus to her chest, a huge incision for such a tiny task. "Lila, Lila," Benjamin said. He sat by her crate, petted her head, brought her water in a small saucer. He was rigorous with her medication, pumping it into her mouth on a precise schedule, and smiling when she took her first timid steps. And it is exactly this—the inconsistencies—that make human loves so snarled. A gentle man? Yes. A blind man? As are we all, sometimes. When Lila was well enough, Benjamin came with me, for the first time, to the Fells, a large wooded area near our house, and we ran with the dogs through the winter woods. Benjamin tied small branches to the dogs' heads, turned them into reindeer, and then we watched as they cantered along, made magic by his hands; these, my husband's hands. For better and for worse.

And the betrayal? I had Musashi neutered behind Ben's back. The night of our neutering fight, I planned my strategy with barely a twinge of guilt. I would wait four months, enough time so that the conversation—the issue itself—was all but forgotten but not so much time that the puppy would have become a dog with observable scrotum, at which point a secret surgery would have been impossible. Lest our vet ever somehow let it slip in Ben's possible future presence, I would bring the dog to a different vet, one we were sure to never see again. Problem #1: Explaining why Musashi had stitches between his legs. I would say he got a deep scrape at the park. Problem #2: Explaining, when the dog finally became fully mature, why he had no testicles. When this happened, as it inevitably would, I decided right then and there that I would feign concern, promise to take him to the doctor, then claim I had and announce that night at dinner that the vet had diagnosed Musashi fully male but with undescended testicles. It all seemed so simple. And, in fact, it was.

Winter turned to summer turned to fall. As planned, Musashi was neutered in a covert operation and when later that evening Ben noticed the small stitches, I gave my rehearsed explanation. It all went by without a hitch. Brilliant. Bad. It seemed a long time went by before the inevitable confrontation, before the day Benjamin finally observed, nearly one year later, that the dog, now fully grown, had no balls. It was summer, and I had just returned from picking flowers on "Poop Hill," the name the neighborhood children had given to the tract of land used by city dogs as an outhouse. Most people, as they approached Poop Hill, gave their animals a long leash, so the canines could find their deposit spot on the grass while their humans stayed safe on the pavement. But I liked Poop Hill because the flowers, so well fertilized, were abundant, bright, and ironically sweet smelling. And there I was, holding a fistful of my bright finds, standing in our hallway, the dogs lapping up water from their dish, a Sunday, and Ben knelt down to give the rare but occasional scritch to Musashi's backside. This time, in response, Musashi lay down, rolled over, and pedaled his paws in the air, a pose Benjamin found especially undignified and from which he would inevitably recoil. But for some reason, he didn't this time. A petal from a flower I was holding floated dramatically down and landed impishly, or accusingly, right at the base of the pup's denuded penis. Benjamin leaned close, picked it off. "Hey," he said, still kneeling, looking down.

"Hey what," I said, although I knew exactly what was coming.

"This dog has no balls," he said.

"No balls?" I said. "C'mon."

"Seriously," he said. "Look here."

I did, of course, look there. "I see some balls," I said. "Right there." I pointed to a place too near the tip where there was a tiny bilateral bulge, a quirk the dog had had since infancy.

"You think those are balls?" Ben said to me. "Are you serious?"

"Well," I said. "Isn't it possible to have, you know, high balls?" I started laughing then, slapping my knee and snorting. "I'm so hilarious," I said. "Aren't I?"

Ben didn't say anything. "Aren't I?" I said again, and now there was a ball in my throat, so swallowing was suddenly difficult.

"What's wrong with Musashi?" Ben said. "Could they have neutered him before you bought him?"

"I doubt it," I said. "I mean, he was practically new born. I'll take him to the vet, check it out."

Which I didn't. But three nights later I said, "So I took him to the vet—" Etc., etc.

"Undescended?" Benjamin said to me.

"Yeah," I said.

"Musashi," Ben said. He gave one of his magnificent whistles then, and the dogs came bounding through their door and into the kitchen.

"Hey, friend," Benjamin said to Musashi. He pulled out his paws then, so the dog slipped gently down, and then he turned the animal over, studied him hard.

"Undescended," Ben then said again, not a question but a statement. He looked from the dog to me back to the dog again. A long time seemed to pass. At last he went, stood by the window. What was it he saw out there?

"Hey," I said, but he either didn't hear or didn't want to listen. Then he left the room.

3: A Baby at One Breast, a Monkey at the Other

If it sounds like our marriage was bad, it wasn't. We shared so many things, I am only telling of the troubles. Benjamin called me

"Pie," short for Sweetie Pie. I loved to hear him sleep talk, long monologues about dolphins and computer code. In 1999 I decided I was ready, and we set about the task of conceiving as though it were exactly that—a task, a military mission. We "succeeded" after battle number three, the bloodless battle, my periods gone. At gestational month four we discovered we were having a girl, a fact that made the prospect only marginally more appealing. In truth the baby was largely Benjamin's idea. My zealous approach to conception arose more in response to challenge than desire. "Look how much you care for the dogs," my friend Audrey kept reassuring me. "If you love the dogs so much, obviously you're a person capable of attachment. You won't have a problem."

But I would. I did. Have a problem. It was easy enough to give voice to my *ambivalence* about having a child; maternal ambivalence is très chic these days; there are lots of books about it, and Oprah did a whole show on the topic, each female guest confessing that, yes, she had a shadow side; that, yes, when it came to babies and feelings about them, it wasn't all cream and talc. None of this comforted me. It seemed to me my ambivalence was of altogether a different sort, or species. A single question circled round and round inside my skull, its serrated edges making a scraping sound that no one else could hear. What I didn't say . . . Okay. What if I couldn't love the baby *as much as* I loved my dogs? Or, what if I found I loved both the baby and the animals *equally?* Can you imagine admitting to that, should it occur? In the hypereducated community that comprises my culture, a culture that boasts more PhD holders per square mile than most other parts of the country, or even the world, such a feeling for one's pets is more blasphemous than having a house decorated with stenciled hearts or printing a tattoo of a serpent on your bicep. In my culture, it's tentatively okay to have a companion animal, but one must avoid the sentimentality associated with it at all costs. One must rigidly remember not to anthropomorphize and above all not to ooze emotion over domesticated beasts, the toys for which consumers stupidly spend over billions of dollars while so many in this world are starving.

So how could I comfortably say, or feel, that I might love daughter and dogs equally? Did I not know the difference between my meats, MacDonald's on the one hand, expensive organic rib eye on the other? *A whole new middle-class, navel-gazing female writer problem*, the critics might write, if they wrote anything at all. *Domesticity diminished to its most insignificant level.* And, yet, were I to claim I valued my dogs and my daughter equally, I would not in fact be making an insignificant statement. I would be in violation of a sacred human stance in place since pets, thousands of years ago, first took up residence in human households.

But that is not the whole story, not by a long shot. If I had known then what I know now, perhaps I could have been comforted. Because there are places and times far, far away from here—there are and were places—where people loved animals as much, if not more, than their own children. And these people represent a vast variety of cultures from all around the world. Explorer Francis Galton, for instance, wrote in his 1883 *Inquiries into Human Faculty and Its Development*, about coming upon aboriginal Australian women who "habitually feed the puppies they intend to rear from their own breasts, and show an affection for them equal to, if not exceeding, that to their own infants."

Another anthropologist of the nineteenth century told how, in Fiji, women and shamans made pets of parrots, fruit bats, and lizards, and, noted James Serpell in his *In the Company of Animals*, they apparently felt such love for their animals that they would masticate for them plants and bananas while their own human babies stayed hungry at their sides. My favorite image is that reported by I. H. Evans in the 1930s. He lived amongst the Semang Negritos of Malaysia and wrote of seeing a woman running down the street in a great hurry, a baby at one breast, a monkey at the other.

My breasts: They grew in pregnancy, the veins bulging blue and a particular deep purple hue. The nipples swelled and sensitized, at the end the size of strawberries, huge and indecent. Around month six I had my amnio—all was well—except the baby on the screen did not look human, nor animal, nor plant. She came, it appeared, from a category not yet created by Linnaeus; all static and blips, she lived inside the Hewlett Packard screen that showed her shape. And the bulge in my belly? What accounted for that? My dreams grew strange. In them I gave birth to a snowman, a two-legged tree, my sister. She tried to wash my hair and the soap stung my eyes. There was grit, burn, push, pull, the moon as tiny as a Cheerio in some strange sky. I woke up, scared and big.

I had the baby. Human birth is an unreasonable proposition; her head was too big for my pelvis; it got stuck in the brackets of bone. Hyenas, however, give birth through the clitoris, so I still count myself amongst the luckier of the beasts on our blue ball. There she was, seven pounds, waxy and wet.

Five days later, C-section healing, Benjamin and I brought our daughter home. We arrived to two dogs howling with joy – hello, hello, hello, kisses and slurps all around, such a long time, so *good* to see you, you too, leaping on hind legs, their short forelegs dangling the way they do, their ears pressed back in pleasure. All the books I'd read emphasized the importance of letting the dogs thoroughly sniff the new family member. I lowered the bundle of baby down. The summer breeze blew in, and halfway to their level, the dogs caught a whiff of the strange smell. They froze. Their eyes turned canine, carnivore, the little dots of yellow in the iris with a wolfish gleam.

"Stop," said Ben. He claims he heard a low growl emanating from Lila's throat. Had I heard it, I would have stopped, of course. I, however, heard nothing.

"Musashi, Lila," I sang. Something was amiss, but what? "This is Clara," I said, and then she was down, this baby so bundled only the disc of her face was visible, the tiny lips, the perfect mini nose, and eyelids scrawled with arteries.

Lila, always the more aggressive, stepped forward. Her snout was wet, her black lips seamed shut; but it was the eyes that gave me pause. Slowly, slowly, she lifted one leg and pawed at the bunting, almost batted it. Playful? Aggressive? Curious? Musashi followed, his blocky head low down and then, before I could stop them, their noses were in the wrappings, the huff huff of their hungry breath, the child screamed, the dogs shot back. Ben grabbed the baby from me, his own face full of canine rage. "How *could* you?" he spit. "They've bitten her."

Understand, I was doped up on drugs, painkillers coursing through my system, the whole world wavy, and I had done what all the books instructed. "No," I said. "No."

We peeled back the wrappings. Our baby was unbroken, everywhere. In an instant she plunged into slumber again. Later on, when we removed her diaper, we saw blood inside it, but that, we knew, was not from the dogs. Female infants shortly after birth often menstruate, if you can call it that, in response to the maternal hormones. Yes, that blood came from me.

I have never brought up, certainly not then, or now, until now, the idea that I might love my animals as much as my child, or children. No one has ever thought to ask, despite the fact that everyone I know, as hypereducated as they all are, understands that meaning is often found in the questions we fail to form. The oversight has freed me to fret privately, and sometimes not at all. While some pluck petals off the daisy—he loves me, he loves me not—my chant is less melodic, as clunky as the conundrum it echoes: *I love her more; I love her less; I love them all the same.* At the end of this exercise, what am I left with? A shredded flower, hands painted with pollen, cupped up and empty. I said nothing, to anyone, ever.

But, as a strategy, silence does not work to tamp the tugs one would rather not feel. As a mother, I *wanted* to feel clearly and cleanly driven *only* to my offspring, that packet of genes and nerves, that person in my pocket for the first nine months of her life, but it didn't happen that way. In the early years of my daughter's life, and then my son's life too, when he was later born, I would sometimes feel a longing for my dogs that overrode every other affection and made no sense to me, given that I had as much physicality from my mate and babies as any person could possibly need. But I wanted to touch *another kind of being.* I wanted snout and paw. Why? The very fact of the connection calms. I love the canine paw, its ridges of interstitial fur, its surface cracked and cratered. I love the shape of the snout, the nostrils, the oblong ears, the teeth, tartared and sharp.

And it was this, this felt biological *need* to connect beyond my human confines, that drew me downstairs, again and again, after my babies were asleep. I'd sit in the kitchen and groom my dogs. Their undercoats were always dense with down; the fur flew, piling up in drifts I swept into big green bags, huge bloated bags that looked heavy but that drifted in the wind on garbage night. I'd stack them on the curb for the next day's trash truck, but the fur-stuffed bags always flew away, flew high above the roofs of our city while over and over again I brushed the pups, until it was very late, and Benjamin came down, tired-eyed, 2 a.m., the first feeding over now. He'd see me on the floor, then and now, as well. "Making love with the pups?" he'd ask, and I say the only thing I could.

Yes.

With one child, and then a second, our lives got busier and then busier still. The children entered a marriage already divided by dogs; our babies sharpened the wedge, and drove it deeper down. We were two parents with full-time jobs and a moderate income, two parents determined to give their kids the best they could— skating lessons, pottery lessons, day camps, Spanish tutoring. As the children grew so too did the needs, and expectations, along with the bills, while time tucked its tail between its legs and went away. We lost time, traded it in for love, but here's the quandary; love and time are hopelessly intertwined.

Benjamin and I worked hard to keep up with the accumulating costs of providing a middle-class education. Because we live in an urban area where the schools are poor, our goal was to save enough for private school, to the tune of $70,000 a year for two, not counting looming college costs. And forget about retirement. We doubted we'd survive the stress.

It was at some point during these difficult years that Ben developed that mysterious arm ailment that defied precise diagnosis. The pain began at first as an intermittent throb, but over time it escalated until, at last, it claimed him almost completely. Thoracic outlet syndrome, carpal tunnel, whatever it was, the ailment resulted from the computer, which he used most moments of his sixty- to seventy-hour work week. Unresponsive to any type of treatment except morphine, the pain, eventually, drained his face, beat in the back of his neck, his burning arms hanging useless by his sides. There were visits to pain clinics, so many I cannot count, each one exactly like the other, hushed and cold, tiled and white. There were visits to pharmacologists, psychologists, neurologists, chiropractors, while for the children there were yearly checkups, dental appointments, ear infections, strep throat, stomach bugs, vomit vomit vomit. If I told you we ever had fun during these years, you would not believe it; neither would I. We did. When Clara was five, we received a reminder card from our veterinarian: time for the canines' various vaccines, the Heartgard medication, time for the toenail clipping, the teeth cleaning, the fecal tests. "We spend," said Benjamin, when Clara was five, "thousands of dollars on these animals. One of these days, I'm going to get a calculator and figure the precise cost."

We were in the kitchen. I was spooning mash into our second-born's mouth. "They're worth it," I said. This a conversation we'd had, in one form or another, since we first wed, both with and without the calculator, going round and round through the course of our marriage, our childrens' lives, never growing stale, this, our old perpetual hot spot.

"To me," I added.

"But to us?" he said.

"These dogs have taught our children a lot," I said, and they had. From them our daughter had learned gentleness (*suavo, suavo*) and a certain perspicacity.

"Yes," said Benjamin. "They have taught our children a lot. I agree." He didn't say anything after that.

"What?" I said.

"They just seem . . . I don't know," he said. "A lot of things. We have limited resources."

"If we can afford cable," I said, "then I think we can afford our pets."

"We can," he said. "But," and then again he stopped. I sensed, suddenly and for the first time, that the conversation was about to change. Benjamin seemed to want to say something hard, something true for him. I could sense him running straight into the hot heart of a feeling, at the last second scuttering to a stop. When he spoke again, he had, to my disappointment, assumed his professorial stance.

"Pets," he said, "are a product of bourgeois culture. Communist cultures abhorred pet keeping, and for a real reason. It is a sign of indulgence to spend so much money on dog food and diamond-studded collars and high-tech medical care when the world has such serious issues. It is wrong. It is a problem of priority. And we only do it because we can."

"No," I said. In fact I said this much later, months later, having by then armed myself with the research I might need in order to defend the dogs and their place in our family. What I found: people rich and poor alike all throughout history have kept pets. Far from being a bourgeois indulgence there have been many plainly impoverished societies where companion animals were prevalent. Writes James Serpell, director of the Center for the Interaction of Animals and Society at the University of Pennsylvania, in his *In the Company of Animals*:

> The existence of pet-keeping among so called "primitive" peoples poses a problem for those who choose to believe that such behaviour is . . . a by-product of western decadence or bourgeois sentimentality. Doubtless, when one looks exclusively at pet-keeping in prosperous cultures such as our own, it is easy to conclude that the practice is a manifestation of some eccentric cultural aberration. The fact that we squander vast resources on the habit is also of little significance since conspicuous waste is a common feature of our society. But this line of reasoning runs into serious difficulties when we contemplate precisely the same phenomenon among, say, the Semang Negritos or numerous Amerindian groups. These people are predominantly hunter-gatherers or subsistence horticulturists . . . and they are not in a position to waste resources on gratuitous luxuries. Nevertheless, they seem to be prepared to invest as much time, energy, and emotion in economically useless pets as the average middle-class European or North American.

I scanned library shelves and tore into cyberspace, looking for—what? The anthropological studies of pet-keeping across cultures and classes has always reliably fascinated me, but I think what I really wanted was some way to justify what it was I was feeling, what

I could not quite say out loud. Looking back, I see that my research had a frantic feel, because at some unspecified point during these years of birthing and raising babies—at some point I cannot locate on my timeline—I think I must have admitted to myself that when it came to hierarchies of caring, I couldn't quite construct them. Perhaps the realization occurred when, one day, in a park, I lost track of my dog and daughter both, and for a split second, before I caught sight of them, I could not quite figure out who to search for first. Or perhaps it happened when Clara was two and I learned with equal horror, and within the same two-day period, of the brutal rape and murder of Samantha Runyon, a five-year-old girl whose abduction was widely televised, and the less televised but to me equally devastating footage of dogs, millions of them being clubbed to death in Beijing for no reason except their status, the panning camera capturing the cracking of canine skulls, the buckling of broken knees, the keening cries of pure unmitigated pain. Yes. I am talking about pain. In the end, pain is pain is pain, and its repetition has no poetic possibilities.

Does this then mean that if forced to choose between my children and my dogs I would have to stop, to consider? If I were to say yes, then who would I be but one of the beasts my husband hates, fit for the soup pot surely. Why is it, I'd like to know, that philosophical questions always come down to this point, the bared bone, the crux we never live in? I am, thank god or Gaia, not forced to make this choice, but nor do I wish to dodge this particular bullet in my high-minded hunt. If forced to make the choice (big sigh) I would, *of course* and *without reflection*, choose my children, my babies, my darling, my doves, but not because I love them more. I would choose them because their humanity comes prepackaged with a particular prize, booby prize: the future. We know it's out there while other animals we think do not. For this reason, I believe the human species suffers more at the sight of the final door.

Chronic pain is its own form of hell. My husband's arms grew gimpy. His hands got spastic and simple tasks—twisting the top off a can—became impossible. Sometimes, in the nights, I would wake up and find Benjamin lying on his back, his flaming arms stuck straight up in the air, staring at the dark through his splayed fingers. The man with the elfin humor—well, eventually he went away and someone distant took his place. I remember the night he stood in the living room holding our young sleeping son. I was in the kitchen, fixing dinner. I heard a crash and came running. What I found: Benjamin standing stricken on the floor, his arms held out in front of him as though they were dripping poison. On the floor Lucas screamed himself blue. "I dropped our baby," Benjamin whispered, tears I had never seen before coming, copiously, from his eyes.

There is nothing that can be said for a situation such as this. My husband stopped working for two years; he was doped on drugs he used and then misused. "Get a job," I said. I screamed. "Doing what?" he said. "Drive a FedEx truck if you have to," I said. "Get disability; do something." Nothing. The pain claimed him completely, was worth nothing to us but the zero balance it brought into our lives. I had my animals and my children. I had, we had, that stolid, solid zero.

Nevertheless, inside every zero is an aperture one hopes to never have to fill. Eventually (so slowly!) I saw small things go into my husband's hole, or perhaps I created these things for my own comfort. After six years of pain he said to me one evening, "I have not had the life I wish I'd had."

What I thought: *I am not what you wished for.* What I said: "For what did you wish?"

"I could have lived in Indonesia," he said. "I could have stayed in graduate school. I could have become an ethnobotanist. I could have—" A sentence he failed to finish.

"I'm sorry," I said. I was stung and small. But I was also grateful for his words, the plain, straight, simple words, words in need of no numbers because they are of the infinite sort.

We both turned forty that year. His birthday was in October, a particularly virulent fall full of fevered trees, delirious leaves of dark wine and ochre. The world was so saturated with pain and color and noise and rush that our white hairs stood out stark and obvious. On a Monday Benjamin took out a calendar and a calculator. "Do you realize," he said to me after some time punching numbers, "we have about 20,000 days left?" On Tuesday, when we had only 19,999 days left, Benjamin gave his great whistle, and the dogs, who once would have bounded over at the sound, stretched creakily and came cautiously trotting. "Lila, girl," he said. He cupped her bony chin in his hand. She turned her brown eyes up to him. "Look," he said. "She's got some gray on the muzzle," and indeed she did. So did her brother. Ben nodded, as though inwardly confirming an obvious but until then unseen fact. Like us, they live and die.

Like us.

There is just one more part to this story, which will go on past this page and end at another point in the future. I came downstairs the next day, our children, growing fast, now in school, Clara in first grade, Lucas in pre-school, and it was then that I found Lila, rushed her to the vet—glaucoma—her eyes marbled over, her face so empty of expression that I saw what so many scientists deny; dogs can scowl, smirk, and smile; their faces are mobile maps of reaction, of *feeling*, yes; the presence and variety of canine expression becomes terribly obvious to humans perhaps only in its absence.

I have not yet said the whole story about the day my dog went blind. That I brought her home, for instance, on a Sunday, in the evening, the streets blue with dusk; that I stopped the car and sat for a while on the side of the road, by the brackish river, where the thick cattails made a hush-sh rush-sh sound; that Lila's ears pricked forward and she turned her head, looking left, then right, smelling skunk, the car windows down and the wind hitting us hard, here and there, the way I wanted it. I wanted her to have as many senses as she could; the smells, the touch, the taste, I offering her my palm, putting it flat against her nose, her tongue, so tentative, taking salt from my skin. How we came home when it was dark and the house blazed in every window and I said, "Home," as if she might somehow, now, learn language, a silly wish. I knew the brain was plastic and capable of rewiring. I knew that eventually her sense of smell would sharpen, as would her ability to hear and perhaps taste, too. What I did not know was that, after a traumatic loss, it is not only the victim whose brain changes. Those around the victim also change, and, at least in our case, in some quite surprising ways.

And so I walked in with our now-blind dog and set her on the floor, and we all called to her and she couldn't come, veering off to the right or walking, instead, into a wall, and then Ben stepped forward. See? I have not yet told the whole story. "Let me try," he said, and then he knelt down and held out his hand and called "Lila, Lila," in a soft, singsong-y way, and Lila, well, she started towards him, and he kept calling, the sound a string between them, his voice reeling her in, and that was the first time I realized he had a hidden fondness for his hounds. "Lilalila," he called, he crooned, and the dog kept coming, his hand held out, and then halfway there she suddenly stopped, sat down, and a rank pool of urine puddled beneath her. Ben's face fell. I brought the dog upstairs, then, and lay with her on the bed, burying my nose in her fur. A little while later Benjamin came in, stood in the doorframe, watching. It was so quiet. "Poor Lila," he finally said, rubbing his arms. "Poor Lila." He paused, held his lame hand up in the air. "Our dog," he said. "*Our* [italics mine] dog has gone blind as a bat."

Bats, of course, have echolocation, but dogs, even with their superior sense of smell, have nothing of the sort. For one week Lila didn't move and because I hated to see her suffer I considered Ben's suggestion that we put her down. When the veterinary ophthalmologist strongly opposed the idea I thought I saw relief in my husband's face. If she could make it, could not also he?

"So we'll give her some time," Benjamin said. He had a startled look in his eyes, white hair on his head: "Give me some time," is maybe what he meant.

And so I did. And something strange began to happen in our house. It all took time, and was subtle and slow, but I saw it, with my own eyes. Benjamin began to watch *our* dog. It was a simple sort of seeing, but different from anything he had ever done before. Suddenly, now, Lila was an object of interest. I caught him standing in the hall, just studying her, his own head cocked like a curious canine's. I caught him holding her chin in his palm and looking into her dead eyes. When she took her first blind steps, we hooted and clapped. *He* hooted and clapped the most.

After that, her changes came quickly. I took her outside on a leash. Ben took to training her and she reaped his edible rewards, his huge chunks of cheese and bread. As for Ben, well, he started to cheer for her, to hope for her in a way he never had before. He put the calculator away. As the months went by it became no longer about how much she cost but rather about how much she'd done. "Did you see her?" he'd ask me, "did you see what she just did?" Blind as a bat, under my husband's tutelage, she learned to shake hands, and to turn on her hind legs. With his help, she braved the front stairs, and then the stairs leading out back. Six months after the glaucoma diagnosis, she started chasing birds she couldn't see, hunting solely by smell and sound. Sometimes her abilities were so precise we swore she had some vision left, but she didn't; *stone blind*, the vet said. "Stone blind," Ben repeated, as though this were some sign of triumph, and in its own way, perhaps it was.

Without a doubt her burgeoning abilities impressed my husband who had jettisoned his own talents, stopped working, and let pain take its prominent place. I remember well the evening he threw a ball into the dining room. Strewn in the path were the objects of chaotic family life: dolls and toy trucks, a sock, a jutting chair. "Ball," Ben shouted, and at the sound of the rubbery smack Lila bounded towards it, like a skier expertly maneuvering the twisted trail; she swerved cleanly around the furniture, sidestepped the toys, and locked onto the ball with her open maw in a series of seconds. She then turned, trotted calmly back to Benjamin, and dropped the ball at his feet, head turned upwards, half coquettish, half challenging, as though she were saying, "See what I can do? Now it's your turn."

And it was. Benjamin, by the way, would deny my interpretation, accuse me of poetic license, and he may be right. But then again, the facts are the facts. "Did I say she was worth 60k?" he asked. "That seems a little low."

"You can always re-figure," I said.

"70k?" he said.

"Maybe there is no number," I said, and he said, he actually said, my husband said, "You could be correct on that."

In my memory of that time, Lila's blindness and her subsequent grace coincides with Benjamin's return to work, which happened about eight months after Lila lost her sight. It coincides with his desire to go beyond his cerebral pursuits, his books and computer code and his calculations, because one day months and months after our dog's demise and return, he told me he would like to have an orchard. "Fruit trees," Benjamin said. There was some subtle shift about his eyes, a look impossible to measure, certainly to prove, a tiny crack in a closed door, the single line of light all the more brilliant because of the darkness that defines it.

Lila returned and proved her courage and Ben went with her. He began to chop wood as a way to strengthen his arms, and find his fire too. He stopped most of his pain medications. I can think of many other examples to set down here, but then I stop. I don't. I want to resist the neat nature of my conclusions, my desire to fuse our dog's recovery with my husband's, but this is what makes me human, as opposed to fish or fowl; I seek my squares of meaning. Therefore, allow me to mention Ben's mysterious desire for a goat that surfaced just as the blind dog was learning to dance on her hind legs. "I need physical activity," Benjamin started to say, he who had sat in a chair for the past several years; and he went walking.

In our educated middle- and upper-middle-class American culture, sentimentality is akin to sin. We judge intelligence by the presence of sentimentality's opposite: irony. Animals, especially of the domestic sort, appear to lack irony, and perhaps this is what makes them ineligible for most academic discourse. And yet, why do we so resist sentimentality and its accouterments? Maybe because at its extreme, sentimentality leads to a dangerous simplicity, the sort of simplicity that allows one to make pernicious and reductive conclusions about the world. The Nazis are a prime example of sentimentality's dark side; they pined for a pure Nordic race in a pure Nordic land lined with lupines and lakes. It is therefore all the more interesting, and frightening, to learn that the Nazis were also avid animal lovers; they burned human beings but kept beautiful zoos. Hitler's palace was populated by dogs he treated regally until at the end of his life, before he killed himself, he snuck outside his bunker so he could walk his dog Blondie, the despot's best-beloved purebred, whom he then later poisoned with cyanide.

I know these facts, along with many others of the same sort, and, therefore, inside my love of dogs I have a guard dog that watches.

The guard dog may not know enough to worry but I do. Therefore, I cannot lie and say that I came home one night in our forty-seventh year and found my transformed mate on the couch, canines draped like breathing bandages over his still-hurting arms, a half sleepy smile on his face. I cannot say he put a picture of our pooches in his office at work, or that he claimed he drew inspiration from their many feats, or that we came to share a love of dogs that had anywhere near equal weight and were thus drawn closer together in a way that mended our beleaguered marriage. I cannot say it is no longer isolating to stand in my marriage, but I can say there is a little more between us than there was before, a strand stretching between two beings who happen to be human.

One of the behaviors that stamp our species apart—that make us human—is the telling of tales, such as the one I have just told you and the one I will tell you now. A few nights ago I told this same story to my children right before they went to sleep. I love this time of the day. I lie on Clara's bed with her, Lucas in his crib right next to us. Clara presses against my back and Lucas, every night, ceremoniously lays his hand over mine in a gesture too elegant and determined for the toddler that he is. The lights are always off, and the door is always open in a burst of yellow from the hallway. And I was telling my children a true story, as I often do, about a discovery made by an archeologist just a few years ago. He had been digging in Israel, in the dry land out beyond the dome and the Via Dolorosa, looking for pottery chips. And this archeologist came across a grave, a surprise grave he had not expected to find. The grave was deep in the dry land, in a time before coffins. The archeologist knelt. He unwrapped the dusty, buried shroud and inside it, remarkably intact, he found the skeleton of a person—man or woman it was impossible to tell. The person, from some point in our Paleolithic past, was curled in a fetal position, and lying next to him was the skeleton of a puppy, the two buried together, lying in the ground this way for all this span of time. Most remarkable, though, was the skeleton's hand. It rested upon the shoulder of the puppy as Lucas's hand right then rested on mine, lightly, the tenderness obvious even in the hardness of bone. Human and canine, living together, buried together, clasped; it has been this way for a long, long while, and so it will go into the future.

And by the time I had finished the story my children were asleep, sweating in their sleep as they often do, and I had forgotten they were there, so immersed was I in the image, in the fact: the fact of skin and fur and how long and short we have been here. So I was surprised to look up and see in the burst of hallway light the man I married there, in the doorframe, listening—since when I do not know. Had he heard it all? Had he heard it at all? Benjamin has copper-colored hair, just like the pups, and he now has old-man whiskers, just like the pups. He sat there on the floor cross-legged, a dog sitting on either side of him, my children long gone, daylight saving time coming soon, this year our forty-seventh circle around the sun, he was bracketed by our animals, in contrast and contact, blurred but distinct, he Indian style, they on folded haunches, all eyes open, each dog alert, their ears pricked forward, his hands hovering over their beautiful heads.

6

The Death of a Wasp

Our new home has ceilings so low the summers are stifling inside, the ample mountain breezes barely able to squeeze themselves through the meager windows of this faux farmhouse. Unlike a real antique, our saltbox was built in the 1970s, which makes its smallness all the more an absurdity. In the olden days, people made their quarters cramped for warmth, but the prior owner built his house tiny in accordance with his wife's penchant for the pretty. Because we haven't yet moved in full time (we're here for whole summers and then for weekends over the rest of the year) we haven't yet had time to steam off heart-patterned wallpaper but knowing we can makes it easier to bear. The ceilings are another story. What can we do about those? At five foot one inch, I can stand up straight and nearly fan them with my fingers, the thick plaster swirled just barely above our heads, its peaked texture like egg whites stiffened with sugar.

The thirty-two acres of land we bought—rolling hills, unprimed woods opening up into grasslands and reservoirs—make the tiny house perched on it paradoxically both harder and easier to handle. Outside stretched fields clotted with black-eyed Susans, and then woods where towering trees, ripped up at the roots from a severe ice storm last year, lie felled like gentle giants on their sides, their canopies crushed under the mammoth weight of the now soft and rotting trunks. Standing in those woods, you look up and see the distant sky crosshatched by what seem like billions of branches: ash, oak, maple, cherry. And then you look down and see the ground gone emerald with moss, creeping up the flanks of the fallen trees; the moss wraps the rot in royal rugs across which dark beetles dart and upon which placid toads squat, staring out at the world with yellow eyes.

Beyond the trees there's more moss, and streams running every which way, and loam which is, says our neighbor, Al, as old as the Pleistocene ice age. "This dirt's been here millions of years," Al told me one day not long ago, cupping a handful of the black fudge that oozed up between the tendons of the trees. I'd never considered the idea of prehistoric dirt before, but why not. "Why not?" Al said to me. "The stones here are glacial and so's the till," and I suppose he's right. Now I hold the till and imagine it teeming with tiny prehistoric creatures, creatures unchanged since dinosaurs roamed and ruled, and as I stare the dirt turns transparent, so I can see in my palm a mini kingdom presided over by microbes and populated with citizens of cells.

Large and small; big and tall; we dwell, it seems, in a land of polar opposites. Winters here are marked by the snow's first descent, the thermometer free falling past zero, the sky breaking up into billions of tiny tatters that, once fallen, revert to a one, a singular white too huge for words. Spring comes as the cracking of ice and by mid-July we've reached some metaphorical boiling point, the fields withered and parched, the pond's crazed cracks on the ground, insects everywhere. We resent the smallest of the predators: mayfly, mosquito; while we fear the largest: the black bear, the coyote, some unseen ones that as of yet have no name. The other night, just into July, we heard an ungodly sound while we slept. It was the sound of murder, or terror, of a beast giving birth. Ben shot straight up in bed. "What is that?" I asked as the kids raced into our room and jumped under the sheets. We four stayed silent, waiting to hear the howl again, I thinking of lions on the loose, knowing it was impossible, but, bears, that could be. "Did you lock the door?" I whispered to Ben. Then the yowl again, this time the sound as if torn from the slaughtered throat of something at once intimate and alien, a beast I could not picture but whose pungent nature I could smell, seeping under our sills. Down stairs, our old dog began to bark, his barks, each one, falling uselessly onto the floor like blunt blades that could never protect us here. Then, a third time, and I could hear, I swear, the sound was slightly simian, and closer; Ben threw the sheets off, moonlight bright on one white leg, that leg, this house, so small, too small, the leg made of god knows what, the house made of cheap wood and single-paned glass; next to me, Clara was crying; Lucas had his eyes squeezed shut. "Don't go," I whispered to Ben, and he didn't, and that disappointed me, even as I hugged him hard, aware of my cold, greasy clutch. We waited and waited. The sound didn't come again. Minutes, maybe even an hour passed. Our bones would not bend. Sleep was a continent away. We stayed up the whole night, and it wasn't until the hills got golden that any of us felt safe enough to rest in our ramshackle country house, while outside, on our thirty-two acres and far beyond that too, beasts roamed, rageful, and rightfully so.

After that, I decided to enlarge the house. Had I been using my common sense I would have thought about fortifying the house, but I wasn't using my common sense. Somehow it seemed to me that if the house were larger we would be safer; we would be making a clear statement; lions tigers and bears OUT THERE; Slater/ Alexander clan IN HERE. Our *in here* needed an exclamation point. Thus, like any good yuppie trying to countrify herself, instead of getting a gun or building a barrack, I called a contractor.

"Cathedral it," the contractor said within moments, it seemed, of walking in our door. On the second floor, he bent his head back to scan our low ceilings, the dangle-down fixtures with their prisms in your hair and, with a sweep of his hand, half dramatic, half dismissive he said, "Cathedral the whole damn second story," and that was that. It seemed easy enough to do. Knock out those poorly plastered ceilings and create a higher heaven. Cheap. Quick. Creative. What could be better?

And in fact it was easy to do. We went at it with hammers, axes, pry bars. A universe opened above us. Tearing down the ceilings was a lot of fun. It was like playing a piñata game over and over again. Wack wack wack with a huge hammer. All of us took turns. We wacked until our cramped ceilings sighed and snowed, until their smashed sternums gave way in heaps of fluff and insulation; we wacked until we were knee deep in the debris of insufficiency, and then we swept it all up and poured our tiny smashed sky in the dumpster we'd rented for just this purpose.

It seems amazing that you can do one thing to a structure and the one thing you do can have so many reverberations. Within a day our pathetic little 1970s saltbox went from kitsch- country to serious, stern, a building with many meaty attic rafters and significant trusses of chestnut and ash, all of it exposed in the soaring shape of an A-frame interior. Now when we looked up, we could see the muscle that had been hidden in our home all this time, and beyond the muscle we could see chinks of sky and patches of white cloud where the roof needed repair. The rain came in on us, but we felt our fortress was stronger, and we slept the damp restful sleep of the seemingly safe.

We loved our cathedral over the summer. The contractor put up planks made of maple, antique maple with a honey hue. We loved that hue, and the steep slope of the ceiling he'd built. We loved that the planks were irregular, not cut to uniform sizes but staggered in width, like an old country floor angling up, over your head. We fixed the roof, put in some skylights, and watched the season pass. We watched storms roll in over Wachusett Mountain, the sky going dark, the rain coming hard, later the stars all sequins. A blistering August brought with it shrill cicadas, hysterical from the heat, and the gardens went limp, the flowers fainting where they stood. At night we could see the massive roof ties of our home at once supporting us in here and sheltering us from what was out there, and we were almost sorry the simian sound of that gigantic wild creature never came again.

Other things came in its stead. The neighbor's cat was killed by a coyote, her mauled body found beneath a tree. End of summer, black bears were sighted in the roads, or crossing people's properties, coming so close to the houses that their dexterous mitted paws were clearly visible, as were the two dark dots of the sow's nostrils. Driving back to Boston, we saw a crumpled car and not far from it a smashed deer, his antlers spearing the air, his head hanging sideways as the blood ran out. "Even the deer are huge here," I remember my husband saying as we sped by, passing the ambulance coming from the other direction.

Indeed it seemed to us that the very idea of the bucolic, at least as it pertained to New England, was a giant misnomer. True, the several states that make up this region are known for their low stone walls and the beauty of the snow settling upon them; for the swards of green where sheep and goat graze side by side; for the genteel farmhouses with their still more genteel porches that shelter folks while they sit in the fading day, dragonflies darting in and out of mud as rich as chocolate. Cows give milk and horses whinny as though straight out of a storybook. That's New England for you, at least from a pamphlet's perspective. But having spent now several summers in Massachusetts's north-central region, in the shadow of a midsized mountain and on fields that sport stone walls older than a century, the bucolic has given way to something rougher, more frightening, something simmering just beneath the skin of our lovely summer days. That simian scream. The fear of going out of doors after dark, because the bears are there, and hungry. Snakes longer than your leg coil beneath boulders, their teeth curved like a canine's, the poison in their split viper's tongue.

Summer ended and we left our country house, otherwise known as our "second home," to come back only on the weekends now. We locked the doors, drove back to the city, dropped our kids off for their first day of school, their second day of school, the city smelling of city, the library's lawn posted with signs: *Danger: Insecticide.* I thought I'd feel safer in the city, but in fact I felt oddly exposed, cramped, everywhere I went lawns being poisoned in preparation for fall.

On Friday, as soon as the kids were out of school, we drove back to the saltbox. Ben, working late, would be meeting us there in an hour or two. The ride was uneventful—the highway, the bathroom breaks, Burger King meals, the car filled with crumpled cups and boxes, the sheen of grease on the steering wheel.

And now—the house. We pulled into the saltbox's driveway. On the outside everything looked just as we had left it. My son's bike was leaning against the chestnut tree, his blue ball precisely where he'd last let it fall. In the darkening day I could see the little light we had kept on in the hallway, giving a glow to one window. We got out of the car. Above us clouds were streaming, surrounded by a cold cobalt blue. I stepped towards the house and, just as I did so, its one light went out, leaving the house sunk in shadows.

"Shhh," I said to the kids, racing around the driveway now. Something in my tone made them stop, abruptly.

"What's wrong? Clara asked.

"The light in the house," I said. "It just went out."

"Well you left it on all week," Clara said."

"I know," I said.

But what I didn't know, what I couldn't put my finger on, was why our house seemed so strange, even as it looked completely the same. It seemed hunched, this house, and when I opened the front door the darkness was deeper than what it was outside; it was bat-black and tangible. And then I heard it, at first barely and then crescendoing to clearly . . . a hiss coming from some inside space. The hallway? The second-story bathroom? I cocked my head. Hissssss. The sound seemed to be nowhere and everywhere at once. Hisssssss. It was low, this sound, both soft and sharp, like the rustling of skirts or flames.

I held the kids back with one arm and snaked my other arm along the wall until I hit a light switch, flicked it on, and in a nano-second the hall and its adjacent rooms were flooded with yellow, warmly glowing, illuminating familiar objects on the one hand, strange vacancies on the other. The shadow space under the desk leapt into life. The wastebaskets were dank and dark inside. I could see the cupboards but the light could not reach that space beneath them, where crumbs and cockroaches go. Hisss-ssss. Now I knew: the sound was coming from upstairs.

"Stay outside," I said to the kids and before they could protest I shut and dead-bolted the door, leaving them on the stoop. Then I made my way down the hall, turning the lamps on switch by switch, the lights each time illuminating objects while underscoring interstices, in every room, everywhere.

—

Houses are filled with holes. You can seal and strengthen, insulate and fortify all you want, but none of these efforts will change the fundamental fact that houses—be they billion-dollar mansions or squatters' shacks—are pocked and torn in too many places to count. The chimney, of course, represents one of the widest points of egress, large enough to let in reindeer and all other manner of mammals, and then there are the smaller chinks, the one's neither you nor I can see with the naked eye, but were our vision bionic, well, would be able to view all the ripped and ragged seams of all our shelters everywhere. We would be able to see the hairline cracks and gaps that practically beckon roommates we'd rather not have.

I climbed the stairs to the second story, still flicking on lights as I went, the hissing growing not so much louder as stereophonic, surrounding me now, over me and below me, beside me, left and right, despite the fact that I still could not see the source of the sound. I checked the kids' rooms, the bathroom, the bathtub; I even lifted the lid of the toilet, let it down, turned around, and then saw, right smack in the middle of the master bedroom floor, a squirming mass of humming . . . wasps, yes they were wasps, dozens, perhaps hundreds in huge, sizzling piles, their plump stingers wagging uselessly as they died, their wings glinting in the low light. I stepped inside the bedroom and heard a wet crunch under foot, and as I listened, and watched, a still living wasp rose from one of the corpse piles and floated drunkenly around the room, ramming its head against the window before falling back into a stupor on the sill, its stinger still pulsing. The window sills in the room were all pinkie deep with dead or dying wasps, and some were stuck to the screens in a desperate bid for freedom.

I ran downstairs and grabbed our shop vac, the one we keep in the basement, its capacity ten gallons, hauled it upstairs, calling to the kids, still outside, "Just a sec," as I, back in the master bedroom, jammed the plug into a socket and started Hoovering my way across the floor, holding the hose hard as it sucked up the dried flakes and crunched corpses of the insects. I vacuumed under the bed, behind the dresser, taking every pile and scrap of wasp I could, regardless of whether it still showed signs of life. When I was done, the shop vac was full to capacity and humming hard.

Disgusted, I banged its black bin once, twice, thrice against the wall, and the sound, as if sliced with a knife, ceased completely. I stood there, then, sweating hard, the night heavy with humidity, I stood there holding hundreds of wasps, some in all likelihood still alive. Suppose they escaped? They could climb out through the hose, could they not? I opened my dresser drawer, took out some socks and stuffed them deep into the tubing and then, just to be on the safe side, I opened a window and hurled the whole vacuum cleaner out into the yard. Dark now, I saw the machine fly through the air and then, oddly, drop onto the lawn with just the softest sound, tumbling down a slope and coming to rest by the red barn. I called to the kids then, and they came in and the bedroom looked as pristine as a princess's so that they would never need to know.

Benjamin arrived about an hour later, and that night, when the kids were asleep, I told him about the infestation, and he, after mulling over it for a moment or so, told me it was probably a one-time occurrence. "How can you be so sure?" I asked, and he explained his surety as he often does, by invoking some statistical principle, the specifics of which eluded me but the gist of which did not. Statistics, I have often found, are for the optimist; those who invoke its rules tend to believe the universe is an orderly, predictable place. I barely passed my statistics courses in graduate school, in part because I'm a numbskull when it comes to math but in part because I'm philosophically disinclined to believe in a universe all organized like some linen closet. My universe is full of wacky objects and cackling midgets and mules with wings. In my universe, nothing is predictable but anything is possible, which is why I was not in fact surprised to find, the following weekend when we arrived back at the house, a whole new crop of dead and dying wasps, hundreds upon hundreds of them in piles. And this time the hissing mounds and drifts were not only in the master bedroom, but in the two other bedrooms as well. While Ben kept the kids occupied outside I once again Hoovered all the rooms, slapping the sluggish live ones with a rolled magazine as I went. It had been an unseasonably warm September and I sweated as I worked, then stopped, stood straight, my hand on my lower back. Through the window of the kids' room I could see the huge bluish mass of Mount Wachusett, its rocky top ringed by coniferous trees, and then further down the slope the trees all turning, and as I watched, and rested, and watched, in through the open window flew a plain pale moth. I've never minded moths and minded them less when compared to wasps. The moth headed straight up for the ceiling light and then settled on the fixture, warming its thorax. I looked away, back towards the mountain now painted with a pink streak, and when I looked up at the light again, the moth was pinned in place by a plump wasp straddling it, holding its wings down while slowly pumping its jointed thorax full of venom. I watched the moth struggle to get free and I saw its struggle slow as what was probably a paralyzing venom went to work, at which point the wasp removed its stinger and began to masticate his meal, the moth fully alive but unable to move. The wings broke into pieces and fell to the floor in flakes of dim glitter.

That night, I found a dying wasp in one of the kid's bed sheets. I crushed it hard and angry between two books and did away with the carcass before either child could see, and then I checked their beds thoroughly before they got in. But when it was time for me to go to bed I didn't want to, and no matter how many times Ben and I shook out our sheets I was still convinced that there was a wasp hiding somewhere in there. "I *hate* wasps," I said to Ben, and I heard a hiss in my own voice, a hiss somehow similar to theirs, which made me hate them all the more. I slept on the couch and the next day called an exterminator.

"When you cathedraled your ceilings," he said, "you removed the barrier between the second story and the attic. And there have probably been wasps overwintering in your attic for years, but when you removed the barrier, well . . ."

I asked the exterminator why so many of the wasps were dead or dying when we found them, and he said, "Trapped. That's why you've got so many on your sills, at your windows. They're trying to get out. They come in for the warmth and then can't find their way out."

"Can you take care of it?" I ask.

"What you really need to do," the exterminator said, "is seal every one of these cracks in your cathedraling, maybe put up seamless sheets of sheetrock instead of these wooden planks with spaces between them. In the meantime," he said, "I can spray."

So the exterminator sprayed. He carried his poison in a backpack and he walked around our house pumping the trigger, spraying here and there, high and low, little lacy arcs giving glisten to the creases and the corners of the house, the odor so slight one could barely detect it, a smell that stung the back of the throat, just barely; and then he was done.

"That's it?" I said.

The exterminator looked at me quizzically. "I did the entire house," he said. "I can come back in six months."

"But aren't you going to do outside the house too?" I asked.

The exterminator looked out one of our windows. It happened to be the large picture window overlooking our thirty-two acres of fields and woods, the mountain looming blue behind it. We could see our pond, with a heron floating, so still he looked like carved clay.

"How far do you want me to go?" the exterminator asked. He gestured with his hand toward the acreage. "I can't very well spray all your land. And even if I could," he said, "I'm not sure the benefits would outweigh, you know, like what they say . . . the risks."

"Of course," I said, and laughed, but inside I was not laughing. I kept seeing that pale moth, the pruning shear mouth, how the wasp had feasted on the juice of its victim. But the exterminator raised a good point. How far would I go to feel safe? Who, or what, would I dispose of in the process?

"I'm not saying you won't see any more wasps," the exterminator said. "But you should see far fewer around here, for now."

His "for now" and "far fewer" hung in the air long after he'd left. I looked up at the planking of our handsome cathedral ceiling. We had tried so hard to make ourselves feel safe against big things, and now the world had been invaded by little things. The fact that the exterminator had already come and therefore supposedly solved the problem only made me feel worse, because the problem didn't feel solved, not at all. All he'd promised us was a reduction, not an annihilation, and it was an annihilation I was after. A completion. And because there was no completion, I heard hisses everywhere in that house, and then I started hearing hisses in my sleep and then the hisses followed me to the city, where I swore I saw a wasp launch off the screen of my computer and swerve through the open window behind it. The world, my world, was all of a sudden abuzz in a most unfortunate way, so that even my clothing felt itchy, suspicious, my senses heightened, as though I had magnifying lenses pressed against my eyes, and I could see. It was as though for the first time I could see all the tiny terrors in the world; I could see the microbes in the packaged chicken parts in the frozen foods section of the supermarket; I could see the intricacy of a web in the corner of a living room and the scum on the furred feet of a blue-black fly. When I peered in places I normally would never look— under our stove, behind our dishwasher, peeling back bark outside, I saw evidence everywhere of a miniature vibrant violent world, a world where black widows liquefied their prey and rats left tracks of scat. I could see my own skin, how spotted and wrong it was, how what appeared as tanned flesh was really, upon closer inspection, a tapestry of swarming cells.

Wasps live in cells and, though they are formally classified as predators who paralyze their prey with venom, they are far more complex than their category allows. I began to read about them as though by understanding them I could somehow get rid of them, or perhaps redeem them, because, I learned, their venom is used for many medicinal purposes; a paralytic, it is a component of most anesthetics, and in its distilled form it is used to make drugs for multiple sclerosis and muscular dystrophy; it is even a component of the drug fluoxetine, more commonly called Prozac, and what are we to make of that? Dozens upon dozens upon dozens of us daily drink down wasp and give it credit for our pleasure. I read the research. I drank it down. And yet even so I could not come to see those insects as anything but a threat: a creature with sticky wings and serrated legs, its belly segmented into three separate sections, its carcass armored like a car. It sings a rusty sound and builds its bloated nest from mud. Where is the sweetness here? Can we even classify a wasp, or for that matter any insect, as an actual animal? Something in me resists the idea, if only because I consider myself an animal lover even as I dislike the creepy crawlies who are, like it or not, a part of the kingdom, at least according to Linnaeus, who spent his life categorizing the planet's living things.

Why is it that we are instinctively disgusted by most insects while we find those higher up the food chain so appealing they can elicit in us the cooing language of affection, and also love? Biologists call the mewing and high pitched voices almost all human beings use in the presence of babies and other furry things—be they human or not—the "cute response." Ethologist Konrad Lorenz explains that the cute response is elicited in almost all people regardless of culture when in the presence of an animal that has certain physical characteristics: a head bigger than its body, short chubby limbs, and large eyes. Given that wasps of any age possess none of these features, one could say that we as a species are preprogrammed to either overlook or outright reject them, regardless of the fact that we rely on the medicinal properties of their venom, and that they are, in other ways, essential to the ecosystem that sustains us all. Given these facts I, for one, would like to overcome my revulsion with rationality, but I can't. I propose that, just as we humans have a "cute response" we also have a "revulsion response," and that it is hard-wired into us and, more problematically, that, were we to look deep down into its dark center, we would find in it the wellspring of human hatreds, the place from which prejudice springs and is sustained, a stinger, of sorts, filled with human venom for which there is no good use.

I remember once, when I had cancer (and I don't anymore) I asked my surgeon if I could see my cells on the slide. She took me to a large, cool room. It was dark inside, the light coming from the tiny bulbs beneath each separate microscope lined up along long counters. Test tubes hung in racks, some filled with blood, others with serum, still others with a liquid I could not identify but that looked to me lipidinous, like fat. On the wall hung an illustrated poster of a man, his skin peeled back in flaps to reveal rib and heart, knee and flank. Next to him, hung on a hook, was an actual skeleton, the screw in the skull that had cracks like continents. "Here," my doctor said, pulling a microscope forward and swiveling a knob. I lowered my head to the oval eyepiece and saw, at first, just a staticky skirmish that looked like insects running every which way, and I recoiled and, as I did so, dropped into a place of despair, but, as the doctor adjusted the knob, the view slowly changed. My cells slowed down, turned around, and then blossomed before me, stained in blues, pinks and purples. There was my cancer and for that moment—a second spliced—it was not ugly, and its colorful clusters allowed me to make of it a metaphor, a living link, my cells massed like hydrangea, which I had at home, in full flower, my load now lightened even as I still had fear, and fear, and fear.

We didn't go back to the house for one week after the exterminator sprayed. September passed into October with the weather still unseasonably warm. The annuals, confused, kept going, putting out new blooms, petunias and nasturtiums growing in masses, overtaking boxes and beds. When we finally returned to the house it was the middle of October, apple season, the time when fruit drops to the ground and rots softly in the sun, the juices drawing everything from hornets to honeybees. Pulling into the driveway, I heard, as always, the satisfying crunch of tires on rubble. The first bats were just appearing; tiny mammalian creatures with webbed wings they swooped low and then hurled themselves high into the sky, their symphony octaves beyond what we could hear, the silence illusory, the air in fact teeming with sonar songs. Benjamin turned the motor off and we all just sat in the car for a few moments, the motor ticking as it cooled, the sky draining itself as the sun set in a crimson puddle.

As always, we had left one light on in the house, and as the day grew darker that light grew brighter, warmer, the window a single square lit amber in the night. Our house looked lovely then, the exterminator having come and gone, the corpses cleaned up, we could, it seemed then, manage this, the inside and the out, this cleansed house and sprawling track of land that, as city goers, we in fact knew nothing about.

That night we opened the home's front door to the sound of complete silence. We slept in our sheets to the sound of complete silence. I awoke at dawn. I felt a finger of sunlight on my face and I heard, outside, what I believed was the soft step of a deer crossing our driveway to drink from our deep pond. Still lying in bed I looked first out the east facing window through which light was now gushing like liquid, so I turned—too much for my eyes— and instead lay on my back, head tilted up towards the skylight to catch some clouds. And that was when I saw. The skylight was blanketed by a moving mass of wasps, their wings erect or flat on their segmented backs, the whole crowd sizzling, a low sybaritic sound, almost alto, maybe mournful. I elbowed Ben. We lay there and watched our wasps, first just covering the skylight, and then, crawling out from between the cracks in our pitched and planked ceiling, crawling out high and low, left and right, the gaps jammed with writhing, the insects marching up and down, going every which way, wave after wave of wasp, the hissing growing louder as their numbers increased, none of them yet flying, although that would happen soon. We got up, left the room, making sure to shut the door—hard—on our way out. We collected our bed-headed kids and our snoozy pooches, and within five minutes we were packed up and, everyone in the car, we headed straight for the city.

Back in Somerville, Benjamin made phone calls, took notes. He spoke at length with the exterminator we'd hired and then called three others for consults. He called the contractor who had put up the cathedral ceiling and came away from that phone call singing. "He'll wasp-proof the ceiling for free," Benjamin announced, and then he flipped open his notebook and drew a deft diagram of how the new vaulted ceiling would, this time, suture shut any gaps from above. "And we don't have to go with sheetrock," Ben said. "We can wasp-proof the place using planks. It's possible."

I looked at his diagram but remained unconvinced, or confused, because I didn't think it would work, because wood moves, first of all, and second of all because I'd been infected by fear and fear is not logical, and what I needed now was a way to keep the wasps out of both my home *and* my head, and he couldn't do that, could he? What engineering solution would solve the problem of a hisss-ssss following me here and there, my senses on the alert, so I could smell more smells and taste more tastes and see more sights, everything all in bits, in dots, like a Pissarro painting, the world was made up of tiny blurs and edges. "Maybe we should sell the place," I said. "We're not farmers—"

"Maybe not you," Ben said, cutting me off sharply, in a way that is unusual for him. "Maybe you're not a farmer, Lauren, but I am, or will be, or . . . ," he said, "at least I want to be."

That night in the shower, I felt a tiny lump on my chest, just to the side of my implant, a small saline-filled bag that took the place where my breast had been. The lump was familiar in my fingers in both its size and its consistency; it was hard, hard as a pinball, the kind of lump you can squeeze and roll between your thumb and first finger. The lump was painless, and yet its implications sent waves of pain and panic. The thought is not, "Oh my god, a recurrence." In times of extreme stress, the mind, my mind, makes metaphors that are the handles on a cup too hot to otherwise hold. Hydrangea. I saw the lace-capped bloom, but before I could lock onto it, it dissolved into Pissarro points and went down some mental drain. I stood there, then, without anything for balance, the bar of soap slipped from my grip and foaming at my feet as the shower shot me, again and again. Steam rose around me and then I felt my body fade back, become tiny. I have always understood my flesh, myself, as a primary player on this planet, but in fact, I could now see, all our bodies are in some senses small; they are, we are, just the random vacant vessels for microbes and all other manner of minutiae with plans that, in all likelihood, not only diverge from ours but trump our intentions in almost every way. When I stepped from the shower I was swaddled in steam and needed to see myself in the mirror. I swiped the fog from the glass. Here I was, my body a host to billions of beings who simply could not care less.

We met with the contractor and picked out new planking, I, hearing everything through the hiss in my head. When I called the oncologist it was with that hiss in my head, so I had to keep saying, "Excuse me, could you repeat that?" so often I wondered if my ears were bound up by wax or otherwise infected with fluid. "She can't see you until the eighth," the receptionist kept saying, and I kept saying, "She doesn't have anything sooner?" and she kept saying, "I've checked; she doesn't," *hsssssss*. In the meantime the planking we picked was cedar, for its aromatic oils and resistance to rot.

The eighth was a Thursday—five days away. Certain tumors are especially aggressive and can grow millimeters in a day, but most proceed along a far more measured path. Tumors can lie dormant in the rafters of your bones for years, only to suddenly take flight and allow sight, the malignancy spreading in accretions too tiny to count, all the way down where quarks and nanos live. Such is the terror of tininess, and our huge super-duper newly planked ceiling seemed to me a sad effort against inevitable seepage. Our bodies, by the way, are all seep, ancient seep, we being made of atoms that were once a part of the Milky Way's stars, atoms as old as the big bang itself; picture it, if you can. Once the whole world was tinier than a teaspoon, the solar systems, the galaxies, all of it folded up into something so compact it was probably not visible. And then someone flicked a switch, or said, *Now!* and the dark, dense dot containing all the universe within it exploded across the sky with such force that it all continues to expand today, pushed outward by its own original velocity. Anyone can look up into the night sky and see the hugeness of streaming space, but how often do we reflect on the fact that everything around us, including the mind-boggling grandeur of the universe, is powered by atoms, and that atoms exist at a scale so small we cannot quite measure them? People wonder: Is there life in outer space? The stars wobble in response. Is it not just as logical to ask, "Is there life in inner space?" Who's to say that there are not entire societies living out of our sight, in another dimension, or simply at a scale so small we fail to see them or to consider their plans?

In the meantime, the ceiling was being sealed with our aromatic "rot resistant" cedar, terms I knew were not absolute, because cedar does rot if you keep it wet for long enough; it's all relative. The size of the lump in my chest was tiny compared to the one that had come back cancerous several years before, but then again large tumors are often pseudo tumors; it's the small ones that aren't playing around. They have to be tough if they're to survive in the dog-eat-dog world of nanoville. It was like I could see that world, a series of swerving tunnels hanging in a mist in the air, everywhere. And then my daughter began to have nightmares, trapped in tunnels, or the great plates of the earth crunching together so beautiful mountains blew their tops and spurted golden magma. Her dreams at night echoed my vision during the day, although I never did I tell her I was stuck with seepage, living in quarkdom, worried about wasps overtaking the home we'd bought.

And no, never did I tell her, but daughters read their mother's minds, the pair hitched by a hook, it's clear. My daughter dreamt she fell down a pin-prick hole, her whole self sucked into something no bigger than the nose of a needle, she fell and fell, passing through layers of earth, the red hot embers of the center rushing up to meet her, and she screamed.

"It's just a bad dream," I said to her, stroking back her hair as she lay in bed. "Don't be scared, there's no need to be scared."

And then, propping herself up with her elbow in bed, so I could see her hair cascading in the darkness, she said, "You're scared. So why shouldn't I be too?"

My daughter was eight, almost nine when she said that, young enough to lie to. "I'm not scared," I said.

"You're scared almost all the time," my daughter said and then she lay back on her bed, staring up at the ceiling to which she'd affixed phosphorescent stars and the perfect crescent of a moon. During the day you couldn't see them but once the light was out in the night they popped into perfect view.

"Sometimes," I now said, staring at her little solar system overhead, "Sometimes I admit I get a little nervous, but that's normal."

"You're scared of the wasps," Clara said, and she was right. For five days the contractor had been out there, installing the new ceiling, and not once had I gone up to check on his progress. And prior to the wasps I'd always insisted we go to the "second home" every weekend, counting down the days until we could get there, my hands missing the ancient till and the pond's cool water, but now I stopped insisting, and we passed our Saturdays and Sundays in the city, where I worked my small plot, pulling weeds and watering my hydrangeas, all of which were in beautiful bloom, some stippled red, others in fat clusters of sky blue. Even when the contractor called to tell us he'd finished our ceiling and the wasps were for the most part gone, their means of egress now nailed shut with rot-resistant cedar, the whole house smelling sweet, no, not even then did I want to go back.

In my life I have had more phobias then I have fingers to count them on. I might go so far as to call myself a professional phobic, except that I've made no money at the job, and it brings me no esteem. Nevertheless, when I start avoiding something, I know just what it is I have to do: its equal but opposite reaction, this cure as sure and steady as the physical law it imitates. If you are afraid of fried eggs nothing will cure you except frying and eating the egg, not even knowing the etiology of the egg fear will help you so don't spend money dreaming on an analyst's couch. Spend your bucks on a flat frying pan and Pam. As for my wasps, who wouldn't be frightened? But my daughter was right; my fear was infectious, even as I felt it stiffen me, constrict me and what I was in the world. We had bought this country house to live in, not avoid. We planned to move there at the end of this school year, motivated by a desire to know the earth more intimately before it disappeared in clouds of carbon and waste. Were there wasps in my childhood? For sure, but who cares? I could not recall a single one. Were the wasps some sort of misplaced fear, their swarming like cells? Of course, but this nonrevelation brought me no bravery. Thursday I had my meeting with the oncologist, but Wednesday was free, and blue and bright, the kind of crisp October day that you wish you could preserve in a bottle.

I did what I knew I needed to do. I did it not out of bravery but superstition. If I was good enough to face what had become a full-blown fear of the house, then maybe my oncologist would palpate the little lump and say, *That? It's just fat,* or some such thing. *Gristle,* or some such thing. So I went up to the house that Wednesday, in the morning, 10 a.m., the roads empty, me in my little car flying down the highway. It was such a pretty day. I rode with the windows down, so the speed had sound, like ripping silk, fields on either side of me, orange tractors pulsing in the strong sun.

I pulled into the driveway, the familiar crunch of its gravel, the apple tree surrounded by fallen fruit, bruised and brown and smelling sweet. The sky was always bluer here, in the country, and today not a single cloud in sight. Overhead hung a transparent daylight moon.

The front door, when I got to it, was open. The contractor had failed to lock it, I suppose, but there's a difference between an unlocked door and an actual open one. There it was—the door—open, just like it might be in a storybook, a fairy tale, the little door open, the golden glow inside, the pull of the place, *go in now*; the necessary hesitation because what else might be in there, what with the open door and all.

By the side of the door hung a copper bell, the clapper going green from the elements. Now I reached up and rung the bell, the sound pure and pealing in the lovely mid-morning, I rang the bell three times, *one*, *two*, *three*, and when no one came to get me, I stepped over the threshold, one hand on my chest, where I often found it these days, pressing the little lump, feeling for its contours and intentions.

The contractor had left the home extremely clean. I could see that immediately. In fact the home was cleaner than we'd ever left it ourselves. The kitchen was shining, the stovetop a wet lacquered black, our old oak table covered with a sprightly red checked cloth. The stairs had been scrubbed down and the whole place smelled of sawdust and pine pitch and cedar.

He had left the place clean, yes, but as I went from room to room the hiss returned—my imagination, perhaps, or was it the fact that I found, webbed in a few corners or simply, seemingly, dead center on some floors, the corpses of wasps, insubstantial in death, they were dried and desiccated and flaked away in the wake of my weight.

Nothing is ever absolute, including revelations or understanding. No one had promised me a complete solution. I studied a few wasps caught in webs, snarled in the silky strands, and then I stood back up, stepped forward and heard a hard *cerrunch-ch* beneath the heel of my shoe.

The crunch was so syllabic, so wet and sharp in the completely quiet house that I jumped, moved back, stared down, and that is when I saw the body of the wasp I'd stepped on. He was still alive, writhing on the floor, his lower body half smashed, oozing red blood. The blood stopped me up short. Do insects have blood, and red blood at that? I knelt down now. It could not be. I pressed my chest where the nodule was. It could not be. Down beneath me there was crimson blood and it was coming not from me but from an insect with, I'd assumed, no significant similarities to myself.

Slowly, I stood back up. I took a mason jar from the window sill and, using a spoon I found on the dresser, I scooped the injured wasp inside. I don't know why. I walked with him out of the house and set him on the hood of my car. Even when wounded he still hissed, his one good wing vibrating with this song he had to sing.

I watched the wasp. My weight had damaged him, a mortal wound for sure. Blood covered the floor of the jar now, and it streaked the walls too. One of his wings was wrangled, all bent and crumpled, and his thorax was partially unhinged. I stood there and watched him as he hurled his torn self against the jar's sides, trying to climb the glass, falling back into blood again, tearing his wing to tatters in the process.

I have always needed to find beauty in what I love, in what I claim for a connection, be it the bodies of my children, or the man I married. There was no beauty here, but there was that blood, which I could not easily overlook, blood as red as any human's, and then I slipped my finger down deep in the jar and drew it back up, dabbed dark now, one single bead of wasp blood sliding down my first finger, caught in the cup I made of my hand, a droplet already evaporating even as it formed, and then I touched it with my tongue. Such a tiny bead, and yet it exploded in my mouth, sheer salt with a tang of sweetness that left before you could lock it in, the blood in the back of my throat now, streaks of salt so pure they stung, and my eyes teared up and then in a simple swallow it was done. Gone. In the jar the wasp, I saw, was still, lying on his side, his one good wing pumping slowly up, then down, up, then down. He'd managed to sting me without once touching me, an insect, an animal, defying the dimensions and coming across.

I tapped three times on the side of the jar and the wasp, well, he turned towards me now, his antennae quivering and then, overtaken by rage or something more primitive still, he began to hurl him-self against the glass, throwing his whole body into it, his humming ceased, the insect utterly silent as he banged his body again and again against this terrible transparency, these slick sides, and I saw in that wasp a willfulness that was terribly familiar to me. I know, I know, it's narrow-minded to anthropomorphize, but how else might we learn to tolerate, to perhaps love, what we have in fact hated? Ani-mal researchers are constantly warning us about anthropomorphiz-ing when in fact it's this that reels in revulsion, this megametaphor we make of a world both too terribly big and also dangerously small. So, yes. I will. Right now. See how he struggles? See how he slows as his wounds widen and the red keeps running out of him? It's not a sadness that we share but some life force, some filament that flows through him and me both, joined, jointed by a fierce need to tri-umph even though we won't; we can't. I see myself in his struggles and, moments later, when the wasp dies, I no longer see myself as I am but as I one day will be.

7

Bat Dreams

1.

When I have trouble sleeping—and even when I don't—I like to go outside in the deepest part of the dark. Everything I fear is out here, the coyotes roaming the rim of the woods, the glades deep enough to drown in, my shadow painted on the pavement. There it is—a self so stretched I can't see past its point of disappearance. What draws me here? When I look back, I see our house, the one we've finally moved to out here in the country, living now closer to cliffs and claws, our door substantial, a weighty wedge of wood, the windows sturdy squares, wrapped in vinyl that no amount of rain will rot. After years and years of searching, I finally have what I have always wanted—a home by the forest, a place called *mine*, where I can stack my books and sip my tea, cups nesting on the shelf I painted primrose blue. Opening the door to darkness is like diving into deep cool pool, the shock of it, the smack of it, reminding me what is real.

2.

Insomniacs have different ways of coping. Some stare at the wall or count cows in their mind; others toss and turn until their sheets are roped around their bodies wet with sweat. Pills come to mind, some tablets, others oblong capsules made of gelatin that dissolve in the mouth and leave some sweetness behind. I've tried all these tricks and found them all, at times, more or less successful. In the end they don't matter. Sleep, as I tell my children, comes to those who wait.

3.

My father, at seventy-four years of age, still struggles with insomnia, his bedside drawer crammed with all manner of questionable cures. Like my sister, of similar temperament, he sleeps with a black gel mask over his eyes and a fan turned on, the white noise blocking the twitches and turns, the pings and guffaws of a planet that never rests. All of us Slaters are sensitive to sound. Our ears, it seems, are magnets, so the whine of a mosquito is multiplied times ten, and the low groan of the crocodile on a bank hundreds of miles away reaches us where we lay, staring at the ceiling, searching for something that cannot be found. No, you don't find sleep. In the end it finds you, and only when you've ceased to scrabble after it.

I have learned not to chase sleep. I have learned that, like a child or a deer, sleep will trot the other way as soon as she sees my outstretched hand. I have also learned, from all those long nights lying in bed, counting cows as they clear my moon—each one, every time—I have also learned that insomnia, at least for me, is in part a fear of precisely what I claim I long for. Yes, sleep entombs us. As soon as I turn my attention away she is there, laying her long body over mine, her cold invisible hand gagging my mouth, her weight so substantial I cease to stir, and thus I lie there, a body in the night, my muscles paralyzed as every sleeper's are, while meanwhile, way up in the globe called my head, dancers are whirling and masked men hold sticks of fire. Houses conflagrate and people drop like leaves from silver skyscrapers, their bodies flocking in the air, which is also packed with letters, A's and X's and Z's all falling with the people, some of whom sprout wings and others of whom fail to find their flight, and thus come to the concrete, crashing.

4.

Human beings have such a long list of fears: nachtophobia—fear of nightmares; pterodophobia—fear of ferns; acerophobia—fear of sourness; cacaphobia—fear of ugliness; venustrophobia—fear of beautiful women; chinophobia—fear of snow; cynophobia—fear of dogs; heliophobia—fear of the sun; leukophobia—fear of the color white; octophobia—fear of the figure eight; belonephobia—fear of pins and needles; chrobophobia—fear of dancing; coulraphobia—fear of clowns; dendrophobia—fear of the woods; astrophobia—fear of stars; caligrophobia—fear of writing; bibliophobia—fear of books; barophobia—fear of gravity; coultraphobia—fear of claws; autrophobia—fear of flutes; nostophobia—fear of returning home; doraphobia—fear of fur and the skins of animals.

5.

Wild animals have no known phobias. Human beings, on the other hand, have 753 phobias on record, fear of sleep amongst them. It seems strange to me that Homo sapiens, which translates into "wise man," is so riddled with so many unwise fears, but stranger still is the fact that, despite all our technological prowess, we nevertheless fear so much more while we suffer so much less than wild animals whose pain is never tamed by morphine, whose hides are never saved by the scalpel. Think, for instance, of arctic caribou, huge lumbering beasts tormented by tiny botflies that crawl up the nose to deposit maggots beneath the skin, maggots that squirm and snack on living flesh. A hunter once showed me an old caribou hide he had hanging on one of his study's walls, the skin stretched and pinned with tiny tacks so you could clearly see the wide infected welts, each one white rimmed and round, with jagged edges that looked to me like tiny teething marks. After seeing such a sight one starts to wonder if what makes an animal wild is not its temper or its teeth but rather it's incredible unmitigated pain, a pain purer than we—who lean on our letters and our lidocaine—can conceive.

6.

Nictophobia—fear of forests and wooded places. These days, when I can't sleep, because I fear sleep, I go outside, into the wooded places. I am not looking to be lulled by the breezes or the natural beauty. One overcomes fear by entering it and, because I can't enter sleep, I do the next best thing. I enter the dew-slick night, the moist forest where millions of mosquitoes dwell, where the carcasses of animals lie deteriorating in the dirt, a half-eaten turkey, meat still clinging to its bones; I pick it up and hordes of beetles drop from its hollows, zig and zag over my bare feet before scuttering into the wall of weeds beside me. Shaken, I turn back to look at our new house and am surprised to see it has somehow shrunk, due to distance or nerves; I think of all its problems. The right-side sill is rotting, ingested by the very insects that right this minute fly in a halo around my head or hide in the heaps of dead grass and decay. The windows, which just days ago seemed so square and solid, look from here all tilted, and they do not properly close, so the weather blows in, sprays of rain in the spring or summer, isolated flakes in the winter. You look up and see those flakes; they land on the bookshelf and melt into a tiny tide pool, lace giving way to water. Every day I consider my lists; so many things to do! So many repairs to make! It seems we close up one gap only to have another open and thus the house is a perpetual project, a lesson it insists we learn, and what lesson is this? There is no way to keep out oblivion; no antidote for annihilation. Put three thousand locks on your doorways and gum-shut your windows with tar and still finality will find its chinks and make its way through, and claim your corporeal being, when the time is right. When the time is right. When the time is right. I repeat that phrase a lot when I'm having insomnia. I lie in bed and stare at my ceiling and think— *When the time is right.*

7.

Benjamin tells me that I've started talking in my sleep, and this makes me still more wary of sleep's strange grip. I don't have secrets

I need to hide. The talking bothers me because it's like having a second self who has slipped past my awareness with her grab bag of tools and tricks she plays on a mind. "What do I say?" I ask my husband. He reports that he can't make out a single phrase. "It's gibberish," he says, "and your voice is high." I have a girl in me, I guess, a girl who has some story to tell, and she emerges in darkness, but ultimately, she, like me, is stymied by the spell of sleep. She tries and tries to talk, but all that happens is a blended mess of vowels and the clunky clunk of consonants tripping over one another.

Thus, I go outside. I take this girl, or rather this girl and I, we go for a walk. The night is not quiet, not quiet at all. Like my body and its busy cells, the night is alive with sounds. Stop now. Stand still. Lean against this tree. To my left, a raucous jay. His song ceases and silence ensues but not for long, because now I can hear, from inside my body, a tick ticking which is the sound of the ancient radiation that lives within me, and you too, our bodies made of astral matter, our atoms as old as the big bang itself. And is that cry across the way from a baby in sleep or a woman in distress, a woman sitting at her kitchen table, one cigarette smoldering in the tray full of ash?

8.

Sleep is annihilation, but it is also the chance for the self to take a break from itself. Who, after all, can be reasonably expected to live with any being, even your own, twenty-four hours a day, seven days a week? Thus there are many beneficial aspects of sleep. We say we wake up refreshed, but what we really mean is released. During the night we are released from the grip of self, and now, upon opening our eyes, we are ready to take on once more our hides and our habits, both of which, after an eight-hour hiatus, seem magically more manageable, freshened, and, maybe just for an instant, interesting, like someone we might want to meet. Separation makes the heart grow fonder, it's true, and thus one of sleep's main functions is to allow the hugely conscious human, with the overgrown frontal lobes, to meet himself anew each morning, when he is who he is, a simple animal, a primate undressed, his hair so sparse, his limbs so pale he'd like to protect this person meeting him in the mirror, and so he—we—throw on our clothes, zip up. Quickly.

9.

Tonight I skirt the woods and go instead for the field, where the grass is crisp from a simmering summer. Out here, bats fly low and I worry one will tangle in my hair. A long time ago, when I was young, bats got into our attic, this despite my mother's considerable efforts to seal shut the house from wanton wind and weather. She was a regal woman, my mother, and she disliked the wayward ways of the world. Our house was kept antiseptically clean, our towels all monogrammed with our initials, as well as the collars of our blouses, as though we might somehow forget who we were without these embroidered reminders.

And yet despite all my mother's efforts, bats came in, probably through the chimney. I don't recall how we discovered them, if someone found a furred corpse or if we heard their silken soars above us. My mother stormed. She sent my father up with a child's butterfly net and obediently (my father was almost always obedient to her) he went. He climbed the three sets of steps, ascending to the attic with a small nylon net hitched to a pink handle, us four children and our clench-faced mother watching from below. We heard our father turn the handle and step into the darkest part of the house and then for a long, long time it was quiet up there. "Papa?" my younger sister mumbled after many moments had passed and he hadn't returned. For some reason I wondered if he'd become a bat himself, joined their ranks, released from the weight of marriage and parenthood, and just as I saw this in my mind's eye we heard from the attic's interior the sound of a mighty struggle, crashing, curse words, something shattering, and then the door burst open and "Papa" returned, red-faced, huffing, one bat captured in that toy net he held pinched closed. He had a scrape above his eye, a slender seam of blood just beginning to show, and his whole face looked odd, stormy, his lips pressed and white. "Just one?" my mother cried. My father said nothing, strode past her,

his anger entirely odd for him, and palpable. Some transformation had happened to him when he went among the bats; with
their webbed wings and silent songs they'd put a spell on him, for
suddenly my father stood straighter and walked with an angry energy we couldn't understand. "Just one," he quipped to my mother,
moving past her.

We followed our father downstairs, us kids did, leaving my
mother to fret alone in the hallway. "C'mon," he said to us, my father said to us, striding through the kitchen, opening the back door
onto the evening. And what an evening it was, the sky all lavender, practically pulsing with late light, darkness creeping towards us
from under the trees and shrubs. "We'll let the little lady go," my
father said and I wondered how he knew the bat was female. We all
went outside, and he held the net up, unpinched the sides, and we
saw the bat soar straight towards the moon, its wings wide, its tiny
furred feet splayed out as it arced heavenward. "What a sight," my
father said, and a sight it was, and we all stood there for a long time,
so long we failed to recognize that the darkness was upon us and
the nighttime had begun.

10.

This is the memory that comes to me as I pace the thatched field,
back and forth, up and down, the darkness deep; I sit down and
then, suddenly, sleep waves her wand because when I next look up
it is somehow, oddly, nearing dawn and the sky is lavender just like
it once was and above me, all around me, dipping and diving, there
are bats, everywhere, small brown bats, crepuscular, some flying so
low I can see their mouse-mouths and the tiny tabs of their furred
ears, and I know it's impossible but I hear it anyway, their sonar
songs; yes, the bats are singing as they traverse the air, as I've tra-
versed the night, and come through, once again, on the other side.

I watch the bats. They are not doing anything special, just being
bats, but that's enough to captivate me, enough to captivate anyone,
really. Mammals who fly. Imagine that. Imagine standing on the
tip of a cliff and spreading your arms. Imagine nursing your young
in a dark cave. Imagine seeing by sound. I stand. I watch the bats

as the sky moves through its morning paces, lavender to lipstick-pink back to violet and finally settling into a pool-bottom blue, the clouds perfect today, fluffed and drifting.

Now the door slams and my daughter and husband step outside, to find me, wet with dew, like the lawn is too. My husband has red hair, just like my father, and I have the shape and shrewdness of my mother, but the similarities end there. I do not have her rage, her huge and negative capacities. I grew up scared, in that place called the Golden Ghetto. I'm still scared now, but I think I know how to hold myself. I've learned how to make a plan, or to ask for directions. Most of all, I have my people, I found my people, it took years but here they are, the ones I can call mine.

"Look," I now say to them—my people, my husband and my daughter and now my son comes too—pointing to the soaring shapes, the webbed wings outspread. Perhaps it's an odor, a smell rising off my skin. Because as my husband and daughter and son come closer, so too do the bats, swooping lower and lower until at last I can feel the black mass of them humming above me—*too close*, I think, but isn't it always that way, the odd, the animal, too close for our comfort? I would run, but my legs seem stuck, like I'm dreaming a bat dream, a bad dream, only the sun is coming up and I am indisputably awake as a bat with an ovoid body swoops so low I can smell the guano, thick and rich, and then he's in my hair, tangled there, while I shrink from the moist touch of nighttime. I shake my mane, flinch forward, and then go crazy, go, finally, wild, yelling, *No no no*, like that's my one and only word. I utter it over and over again, my single primitive syllable, and as I speak it I raise my arm and grasp the body of the bat, surprised to find how hot he is, all throb and twist, and then I lift him with my hands and hurl him, hard, back to the heavens.

And he goes. He catches a current and soars straight up a shaft of crystalline air, and as he rises I hear the sound of something ripped from my head, a thatch of my hair he has, carrying it clasped in what must be his mouth; it's hard to tell. I reach up to rub, surprised by the space I can feel on my stinging scalp. I'll have a small bald spot there until the fuzz grows in, but that won't be for weeks. And when I look way up, I see my bat is indeed holding a hunk of my hair, so I am, for just a moment, with him, of him (or is it her, the little lady?), and this is how it comes to be that I am—a part of me is—streaming through the sky, and then I soar one step further and am winged and singing in a key no human can hear. This my daylight dream, while below me are my bones and the landscape dotted with houses and horses and strange pale *people they're called*, the only animals with 753 fears. The bat knows this and nods. And then, because he needs his mouth to sing sonar, the bat quickly lets my locks go. I watch as all my strands circle the sky and then, at last, drift down—falling, falling, like you do in a dream, down stairs and steeples and saddles and swords, immobilized by fear as you fall—

11.

Except this time, grown up and long gone (I have my own home now. Come visit me here and we'll have a cup of tea), I step forward and catch myself in my cupped hands.

Acknowledgments

Thanks to Helene Atwan of Beacon Press for her unwavering support for this book. Thanks to Angela von der Lippe of W. W. Norton for believing in the project for as long as she did; to Betsy Lerner of Dunow, Carlson & Lerner for ferrying the book through its labyrinthine course; to Dorian Karchmar for being there during the absolute hardest parts; and to Kim Witherspoon for suggesting the idea in the first place. Thanks to my inimitable writer's group—Karen Propp, Pagan Kennedy, and Audrey Schulman—a twenty-five-year-old constellation of friends and critics who heard portions of this book well past their bed times, and to my husband, who (and if you've read the book know this by now) put up with this project and did so with good humor. Thanks to Evans Huber, who dove in and took charge when things started coming undone. Thanks to my children, Clara and Lucas Alexander, who are inspirations and sources of solace when the going gets tough (and it did). And thanks, of course, to my canine companions, especially Lila and Musashi, with whom I shared thirteen and seventeen years respectively, who I will never stop missing, and whose gentleness, grit, mirth, and courage remain for me models of how one can live with grace and goodwill.